Mary, the Beloved

MARY, THE BELOVED

Keith Berube, M.A.

En Route Books & Media
5705 Rhodes Avenue, St. Louis, MO 63109
Contact us at contactus@enroutebooksandmedia.com

Cover design by TJ Burdick

Cover credits:
Bloch, Carl Heinrich, The Meeting of Mary and Elisabeth, via Wikimedia Commons: https://commons.wikimedia.org/wiki/File:%27The_Meeting_of_Mary_and_Elisabeth%27_by_Carl_Heinrich_Bloch.jpg

Bloch, Carl Heinrich, The Annunciation, via Wikimedia Commons: https://commons.wikimedia.org/wiki/File:Carl_Heinrich_Bloch_-_The_Annunciation.jpg

W. Bouguereau, Virgin Mary, Child Jesus and John the Baptist via Restored Traditions: http://restoredtraditions.com/products/virgin-child-detail-bouguereau

Hardback ISBN: 978-1-63337-156-9
Paperback ISBN: 978-1-63337-155-2
E-book ISBN: 978-1-63337-157-6

Printed in the United States of America

The celestial traitress play,
And all mankind to bliss betray;
With sacrosanct cajoleries,
And starry treachery of your eyes,
Tempt us back to paradise

–Francis Thompson

To Mary and her little Son, my Beloveds,
and to the six beloveds they gave to me:
Pam, Maria, Matthew, Anna, Sophia and Liliana.

Contents

Introduction

> "...there is something deeper at work. I think she is, in a sense, closer to us nowadays than she was to earlier generations of Christians. She is something more to us than a theological symbol; nor do we think of her, in the manner of the Middle Ages, as the patroness of this or that institution, a religious order, or a parish, or a guild. Rather, to each of us, she is a personal romance. Because a natural instinct makes us unwilling to discuss such things in public, I will leave it at that."
>
> –Monsignor Ronald Knox

"To each of us she is a personal romance." What does this mean? It means she is the Beloved—God's, mine, yours. After the love of the three Divine Persons for each other, Mary is the first love of the Holy Trinity *ad extra*. She is not an abstraction, nor some idea we toy with. She is not merely a group of doctrines we learn nor theology we wrangle with. She's not a ghost, nor simply a holy soul in Heaven. Scripture and Tradition; Marian doctrine and dogma; the Mariology of the Saints; the apparitions of Mary: these are ways of getting to know a real flesh and blood Lady who loves us and longs for us to return her love. Her entire being is beauty beyond telling, sweetness surpassing description, a burst of God's love concretized in a human person. She is truly our Mother, but she is to us more than any mother, and we come to God through her and with her. When an artist creates a work that is his masterpiece, he puts something of himself into it—"his heart is in it," we say. We see the artist reflected in his art, and in some way we come to know him better through his art. And of course, the honor paid to the art is paid to the artist—to ignore his masterpiece or downplay it would be an incredible insult. If Michelangelo asks you over for a visit to show you his newest sculpture, and you say, "Ah, no, I'm just here to see you," his reaction can be well imagined. This is so with God and His masterpiece as well, but on a much deeper level: when we see God's Masterpiece, Mary, we see Him reflected there in a special way not seen in any other human person; only Jesus, a Divine Person, exceeds her in this reflection. The masterpiece points back to the artist and she brings us to Him because she lives only in union with Him.[1]

Our primary end and focus then is Christ, and our secondary end is Mary, but it must be understood in the right way: the primary does not exclude the secondary, but rather leads to it, and even this leading to and focus on the secondary end is a participation in the primary end. To love Michelangelo's sculpture alongside him is directly loving and participating in a friendship with Michelangelo. With Mary we go to Jesus, and the closer our union with Him becomes, the more His dispositions become our own—our heart begins to be fashioned like to His Heart, and after God, Jesus' Heart is on fire with love of Mary, so much so that He totally gives Himself to her and becomes incarnate within her. His love becomes our love, and where He is we are. Thus union with God always means union with Mary.

In Scripture, God cannot help but talk about Mary. She is present in Scripture from beginning to end as uppermost in God's mind from eternity. And since God does not change, this means that Jesus, the Second Person of the Trinity, must as God have had Mary uppermost on His mind during His entire life on earth. "Mary most holy was predestined by God from all eternity 'in one and the same decree' with the Word Incarnate, as the bull *Ineffabilis Deus* affirms,"[2] and we also were destined with Jesus in that one decree. Putting on Christ[3] then necessarily implies that Mary is to me what she is to Jesus. And after God, she is everything to Jesus. She is His Mom, His sister, His mystical spouse, His most precious daughter. We will never comprehend fully either Mary, that finest of all masterpieces, or God's love for her. It's not only for us that she's "a personal romance," she is God's "personal romance" first and foremost! And God's love for her is the model and matrix of every love that men and women have ever borne toward a woman, whether she be mom or sweetheart, sister or daughter.

In the Old Testament we begin to know this masterpiece in prophetic form, a form that will be fulfilled in the New Testament; but the Old Testament in itself presents profound characteristics of this Woman. And this makes complete sense: the Old Testament is a sort of *commentary* on the New Testament, whereby we understand better what God is revealing in the New Testament.[4] But it should also be kept in mind that there is one whole Bible; that is, one whole Salvation History with distinct sections. Within this schema, there are the Old and New Testaments; within those Testaments are distinct books; within those books are distinct scenes. But all of this comprises one book that is one portrait, with varied colors, nuances and shades of beauty such as any good artist employs in his paintings. Thus the Old Testament simply flows into the New as one complete and integrated story where we find a cohesive (though not comprehensive) portrait of Mary. In the Old Testament we are, so to speak, told all about her by God, then introduced to the beautiful young Lady of God's dreams and ours in the New.[5]

From Scripture and Tradition dogmas and doctrines flow as the Magisterium correctly interprets divine Revelation. The portrait becomes still more detailed as these layers of loveliness are added. As the Marian saying goes, *de Maria numquam satis*: "of Mary there is never enough." It is upon Scripture, Tradition, and the Teaching of the Church (dogmas and doctrines) that consecration to Mary is understood. God creates His Beloved and He gives us to her and her to us…consecration is accepting this "romance" fully in a total gift of self to Mary and a total reception of Mary to oneself. After all, it would be absurd to have a beloved and be a beloved and do nothing about it. In Shakespeare's *The Merchant of Venice* Bassanio is in love with Portia, the beautiful Lady of Belmont, and she loves him. But the play would have suffered an abrupt and unpleasant ending had Bassanio's reaction been, "It's nice and all that we are passionately in love with each other, but I think I'll just go watch a play, eat an early supper and head off to bed." Such a reaction would be what philosophers call an inappropriate "value response" in light of the good that is authentic love; preferring to be alone when confronted with love would be a disvalue. When God gives us to Mary and Mary to us that we might live in deepest bonds of union with her, and through her with God, it would be the epitome of a disordered value response to live as though one is oblivious to the reality.

It is for these reasons that this book is ordered the way it is: from Scripture and Tradition (where we are presented with the Beloved) we move to dogma and doctrine (where we are given more detail about her), and then follows an outline of what an acceptance of this gift looks like (consecration to Mary). It is only after this that apparitions of Mary (those approved by the Church) are brought into the picture; what we know of her is based primarily on public Revelation, which ended with the death of the last Apostle, but subsequent, truly supernatural visits of Mary enhance what we already know—Mary helps us understand God's public Revelation better (she never adds any new material to public Revelation *qua* public Revelation) and she acts as the Mother and Beloved she is to us by gently warning, encouraging, guiding and consoling. Her visits are meant to strengthen our relationship with her and her Son, just as the visit of one's beloved after an absence brings joy, consolation and a deepening of love and union.

A Word on What this Book is and is Not

There are a great many Marian passages and elements in this book, and yet, there are many that are not, and no doubt the question would arise but for this *nota bene*, "Why did he not include_____?" But this volume is not meant to be a thorough *compendium* of introductory, general, or advanced Mariology. It is a theological and philosophical portrait that is both simple and complex, with shallows and deeps, incorporating a variety of elements in order to craft an overall and specific portrait of Mary as the Beloved. This portrait is one small piece of a puzzle that is Mary, one fragment of a mirror that refracts her image. Given this, I am not presenting a full treatment of each Marian Scriptural prophecy and event, nor of each doctrine and dogma, and while some aspects covered are basic, others are more complicated. Certainly the verses and passages could be multiplied *ad quasi infinitum* concerning the theme of this book, and it is my hope that I and others will write more books with still more details based on the reality of Mary as Beloved. May we, in the very depths of our hearts, always be ravished by her gentle, charming love.

A Note Concerning Scripture Passages

Pondering the Scripture passages pertinent to Mary wonderfully expands one's knowledge, understanding and love of her. Given this, I have included copious Scripture passages to ponder. But further, concerning the Old Testament passages, these are Scriptures that Mary read too. What is included herein then is both the Word of God and also, as historical point of fact, *Mary's reading material*! You are reading her books and pondering what she pondered. Friends and lovers will often read the same novel together as a way of nurturing their bond. This is truly what is happening in regard to us and Mary when we read these Old Testament passages. If you asked her what she was reading and she handed you some books, some would be books of the Old Testament. This is how Scripture should be read: as love letters from God that we ponder with Mary by our side, and indeed in her arms and by her Heart.

Finally, most Scripture passages are taken from the *Douay-Rheims* Bible. This biblical translation faithfully and literally translates the words of the original languages, often giving this version a depth that other versions lack; however, no translation can completely convey what the original words mean, and so at times, in order to bring out various aspects, the Revised Standard Version Catholic Edition (*RSVCE*) is used, and this is noted in the text or endnotes.

—Notes—

1. Perhaps one of the most consoling aspects of Mary's love is that it is morally impossible that a soul *truly devoted* to her will be lost, as St. Alphonsus Liguori writes in his book, *The Glories of Mary*. But it's important to make a distinction: "truly devoted"=trying to be holy, and getting up if there is a fall. False devotion, a species of the sin of presumption, is using devotion to Mary as an excuse to sin or persist in sin.
2. Fr. Stefano Manelli, *All Generations Shall Call Me Blessed, Biblical Mariology*, p. 105
3. Romans 13:14 "But put ye on the Lord Jesus Christ, and make not provision for the flesh in its concupiscences." We might note here too that along with putting on Christ, one must be pure, not lustful; making no provision for the flesh implies not only that Christ is pure and so must we be, but Mary is as well. To be one with Christ is to be one with Mary, as both she and Jesus are "predestined by God from all eternity 'in one and the same decree'…"
4. Scott Hahn, *Consuming the Word*, p. 4
5. Venerable Fulton Sheen, *The World's First Love*, chapter 1

—Section One—

The Old Testament
A Sketch of the Beloved

"We can affirm, then, at once that the Mariology of the Old Testament has all the essential characteristics of a Mariology at its 'roots.' In that Mariology are contained in fact the 'roots' of that unique, precious plant that is Mary most holy. From those 'roots' has sprung, in the New Testament, the one 'full of grace,' the Mother of God and of the new humanity."

–Fr. Stefano Manelli, FI,
All Generations Shall Call Me Blessed, p. 111

Chapter One
Beauty and Strength

The Golden Thread

It is often said that Mary is little mentioned in Scripture. Yet this leads to a pertinent question: if the Marian maxims are true (which they are), "There is no Jesus without Mary, and no Mary without Jesus," and *De Maria numquam satis* ("Of Mary there is never enough"), and if what St. Alphonsus Liguori says is true—that true devotion to Mary equals a moral certainty of salvation[1]—then *why* is there so little of Mary in Scripture? Or perhaps the question should be, "Is there more of Mary in Scripture than I realized?" A distinction here needs to be made. It is true that there is very little *explicit* mention of Mary in Scripture. There are indeed rather few direct references to Mary in the New Testament (though packed with more information than many realize), but that does not mean God has not spoken of Mary in other books of the Bible in an *implicit* way. In fact, it would be remarkable that Mary, so utterly involved with our redemption, the Mother of God and our spiritual Mother, the one without whose "yes" God would not become incarnate, would be barely mentioned in Scripture. Further, the Saints tell us that God was so enamored of Mary's beauty that He was captivated by her.[2] It would be incredible then if God were to speak almost nothing of this Woman in His own Book! After all, how important must she be if God Himself is literally captivated by her, and since that is the case would He not speak of her…a lot? The logical conclusion is that there is a deep Marian treasure mine in Scripture, and indeed a little digging reveals that Mary is like a golden thread that is woven from the beginning to the end of this sacred tapestry, a golden thread that is found in the very warp and woof of the fabric. This reality is so vivid that we could coin a new name for her: Mary, the Golden Thread. Of course, a garment is nothing if there is only thread and no cloth; so, too, Mary is nothing without Jesus and without Jesus there is no salvation. However, not by necessity but by God's will He has determined that the garment of salvation will not be woven without the Golden Thread. This Thread we pick up at the beginning of Scripture, in Genesis, and we begin, fittingly, with a beautiful woman…

Eve

What are we to make of feminine beauty? We could look first to Adam's reaction: "This now is bone of my bones, and flesh of my flesh; she shall be called woman, because she was taken out of man."[3] But we have to put ourselves in Adam's place to conjure in our imaginations the right tone of his voice—an ecstatic, astonished, smitten, "Wow!" All Adam had seen before was animals, no person, no place where beauty was concentrated in a human person. There had been no one who was fit for him, no one who stood in complementary contrast to him…and suddenly he sees pure feminine beauty—Eve. If you are a man, you have no doubt pondered the beauty of women, and have also said on occasion, "Wow" (and you may have married her too), and if you are a woman you have probably wondered about the mysterious power your beauty has upon others.

To understand the beauty of women, we have to take into account what God said of Eve: "And the Lord God said: It is not good for man to be alone: let us make him a help like unto himself."[4] So, she is a helpmate. But help for what? To cook meals? To bring Adam a drink? Encourage him with a kiss? All true, but Adam could have encouraged her as well in this way. Rather, her role is much more fundamental than these things. As helpmate, not only by her talents but by her loveliness and charm, her sweetness and virtue, she was meant to lead Adam to God, his Father and hers, and encourage him to fight the devil that had appeared in the Garden. Beauty is meant to lead to God, thus Woman was meant to lead others to God.[5] That is her primal role. She is *by nature* mediatrix, not only mediating new human life by bearing and nourishing her children, but she is mediator also by mediating in the sense of lifting man up to God, as the goodness of her beauty is a reflection of His.

The split between men and women due to the fall thus is a chasm. Woman became an anti-mediatrix: instead of encouraging Adam to die for God his Father and to protect Eve, his bride, she encouraged him to listen to the devil. Nevertheless, we do see the great strength of woman in Eve. Adam stood there silent; Eve made the mistake of engaging the devil in conversation, but at the very least she held her ground against the monster as best she could, while Adam let his fair love tangle with the dragon. Here then we find a trait that is complementary to her beauty: tenacious durability amidst all manner of difficulties. This concatenation of traits is remarkable, and somewhat unexpected. Women possess refined, elegant beauty, yet that delicate, charming creature is strong: strong enough to care for husband and children, strong enough to follow the Savior to the Cross and remain there with Him as He is crucified—and here we do not mean only Mary, who, we shall see, is *the* Strong Woman, but the other women with her. Opposed to those women, there was but one man, St. John, and no doubt if it were not for the Mother of God he wouldn't have been there.

Immediately following this horrific instance of anti-mediation in Genesis, where beauty, that special image of God's own beauty, is used to lure man away from God instead of to Him, we find woman again, but this time in a hint at a new creation: "I will put enmities between thee and the woman, and thy seed and her seed: she shall crush thy head, and thou shalt lie in wait for her heel."[6] This Woman, however, is clearly not Eve. "Enmity" means irreconcilable, absolute opposition, and there is no possibility of Eve claiming enmity since she has transgressed and gone over to the devil's side. And sin puts one in the opposing camp. Eve is against the devil later, but by its very nature "enmity" is ruled out as something Eve could possess post-fall. This Woman, who will with her seed crush the serpent, could only be a different and altogether unique woman: this woman will not only be at enmity with the devil, she will, while a mother, yet be and remain virginal—notice there is no mention of a father, because the Messiah has only God for His Father. Yet there is a parallel between the Woman who is at enmity with the dragon and Eve: as Eve was instrumental in man's fall, so this promised Woman will be instrumental in the work of man's restoration.

The word "enmity" can tell us more though. Enmity is radical. Think of God: He is at enmity with the devil; God is absolutely good, "Our Father," Who gives life in abundance, while the devil is a murderer from the beginning, the father of sin and death. There is in God not even a shadow of evil. The only other person in the history of the world who shares this radical opposition with God is the Woman mentioned in Genesis 3:15. In other words, after God, there is no one more holy than this Woman. Thus the Church states, "The 'splendor of an entirely unique holiness' by which Mary is 'enriched from the first instant of her conception' comes wholly from Christ: she is 'redeemed, in a more exalted fashion, by reason of the merits of her Son.' The Father blessed Mary more than any other created person 'in Christ with every spiritual blessing in the heavenly places' and chose her 'in Christ before the foundation of the world, to be holy and blameless before him in love.'"[7] In other words, she is "All-Holy."[8]

And so Scripture begins with two women who are each mediatrix to a spouse: the first is beautiful, immaculate, and strong enough to at least attempt to confront the evil one. She is not, however, "full of grace," she is not *the* Woman, and in the combat Eve falls, becoming an anti-mediatrix. This first woman, spouse of Adam, is a foretaste of *the* Woman, who will be still more beautiful, and whose strength, flowing from her total holiness, is such that she will not only confront the devil, but will utterly crush his head. This second Woman will be both Mother and mystical spouse of the New Adam, and she will assist Him in defeating the devil, thereby mediating salvation, not death, to mankind.

And this is not the only time in the Old Testament we will find mention of the Woman and her confrontation with the devil; there will be another vision of enmity in the book of Proverbs, where we will meet the Woman and her Seed in a sort of eschatological show-down with the evil spirit. Prior to the vision of that Lady's character and strength, however, let's follow the pattern set in Genesis, which is in accord with our human nature. Adam was not first confronted with Eve's *strength*, but with her ravishing beauty that he sees with his eyes and that draws him to Eve, and that was meant to draw him to God.

—Notes—

1. *The Glories of Mary*, Part I, chapter viii, "Mary Delivers her Clients from Hell," p. 220
2. St. Alphonsus Liguori, *The Glories of Mary*, from discourse IV on the Annunciation: "…the Holy Spirit so much praised the beauty of this his spouse for her eyes, which were like those of a dove: 'How beautiful art thou, my love! how, beautiful art thou! thy eyes are like doves eyes;' because Mary, looking on God with the eyes of a simple, humble dove, he was so much enamored of her beauty, that with the bands of love she made him a prisoner in her virginal womb."
3. Genesis 2:23
4. ibid 2:18
5. *Catechism of the Catholic Church*, 341 "The beauty of creation reflects the infinite beauty of the Creator and ought to inspire the respect and submission of man's intellect and will." There are lev-

els of beauty. In the realm of physical beauty, a bird has a certain beauty, as does a tree. There is a certain beauty when we see a mother duck care for her ducklings. A beautiful woman, however, exceeds them all, as does a woman caring for her little ones. Woman's reflection of God's beauty thus inspires mankind all the more to submit himself to God in love, from Whom all beauty flows.

6. Genesis 3:15. The *RSVCE* has a different, but also correct, variation: "I will put enmity between you and the woman, and between your seed and her seed; he shall bruise your head, and you shall bruise his heel." In the *Douay-Rheims*, the Woman crushes the devil, and this happens in three ways: 1) she crushes the devil by her Immaculate Conception, where she overcomes sin; 2) she crushes the devil by her Assumption, where she overcomes death; 3) and she crushes the devil of course as she brings forth the Messiah. Hence the *RSVCE* is also correct: Mary, by her seed, Jesus, crushes the devil.
7. *Catechism of the Catholic Church*, 492
8. ibid, 493

Chapter Two
Mary's Type of Beauty

God created human beings with an elemental need and desire for beauty. We also have an innate need and desire to be loved unconditionally and nurtured, and we naturally long for union with beauty—we want to melt into it, become part of it, not to the loss of self but to a oneness, much like wax, melting from two different candles that are sitting side by side, flows down and becomes one mix of wax, yet both sets of wax remain distinct. We notice this desire when we gaze at natural beauty such as sunsets, and particularly when we encounter a beloved person. Indeed, our hearts deeply desire that the one by whom we want to be nurtured and with whom we want to be one be…lovely. Of course, the greatest, most intense beauty is found most potently in persons; this is no surprise (though it is a mystery to ponder), since the Holy Trinity, the ultimate font of beauty, Who is Beauty, is a Holy Trinity of *Persons*. But what of human persons? It is through Mary that God fulfills the human heart's desire in regard to beauty in a unique way, a way that is only exceeded by God Himself, and it is in Mary, the Woman, that He especially wants to demonstrate His nurturing and beauty in a human person, a human person of absolute beauty of soul and body, a whole human person who is a sort of incarnation of God's love. Scripture alludes to the incredible rarity of fairness this Woman possesses by telling us in Ecclesiasticus 13:32 that, "The token of a good heart, and a good countenance thou shalt hardly find, and with labour." Where can both total feminine loveliness coupled with total goodness be found? Hardly anywhere—only in one place, though there are a few examples, "types" of Mary, who are so amazing that God holds them up as a sort of preview of *the* Woman to come.

Types

A "type" is like a charcoal drawing of a person: it is a dim presentiment, a likeness merely, but one that points to a reality that absolutely supersedes the model, or "type." In other words, a "type" is a prophetic "rough sketch" that will be surpassed by the painting itself. Aside from Eve, there are several types of Mary in the Old Testament, and seven will be considered here, though two have no proper name and one type is not a person: Rebecca, Rachel, Judith, Esther and Bathsheba, the Bride in the *Canticle of Canticles* (*Song of Songs*) and *the Ark of the Covenant.*

Rebecca

Scripture tells us she was,

> An exceeding comely maid, and a most beautiful virgin, and not known to man: and she went down to the

> spring, and filled her pitcher and was coming back. And the servant ran to meet her, and said: Give me a little water to drink of thy pitcher. And she answered: Drink, my lord. And quickly she let down the pitcher upon her arm, and gave him drink. And when he had drunk, she said: I will draw water for thy camels also, till they all drink. And pouring out the pitcher into the troughs, she ran back to the well to draw water: and having drawn she gave to all the camels.[1]

The spring is a symbol of life-giving water, and the pitchers are reminiscent of the huge jugs of water at Cana that Jesus transforms into wine. Rebecca's beauty is evident, both of body and of heart: she is virginal, pure, humble, and selfless.

Rachel

"Rachel was well favoured, and of a beautiful countenance. And Jacob being in love with her, said: I will serve thee seven years for Rachel thy younger daughter."[2] Rachel is also taking care of a flock, in this case her father's sheep. She is of incredible beauty, such that she is worth Jacob serving someone for seven years in order to obtain her as his wife. Seven is a perfect number, the number of completeness: creation is complete after seven days, there are seven Sacraments, and so on. Rachel is worth perfectly preparing for, and the number seven here also reflects upon Rachel herself. Only a woman of astonishing winsomeness of character and body would be worth waiting a *perfect* amount of time for.

Judith

And she was exceedingly beautiful, and her husband left her great riches, and very many servants, and large possessions of herds of oxen, and flocks of sheep. And she was greatly renowned among all, because she feared the Lord very much, neither was there any one that spoke an ill word of her.[3]

And she washed her body, and anointed herself with the best ointment, and plaited the hair of her head, and put a bonnet upon her head, and clothed herself with the garments of her gladness, and put sandals on her feet, and took her bracelets, and lilies, and earlets, and rings, and adorned herself with all her ornaments. And the Lord also gave her more beauty: because all this dressing up did not proceed from sensuality, lent from virtue: and therefore the Lord increased this her beauty, so that she appeared to all men's eyes incomparably lovely. And she gave to her maid a bottle of wine to carry, and a vessel of oil, and parched corn, and dry figs, and bread and cheese, and went out.

And when they came to the gate of the city, they found Ozias, and the ancients of the city waiting. And when they saw her they were astonished, and admired her beauty exceedingly. But they asked her no question, only they let her pass, saying: "The God of our fathers give thee grace, and may he strengthen all the counsel of thy heart with his power, that Jerusalem may glory in thee, and thy name may be in the number of the holy and just."[4]

> And when the men [the Assyrian watchmen, enemies of God's people, to whom Judith went in order to slay the general of their army] had heard her words, they beheld her face, and their eyes were amazed, for they wondered exceedingly at her beauty.[5]
>
> ...and they admired her wisdom, and they said one to another: There is not such another woman upon earth in look, in beauty, and in sense of words.[6]
>
> She anointed her face with ointment, and bound up her locks with a crown, she took a new robe to deceive him [Holofernes, Assyrian army general]. Her sandals ravished his eyes, her beauty made his soul her captive...[7]

Such is the description of this woman—at that time, there was no one fairer. This acclamation pertains not only to her physical beauty, but in a vivid way to her character as well. The rest of the last quoted Scripture verse goes like this: "...her beauty made his soul her captive, with a sword she cut off his head." It is in this way that Judith saves her people: she smites the head of her enemy, like cutting the head off a snake, thus connecting this forerunner of Mary with the prophecy of the purely beautiful Woman of Genesis 3:15: "...she shall crush thy head..." And it doesn't end there! The image of Mary we see in Judith becomes still more apparent:

> And when she had said this, she went to the pillar that was at his bed's head, and loosed his sword that hung tied upon it. And when she had drawn it out, she took him by the hair of his head, and said: Strengthen me, O

> Lord God, at this hour. And she struck twice upon his neck, and cut off his head, and took off his canopy from the pillars, and rolled away his headless body.
>
> And after a while she went out, and delivered the head of Holofernes to her maid, and bade her put it into her wallet. And they two went out according to their custom, as it were to prayer, and they passed the camp, and having compassed the valley, they came to the gate of the city. And Judith from afar off cried to the watchmen upon the walls: Open the gates for God is with us, who hath shewn his power in Israel. And it came to pass, when the men had heard her voice, that they called the ancients of the city. And all ran to meet her from the least to the greatest: for they now had no hopes that she would come.
>
> And lighting up lights they all gathered round about her: and she went up to a higher place, and commanded silence to be made. And when all had held their peace, Judith said: Praise ye the Lord our God, who hath not forsaken them that hope in him. And by me his handmaid he hath fulfilled his mercy, which he promised to the house of Israel: and he hath killed the enemy of his people by my hand this night.[8]

Despite the overwhelming odds, this handmaid of the Lord holds to faith and hope, and because of her "yes" to God she utterly defeats the enemy. In a word, here in the book of Judith we find a sort of implicit, yet vivid, pre-enactment of the Annunciation, where, hundreds of years after Judith, Mary, the pre-eminent handmaid, gives her "yes" to the Lord, and with a faith far exceeding

Judith's. Mary's "yes" results in the Incarnation of God the Son, with Whom she will crush the ancient serpent's head, the general of the fallen angels. And just as St. Elizabeth's "Blessed are you among women," follows Mary's "yes," so Mary's type, Judith, has a similar experience after her victory over the Assyrians:

> ...Blessed art thou, O daughter, by the Lord the most high God, above all women upon the earth. Blessed be the Lord who made heaven and earth, who hath directed thee to the cutting off the head of the prince of our enemies. Because he hath so magnified thy name this day, that thy praise shall not depart out of the mouth of men who shall be mindful of the power of the Lord forever, for that thou hast not spared thy life, by reason of the distress and tribulation of thy people, but hast prevented our ruin in the presence of our God.[9]
>
> And Joachim the high priest came from Jerusalem to Bethulia with all his ancients to see Judith. And when she was come out to him, they all blessed her with one voice, saying: Thou art the glory of Jerusalem, thou art the joy of Israel, thou art the honour of our people: For thou hast done manfully, and thy heart has been strengthened, because thou hast loved chastity, and after thy husband hast not known any other: therefore also the hand of the Lord hath strengthened thee, and therefore thou shalt be blessed forever. And all the people said: So be it, so be it.[10]

And so, with Judith we find a mixture of exceeding loveliness and brave faithfulness.

Esther

With Esther a slightly different facet comes into focus: beauty and intercession while in the throes of great agony. She "...was exceeding fair beautiful"[11] and "...her incredible beauty made her appear agreeable and amiable in the eyes of all."[12] The king was no less affected. One risked death by appearing before him unbidden, yet,

> ...when he saw Esther the queen standing, she pleased his eyes, and he held out toward her the golden sceptre, which he held in his hand: and she drew near, and kissed the top of his sceptre. And the king said to her: What wilt then, queen Esther? what is thy request? if thou shouldst even ask one half of the kingdom, it shall be given to thee.[13]

A second time Esther intercedes:

> What is thy petition, Esther, that it may be granted thee? And what wilt thou have done: although thou ask the half of my kingdom, thou shalt have it.[14] She had "...a rosy colour in her face," and "...gracious and bright eyes," although these "hid a mind full of anguish, and exceeding great fear."[15]

Esther is a portrait of Mary as Queen-Advocate between us and God, and in her we find, like Mary, beauty, holiness, sorrow, and intercession. As Esther intercedes for the Jewish people with the entirety of her selfhood, so Mary will do at the Cross.

Bathsheba

In the meantime it happened that David arose from his bed after noon, and walked upon the roof of the king's house: and he saw from the roof of his house a woman washing herself, over against him: and the woman was very beautiful. And the king sent, and inquired who the woman was. And it was told him, that she was Bethsabee the daughter of Eliam, the wife of Urias the Hethite.[16]

And the days that David reigned in Israel, were forty years: in Hebron he reigned seven years, in Jerusalem thirty-three. And Solomon sat upon the throne of his father David, and his kingdom was strengthened exceedingly. And Adonias the son of Haggith came to Bethsabee the mother of Solomon. And she said to him: Is thy coming peaceable? he answered: Peaceable. And he added: I have a word to speak with thee. She said to him: Speak. And he said: Thou knowest that the kingdom was mine, and all Israel had preferred me to be their king: but the kingdom is transferred, and is become my brother's: for it was appointed him by the Lord.

Now therefore I ask one petition of thee: turn not away my face. And she said to him: Say on. And he said: I pray thee speak to king Solomon (for he cannot deny thee any thing) to give me Abisag the Sunamitess to wife. And Bethsabee said: Well, I will speak for thee to the king. Then Bethsabee came to king Solomon, to speak to him for Adonias: and the king arose to meet her, and bowed to her, and sat down upon his throne:

> and a throne was set for the king' s mother, and she sat on his right hand. And she said to him: I desire one small petition of thee, do not put me to confusion. And the king said to her: My mother, ask: for I must not turn away thy face.[17]

With the coming of Bathsheba (in the *Douay-Rheims* "Bethsabee"), we find again great beauty and greater and more clear intercession: she sits at the right of the king (her son, Solomon), she intercedes, and people know they can go to her and that she will listen to them and present their petitions to the king as she deems the best way to do so, because she knows the king better than anyone—after all, he is her son.

In considering these types of Mary, from Eve to Bathsheba, an interesting progression presents itself: with Eve we learn little, directly, of her beauty and character; when we come to Rebecca there is more detail; Rachel is worth waiting a perfect fulfillment of time for; Judith is stunning, brave and full of faith; Esther is an intoxicating combination of physical beauty, holiness and sorrow that the king cannot resist; and Bathsheba is not only so lovely as to attract David, from whose line will come the Messiah, she is also an incredibly clear type of Mary as Queen Mother. In fact, there are several progressions here, pertinently including the responsibility these women have:

1) Rebecca: beautiful, *tends to flock of camels*, becomes wife of Isaac, mother of Jacob (his sons the progenitors of the twelve tribes of Israel).
2) Rachel, still more beautiful, *tends to flock of sheep*, becomes wife of Jacob and mother of Joseph (exiled to Egypt and saves

his people during the famine).

3) Judith *owns her own flocks*, is "exceedingly beautiful" and captivates an enemy general, whose head she bravely cuts off.
4) Esther wins the heart of a king, becomes a queen, and saves her people by her beauty and tender holiness in interceding for the Jews with the king. *She tends to her people.*
5) Bathsheba enchants David, not just any king, but king of Israel from whose line will come the Incarnate God, and she becomes not merely a queen, but *Queen Mother of Israel.*

Then we come to Mary. As amazing as the above women were, they are as sign posts that point to the coming destination, the main objective. Mary is not merely beautiful, she is Immaculate in her humanity (body and soul). God Himself will take His flesh from her, not from muddy clay, but from Immaculate soil. Mary captivates not a merely human king, but God Himself! As St. Alphonsus Liguori writes, "For Mary, looking at God with the eyes of a simple and humble dove, enamored him to such a degree by her beauty, that with the bands of love she made him a prisoner in her chaste womb."[18] She becomes the Mother of the King of Kings; she is the Daughter, Mother and Spouse of God. She becomes our Mother as well, *the Mother and Queen of all*, not the Jewish people only. And her intercession is unfailing, for all: "…never was it known that anyone who has fled to thy protection, implored thy help or sought thy intercession was left unaided…"[19] There is thus a distinct advance from one type of Mary to another, and from those types to Mary herself, in beauty, in responsibility, and in proximity to the Messiah. If the people who saw Judith were stunned to see her, we can hardly imagine what it must have been like to see Mary walk by. Yet, two more types must be mentioned…

The Bride in the Song of Songs (Canticle of Canticles)

The *Song of Songs* is a love song about a bride and a bridegroom. Yet we have to ask a crucial question: who is the bride, and who is the groom? We could say that at its heart this book is a love letter from God about Mary, yet we are implicated in this book as well. Notice that this book is right in the middle of the Bible! Why? Because it is a sort of summary of the life of union that each soul is meant to have with God; after all, the goal of love is union. The groom can be God and each of us by analogy the bride. The groom can be the Person of the Son and the bride the Church. But there is something more here; as Fr. Manelli points out, the *Song of Songs* is "Mariologically watermarked,"[20] and the description of the bride is a sort of summary of all we have read thus far. Most especially, the bride is Mary. In a way that will become more clear in the section on consecration to Mary, we can also say that the groom is the soul, you and I, in the sense that we are one with Christ and in the sense that this is the love that Mary has for each of us—she loves us, the rest of her children, as she loves Jesus. Given these theological realities, the *Song of Songs* provides a still more filled-in sketch of Mary, shading it in hitherto unsuspected elements of her rare beauty and beginning to add color to the sketch—a vivid red, for the love that burns in her Heart hotter than all the stars put together.

The focal point of this book is certainly on the bride. Think of any wedding—no one says, "Great Scott, look at the groom, how stunning!" As with Adam and Eve, the "wow" in this book is directed at the bride. It's her day. One line, however, concentrates into a few words the many wondrous details of the bride in this book: "O fairest among women."[21] The rest of the book unpacks this, exclaiming her beauty in myriad ways...

Beauty that we see

Her "cheeks as beautiful as the turtledove's," her "neck as jewels."[22] "How beautiful art thou, my love, how beautiful art thou! thy eyes are doves' eyes, besides what is hid within."[23] The holy author goes on to praise her perfect hair ("thy hair is as flocks of goats"—i.e. beautifully, luxuriously flowing) and her perfect teeth ("as flocks of sheep, that are shorn which come up from the washing, all with twins, and there is none barren among them"—i.e. totally white, and none are missing; perfect teeth even in our days of modern orthodontics are tough to come by!).[24] And "Thy lips are as a scarlet lace: and thy speech sweet. Thy cheeks are as a piece of a pomegranate."[25] "As the lily among thorns, so is my love among the daughters."[26] "Thou art beautiful, O my love, sweet and comely as Jerusalem: terrible as an army set in array" (not only is she ravishingly, softly beautiful, she is strong—her absolute purity gives her total defeat over all that is impure).[27] So striking is she that Solomon has to keep searching for better ways to express her, and so he goes on to compare her, as any man would his beloved, with the heavens: she "cometh forth as the morning rising, fair as the moon, bright as the sun."[28] Sunsets and sunrises, the moon and the sun and all the stars, present some of the most incredible beauty of the natural world. In fact, the colors of sunsets and sunrises are so beautiful they can convert hearts to God, since confronted with such beauty the mind often says, "Such beauty can't come from nothing, nor from anything other than a Being Who is absolutely good." The silvery moon and the twinkling stars can also have this effect, one we often miss with city lights. But in the country they can still be seen and hold one enraptured. It is to these displays of beauty that Solomon compares the bride. If he could have found better analogies to his bride, he would have used them. And he does go on, this time raving about her by a description from tip to top (the *RSVCE* is somewhat clearer in its translation of this description):

> How graceful are your feet in sandals, O queenly maiden! Your rounded thighs are like jewels, the work of a master hand. Your navel is a rounded bowl that never lacks mixed wine. Your belly is a heap of wheat, encircled with lilies. Your two breasts are like two fawns, twins of a gazelle. Your neck is like an ivory tower. Your eyes are pools in Heshbon, by the gate of Bath-rabbim. Your nose is like a tower of Lebanon, overlooking Damascus. Your head crowns you like Carmel, and your flowing locks are like purple; a king is held captive in the tresses. How fair and pleasant you are, O loved one, delectable maiden! You are stately as a palm tree…

There are some key phrases here, and while Solomon praises her physical attractiveness, even how she holds herself ("stately as a palm tree"), it shouldn't be taken in a carnal sense (something that has to be reiterated in these times when people, obsessed with the carnal aspect of life, speak of food, books, movies, art, and everything else as "sexy"—that is not what is meant here, though the physical attractiveness, as well as the spiritual, is literally true). And so Solomon starts from the ground and works his way up, from her feet to her hair. This is a portrait of someone who is purity and beauty itself. That is what Solomon is getting at and why he writes of her that she has "*graceful* feet," a "neck like an *ivory tower*," that she is "*fair*," and in other places that she is "all fair, O my love, and there is not a spot in thee" (*Songs* 4:7), a "lily" (*Songs* 2:2), and "a garden enclosed, a fountain sealed up" (*Songs* 4:12). The whole of the *Song of Songs* tells of an all-pure Lady, and she must be absolutely, uniquely pure since Solomon includes in his description, for example, her feet (not normally part of a description of beauty *and* purity).[29] But there is much more. She is made by a "master hand," the impression being—along with phrases that tell us she is absolutely unique amongst all other women—that God made her as a special masterpiece. Her belly—her womb—is a "heap of wheat": she is *fruitful* (how can he know this before marrying her? Again, this points to the fact that what is meant here is not to be taken in a carnal sense, but in the sense of a womb fruitful with eternal life Incarnate), and is "encircled with lilies." Lilies, the flower of purity; her womb is *pure*. Stepping back a phrase, he also says that her belly never lacks "mixed wine"—this is a truly astonishing phrase, and hold on to it, because it will be better understood when we come to the meal of Lady Wisdom a few chapters from now. So her womb is fruitful, pure, and won't lack mixed wine.

The rest of this description is also powerful. When God makes His own Mom, He does it right. She will be the picture of utter feminine elegance, and that beauty includes her breasts—and it's not simply a fact of her beauty, it is important for a mom and her baby! St. Francis De Sales speaks of this at the spiritual level, saying in one of his homilies about Mary, "Although in reality she has borne only Him in her womb, she has nevertheless borne all Christians in the Person of her Divine Son… Blest is the womb that bore You and the breasts that nursed You! We have all been fed from these sacred breasts, for our Lord nursed and took His nourishment from them…"[30] So again, this passage is not to be taken in a carnal sort of way; the simple fact is God made women to be special reflections of His beauty, His nurturing of His creation and His gentleness[31]; Solomon then goes on to speak of her eyes again—pure reflections of her soul, like a deep pool reflecting the heavens at night. Even her nose is beautifully sculpted, and her hair is "like purple"—not literally purple, but a woman's hair is her glory, and this woman's glory is shaded purple—and purple is the color of royalty; thus, Solomon is speaking of a woman who is queen, the spouse of the king. And further, so beautiful is her hair that she holds the king captive in her tresses!

In a word, God desired to make this Woman of whom He has thought of from eternity so like Himself in beauty and holiness that she is irresistible (not that God could not resist her, but He wanted to make her such that He would not resist her, finding in her nothing to resist because finding in her an image so like Himself that if she were any closer to God she would be God—she, a human person!).

Thus, the bride as type of Mary is a sort of mosaic image made up of all the previous types of Mary, one grand image-type! But Solomon is not done yet…

Beauty of scent

It is said of some Saints, such as St. Joseph of Cupertino, that they could smell sin. What then must someone who is immaculate and full of grace, all fair, smell like? A bouquet of roses, lilies and lilacs conjures the heavenly scent of Mary to our imaginations, and this is certainly true. Solomon, however, goes into more detail, so much so that he leaves us with the notion of a perfume that arises from Mary's innermost being, passes from soul to body (because the two in her exist in perfectly integrated unison due to her Immaculate Conception), and tantalizes all who encounter her.

She "goeth up by the desert, as a pillar of smoke of aromatical spices, of myrrh, and frankincense, and of all the powders of the perfumer"[32] "…the sweet smell of thy ointments [is] above all aromatical spices."[33] She has the scent of "pomegranates with the fruits of the orchard. Cypress with spikenard. Spikenard and saffron, sweet cane and cinnamon, with all the trees of Libanus, myrrh and aloes with all the chief perfumes."[34] Her breath has the scent of apples.[35]

Wow

What else can Solomon say of this woman? In the middle of the book, he puts everything he just said into a concise paragraph, like a New Adam confronted with the New Eve, and in fact, since a primary understanding of this book is Jesus as groom and Mary as bride, this is precisely what is happening—a recapitulation of Adam's "wow":

> You have ravished my heart, my sister, my bride, you have ravished my heart with a glance of your eyes, with one jewel of your necklace. How sweet is your love, my sister, my bride! how much better is your love than wine, and the fragrance of your oils than any spice! Your lips distil nectar, my bride; honey and milk are under your tongue; the scent of your garments is like the scent of Lebanon [frankincense]. A garden locked is my sister, my bride, a garden locked, a fountain sealed. Your shoots are an orchard of pomegranates with all choicest fruits, henna with nard, nard and saffron, calamus and cinnamon, with all trees of frankincense, myrrh and aloes, with all chief spices—a garden fountain, a well of living water, and flowing streams from Lebanon. Awake, O north wind, and come, O south wind! Blow upon my garden, let its fragrance be wafted abroad.[36]

Love

The exclamation of being overcome with love is not all on the part of Solomon either. In the bride we find a woman who loves passionately and wants to be loved. The first line of the book in fact is the bride telling of her love for the groom: "O that you would kiss me with the kisses of your mouth! For your love is better than wine, your anointing oils are fragrant, your name is oil poured out; therefore the maidens love you. Draw me after you, let us make haste."[37] "Shew me, O thou whom my soul loveth, where thou feedest, where thou liest in the midday…"[38] Quickly the love of the bride builds to a crescendo, where she reveals in one pin-point sentence her love and desire to be loved: "Stay me up with flowers, compass me about with apples: because I languish with love."[39] And she is ever listening for him: "The voice of my beloved... Behold my beloved speaketh to me..."[40] But she can't find him! She goes seeking for him, simply smitten with love, braving the dangers of the nighttime city: "In my bed by night I sought him whom my soul loveth: I sought him, and found him not. I will rise, and will go about the city: in the streets and the broad ways I will seek him whom my soul loveth: I sought him, and I found him not. The watchmen who keep the city, found me: Have you seen him, whom my soul loveth? When I had a little passed by them, I found him whom my soul loveth: I held him: and I will not let him go..."[41] She doesn't stop there—the dangers she faces in trying to find him increase, but her love drives her on: "My soul melted when he spoke: I sought him, and found him not: I called, and he did not answer me. The keepers that go about the city found me: they struck me: and wounded me: the keepers of the walls took away my veil from me. I adjure you, O daughters of Jerusalem, if you find my beloved, that you tell him that I languish with love."[42]

Union

And so we say in love, in awe, in exultation, as does all of Heaven: "Who is she that goeth up by the desert, as a pillar of smoke of aromatical spices, of myrrh, and frankincense, and of all the powders of the perfumer?"[43] Who is this woman who is so intriguingly beautiful, so utterly in love? And in ecstatic joy, every heart of every soul and every angel replies in love, "Mary!" And Mary replies, "Put me as a seal upon thy heart, as a seal upon thy arm, for love is strong as death."[44] And it is the groom, and those who share the life of the groom, and only those, who have access to this pure Garden. "Let my beloved come into his Garden," says the bride, "and eat of the fruit of his apple trees."[45] The bride continues this theme of living an intimate life with her, and toward the end of the book she says something that hints, again, that the bride is Lady Wisdom, who we will soon meet, and again the bride mentions wine, but this time she is more specific: "...I will take hold of thee, and bring thee into my mother's house...and I will give thee a cup of spiced wine and new wine of my pomegranates."[46] She is alluring the groom into a house where she will give him this special wine. And there is no time like the present to go there: she ends saying, "Make haste, my beloved..."[47] And not just any haste—haste "like to the roe, and to the young hart upon the mountains of aromatical spices."[48] Deer run *fast*—and that kind of speed will be to our benefit; again, this will become clear with Lady Wisdom, because eventually we will see that to get to the bride's house and live this life of blissful union we have to pass by an extreme danger.

When she comes...

When the bride comes, the dawn comes, a new day, a bright day, a beautiful day. When she comes, everything will be well. This applies to Mary in various ways. First, when she comes, Jesus comes—our redemption! The time of slavery to the devil and sin is over. Second, when she comes into each individual life, Divine Life comes. Third, when she comes, it means Jesus is soon to return. Solomon puts it this way: “For winter is now past, the rain is over and gone. The flowers have appeared in our land, the time of pruning is come: the voice of the turtle is heard in our land: The fig tree hath put forth her green figs: the vines in flower yield their sweet smell.”[49] When she comes, “the day of the joy of his heart” comes,[50] because her kisses are like the best wine,[51] and she is simply “flowing with delights” as the beloved pours her love out upon her beloved.[52]

The Ark of the Covenant

Between the wings of the angels who rested upon the top of the Ark, the presence of God resided in a special way. There are various important elements in consideration of the Ark as a type of Mary, but one in particular is crucial in regard to Mary’s beauty: that the Ark is made of incorruptible wood. In the Septuagint (ancient Greek version of the Old Testament), we read, “And thou shalt make the Ark of testimony of incorruptible wood...”[53] In the *Douay-Rheims* version of this passage we read, “Frame an ark of setim wood,” and in the *RSVCE* the translation is, “They shall make an ark of acacia wood.” Each translation is saying the same thing: setim/acacia wood is a sort of an incorruptible wood—it is hard and has such a high oil content that it resists water, rot and bugs (hence it is used to this day for outdoor furniture).

Due to her Immaculate Conception, Mary was free from the punishments due to original sin, excepting those things that are common to all humanity and that Jesus, too, accepted (suffering from thirst, hunger, cold, heat, weariness); she did not suffer from the ravages of old age, wherein our bodies begin to fall apart as we decay even as we are yet alive (our skin, eyesight, hair, organs and so on all begin to suffer at some point due to material breakdown with ever-increasing age). Like the gold-covered Ark, she held the presence of God, and in a passage that combines elements of the gold-covered Ark with elements of the *Song of Songs* and descriptions of Judith as blessed amidst all the people, we read in Psalm 45:9-17 (*RSVCE*),

> ...at your right hand stands the queen in gold of Ophir. Hear, O daughter, consider, and incline your ear; forget your people and your father's house; and the king will desire your beauty. Since he is your lord, bow to him; the people of Tyre will sue your favor with gifts, the richest of the people with all kinds of wealth. The princess is decked in her chamber with gold-woven robes; in many-colored robes she is led to the king, with her virgin companions, her escort, in her train. With joy and gladness they are led along as they enter the palace of the king. Instead of your fathers shall be your sons; you will make them princes in all the earth. I will cause your name to be celebrated in all generations; therefore the peoples will praise you for ever and ever.

It is Mary, and because she is Immaculate and "full of grace," who will be the true Ark, the place where God is present in an ultimate way.

In sum...

In the passages of Mary's types, what first allures is the young woman's physical beauty, and this, as we know, is true to life. We first *see*. The vision of beauty is followed by the sound of the voice, and then scent as one comes closer. But one comes closer not merely due to physical beauty, gentle voice and fragrant scent, but due to a discernment of character—loveliness is not only seeing, hearing, smelling; loveliness requires that character be imbued with love and all the attendant virtues of love. It is her heart, shining through her sensate beauty and enhancing that beauty that we take in with our senses, that charms us. The types of Mary in the Old Testament have all of those elements, and were Mary herself simply to possess all of those elements, she would be stunningly beautiful; but she far surpasses her types both in *perfection* and in *number* of all manner of inner and outer facets of loveliness. Whatever trait of loveliness can be conceived of, Mary has it in perfection; all other women have the honor of possessing in a limited and imperfect way a bit of Mary's loveliness, as many reflections of one mosaic.

Shakespeare comes closest perhaps to saying what we all would like to say reading of Mary in the Old Testament. Writing of Portia, his own type of Mary, he says,

> In Belmont is a lady richly left;
> And she is fair, and, fairer than that word,
> Of wondrous virtues: sometimes from her eyes
> I did receive fair speechless messages:
> Her name is Portia, nothing undervalued
> To Cato's daughter, Brutus' Portia:
> Nor is the wide world ignorant of her worth,

For the four winds blow in from every coast
Renowned suitors, and her sunny locks
Hang on her temples like a golden fleece;
Which makes her seat of Belmont Colchos' strand,
And many Jasons come in quest of her.
O my Antonio, had I but the means
To hold a rival place with one of them,
I have a mind presages me such thrift,
That I should questionless be fortunate![54]

The beauty we encounter in Mary via the Old Testament types draws us to her, and her beauty and love create a longing for union—the natural destination of love. Scripture gives us a picture of this union as well—it doesn't only create the desire. Where is this picture? One might be inclined to think, "Now we go to the New Testament!" But not yet! Rather, the Old Testament gives us a *thorough* sketch—it doesn't leave us hanging—it progresses from beauty, to love…to *Lady Wisdom*, where we find the culmination of love: ultimate union with the Lady and with God through her and with her. And we first meet Lady Wisdom, who is a compilation of every type of Mary thus far, at the very beginning of the world, and even prior to that.

—Notes—

1. Genesis 24:16-20
2. ibid 29:17,18
3. Judith 8:7,8
4. ibid 10:3-8

5. ibid 10:14
6. ibid 11:19
7. ibid 16:10,11
8. ibid 13:8-18
9. ibid 13:23-25
10. ibid 15: 9-12
11. Esther 2:7
12. ibid 2:15
13. ibid 5:2,3
14. ibid 7:2
15. ibid 15:8
16. 2 Kings 11:2,3
17. 3 Kings 2:11-20
18. *The Glories of Mary*, Disc. IV, The Annunciation of Mary, end of part I
19. Memorare
20. *All Generations Shall Call Me Blessed*, p. 109
21. *Song of Songs* 5:9
22. ibid 1:9
23. ibid 4:1
24. ibid 4:1,2
25. ibid 4:3
26. ibid 2:2
27. ibid 6:3
28. ibid 6:9
29. We see this signified in Mary's appearance at Lourdes, where she has a golden-pale yellow rose on each foot.
30. *Our Lady, Sermons of St. Francis de Sales*, chapter 2, "Our Lady of the Snow"
31. St. Maximillian Kolbe writes, "A human mother is an image of our Heavenly Mother (the Immaculata), and she in turn is the image of God's own goodness, God's own heart," p. 23 of *Immaculate Conception and the Holy Spirit*, by Fr. H.M. Manteau-Bonamy.

Important to note is that all women are "mother" in one way or another, in a spiritual sense (single women, nuns, etc., who pray for souls and the like) or in a physical sense (which does not exclude the spiritual).

32. ibid 3:6
33. ibid 4:10
34. ibid 4:14
35. ibid 7:8
36. *RSVCE Song of Songs* 4:9-16 While the *Douay-Rheims* passage has its own benefits here, I prefer this version of this passage. For example, the *Douay-Rheims* has "wounded my heart," the *RSVCE* has "ravished my heart." Here, "ravished" seems to bring out a bit more clearly what is meant: the Bride's beauty has "stolen" the Bridegroom's heart. "Ravish" implies a beauty that is so enchanting, charming and striking that one's heart could easily be captured…and this Bride is such that she ravishes the Heart of God! What then of us?
37. *RSVCE* ibid 1:2-4
38. *Song of Songs* 1:6
39. ibid 2:5
40. ibid 2:8, 10
41. ibid 3:1-4
42. ibid 5:6-8
43. ibid 3:6
44. ibid 8:6
45. ibid 5:1
46. ibid 8:2
47. *RSCVE Song of Songs*, 8:14
48. *RSVCE* ibid 8:14
49. *Song of Songs*, 2:11-13
50. ibid 3:11
51. *RSVCE* ibid 7:9
52. *Song of Songs*, 8:5

53. Exodus 25:10
54. *The Merchant of Venice*, Act I, scene 1. It is beyond the scope of this book to go into detail, but many facets of the character of Portia lead one to believe that Shakespeare had Our Lady in mind. To name but three of several coinciding features in this regard, aside from the obvious claim that she is, "fair, and fairer than that word,"—a close resemblance to Solomon's description of the bride—we also note that her name in itself points to Mary: "Portia" means gate, and Mary is the gate of Heaven. Further, Portia lives high above Venice in "Belmont," which means "beautiful mountain," and in the play it is clear that to be with her requires one to be on one's best behavior—she is completely pure, and those who would be in Portia's presence must endeavor to be likewise. But we also see in the play that she is filled with mercy, even attempting to guide the wicked Shylock out of his evil ways as Portia literally acts as an "advocate," a lawyer.

Chapter Three
Lady Wisdom and Creation

To find Lady Wisdom in her first appearance, we must travel back to the beginning of the world. Intriguingly, this type of Mary is present, in some mysterious manner, *while God creates*! In other words, she was "on His mind," even as He laid the foundations of the world, and she thus colors, so to speak, God's creation. God allows Himself, we could say, to be influenced by the thought of this Woman as He brings the world into being. As we read of Lady Wisdom in Sirach (Ecclesiasticus), "From the beginning, and before the world, was I created, and unto the world to come I shall not cease to be, and in the holy dwelling place I have ministered before him."[1] In the passage of Proverbs 8:22-31, Lady Wisdom puts it like this:

> The Lord possessed me in the beginning of his ways, before he made any thing from the beginning. I was set up from eternity, and of old before the earth was made. The depths were not as yet, and I was already conceived. Neither had the fountains of waters as yet sprung out: The mountains with their huge bulk

> had not as yet been established: before the hills I was brought forth:
>
> He had not yet made the earth, nor the rivers, nor the poles of the world. When he prepared the heavens, I was present: when with a certain law and compass he enclosed the depths: When he established the sky above, and poised the fountains of waters: When he compassed the sea with its bounds, and set a law to the waters that they should not pass their limits: when he balanced the foundations of the earth; I was with him forming all things: and was delighted every day, playing before him at all times; playing in the world: and my delights were to be with the children of men.

Given this, we see here a new detail concerning the creation account in the beginning of Genesis, and we come to a more thorough understanding of why creation is so beautiful. Yes, it is beautiful because it comes from God, and certainly that is the ultimate reality; but Mary, aka Lady Wisdom, also plays an intriguing role here. Since she was uppermost in His mind when He created the world of space-time, it makes sense there would be an intersection between the Holy Trinity's creation of the natural world and His masterpiece of creation, Mary. This conjunction of creations, Mary and the world of matter, is inherent in the very fabric of the universe, and there is an eschatological aspect of God's direct creative activity that becomes clearer and more refined inasmuch as it points to what the Church tells us are the *primary end* and the *secondary end* of the human person[2]: God and Mary. That is, the natural world has an *extra*, also sweet and subtle, layer to it.

In this passage, Lady Wisdom is "seen as an intermediary, at home with God and man (vv. 30-31)"[3] and "remains distinct from God, though his own 'issue' in some mysterious way."[4] In fact, the way Lady Wisdom is described may "indicate the sense of being the best and most valued of all things God created."[5] What is of great interest here is that, "Wisdom is a female offspring. The poem breaks with social convention that often placed a greater value on the male."[6] The *Catechism of the Catholic Church* supports the use of this reading as pertaining to Our Lady,[7] and with this same understanding Venerable Fulton Sheen writes, "She existed in the Divine Mind as an Eternal Thought before there were any mothers. She is the Mother of mothers—*she is the world's first love*."[8] At this point Sheen cites Prov 8:22-35 in its entirety, and concludes, "But God not only thought of her in eternity; He also had her in mind at the beginning of time,"[9] that is, when He was creating the natural world.[10]

St. Alphonsus, in his book the *Glories of Mary*, points to Proverbs 8:22 as referring to Our Lady in a variety of ways:[11] she was "always possessed by her Creator; and this she in reality was, as we are assured by herself: *The Lord possessed me in the beginning of His ways.*"[12] He further relates that St. Bonaventure applied the words of Proverbs to Mary, words that are, "applied by the Church to Mary: *I was with him forming all things.*"[13] It is here that St. Alphonsus provides an answer to how Mary participated in creation, being as she was uppermost in God's mind when He created the world but while she did not yet exist concretely:

> In fine, O sovereign Princess, from the immense ocean of thy beauty the beauty and grace of all creatures flowed forth as rivers. The sea learnt to curl its waves, and to wave its crystal waters from the gold-

> en hair which gracefully floated over thy shoulders... The morning star itself, and the sweet stars at night, are sparks from thy beautiful eyes... The white lilies and ruby roses stole their colors from thy lovely cheeks. Envious purple and coral sigh for the color of thy lips.[14]

St. John Eudes posits the same answer, in a different way. In his book, *The Admirable Heart of Mary*, he writes that "God did not create the natural sun, our wonderful luminary, merely to enlighten our material world; He made it also to be a representation of the excellent perfections which shine in the luminous Heart of the world's Sovereign Lady."[15]

Thus, nature is a reflection of God's beauty, and second, it is a reflection of God's masterpiece, the world created with Mary in mind, a reflection of *the Reflection* of God's beauty. "I was set up from eternity, and of old before the earth was made. The depths were not as yet, and I was already conceived... I was with him forming all things..."[16]

We could think of it this way: when a person is writing a letter to a beloved person—say Mom or sweetheart—one writes as clearly and as beautifully as possible, adding flourishes both in the language and in the handwriting, forming letters with beautiful curves and lines. Why? Because as one creates the prose, this person is upper most on the writer's mind. Or we could imagine a man walking down the street, thinking of the woman he is about to marry, and he is going to meet her. He is well-dressed, he walks with a spring in his step, his whole being is affected. Now, God is unchangeable, but there is no change implied here: He has *from eternity* had Mary in His mind as the epitome of creation, His masterpiece. Not by strict necessity but by His will He desires to "color" creation by shining

His beauty through Mary, aka Lady Wisdom.

This "in-loveness" of God with Mary, His masterpiece, explains why He would create in this way. Recall His ecstatic "Wow" from the *Song of Songs*:

> How beautiful art thou, my love, how beautiful art thou! Thy lips are as a scarlet lace: and thy speech sweet. Thy lips, my spouse, are as a dropping honeycomb, honey and milk are under thy tongue; and the smell of thy garments, as the smell of frankincense. My sister, my spouse, is a garden enclosed, a fountain sealed up. There are maidens without number. One is my dove, my perfect one.

This reality imbues the natural world with a *double eschatological reality*: simply put, the natural world leads to God, and part of its beauty is that of Mary, whose beauty is a pure reflection of God's own beauty, poured into her and then imprinted into the natural world, and thereby the cosmos points both to God as our primary end and also to Mary as secondary end and guide to God.

We could apply, after a fashion, the words of the song "The Very Thought of You" (best sung by Nat King Cole) to God (and also to ourselves):

> *I see your face in every flower,*
> *Your eyes in stars above.*
> *It's just the thought of you*
> *the very thought of you*
> *my love.*

Now, the end of Proverbs 8 is striking, because it moves from Lady Wisdom's presence in the mind of God and the influence God allows her to have upon the created world to the absolute necessity of finding her:

> Now therefore, ye children, hear me: Blessed are they that keep my ways. Hear instruction and be wise, and refuse it not. Blessed is the man that heareth me, and that watcheth daily at my gates, and waiteth at the posts of my doors. He that shall find me, shall find life, and shall have salvation from the Lord: But he that shall sin against me, shall hurt his own soul. All that hate me love death.[17]

Why the urgency, and why does this come immediately after creation? To reject Lady Wisdom is in some real way to reject God Himself; it is as if she is indispensable: "...and love is the keeping of her laws: and the keeping of her laws is the firm foundation of incorruption: And incorruption bringeth near to God. Therefore the desire of wisdom bringeth to the everlasting kingdom."[18] Such is her union with God, in fact, Scripture records that "she is a vapour of the power of God, and a certain pure emanation of the glory of the almighty God: and therefore no defiled thing cometh into her. For she is the brightness of eternal light, and the unspotted mirror of God' s majesty, and the image of his goodness."[19]

Now, although granted she is a reflection of His beauty and goodness, and although granted she is in a mysterious and unimaginable union with God, *how*, precisely, is it that she gives us divine life? And if she does, what are we to do, specifically, in her regard? We must, says she, listen, wait beside her doors, and find her, and then we will have that life. Yes, but *what does she say, where are her doors, and what is she doing behind those doors?* We already know she is fairer than fair, we know she is good, and we know she is in love with God and us. Whatever she is saying, wherever she lives, whatever she is doing, it must be extravagantly, lavishly, ineffably good…beyond our wildest dreams. "I am the mother of fair love, and of fear, and of knowledge, and of holy hope," she tells us. "In me is all grace of the way and of the truth, in me is all hope of life and of virtue. Come over to me, all ye that desire me, and be filled with my fruits."[20]

—Notes—

1. 24:14
2. Fr. Matthias Scheeben, *Mariology*, p. 226: "…Mary, next to God and Christ, is the end to which the entire rational and irrational creation is directed."
3. Cox, p. 155
4. Cox further writes on p. 156: "Wisdom is "at once divine and human, stands as a communicator between humanity (invitation is universal) and the created world, for she reveals to men the key to the ultimate meaning of the universe. Access to God and to the created world is found in a relationship of love with Wisdom (vv. 17 and 21)."
5. ibid
6. ibid, pp. 143-144: "The firstborn son in Israelite and Jewish society held a privileged rank (Gen. 43:33) and received a double portion of the family estate (Deut. 21:17). He was expected to become the head of the family eventually, after the death of his father…" So the change here to a female heir is most unusual.
7. CCC 721

8. Sheen, *The World's First Love*, pp. 17-18
9. ibid. Simarly, St. John Eudes, a Doctor of the Church, writes that,

    > The all-surpassing love of God for Mary causes Him to become entirely hers: "My beloved to me," by His thoughts, words and actions. By His thoughts, because she has been from all eternity the first object of His love, after the sacred humanity of His Word, and the first and worthiest subject of His thoughts and designs: "The Lord possessed me in the beginning of his ways" (Prov. 8:22).

10. The Fathers of the Church, various bishops, and the *Catechism of the Catholic Church* provide explicit mentions of Proverbs 8:22-36 as applying to Jesus, the Holy Spirit, and Our Lady. Wisdom has also been interpreted by the Church as the Holy Spirit. St. Irenaeus, another Doctor of the Church, while in agreement that Wisdom is Jesus, also, "equated divine Wisdom with the third person of the Holy Trinity, the Holy Spirit" (Steinmann, *Concordia Commentary: Proverbs*, 221). Of interest here is the unimaginable unity the Holy Spirit and Mary share, as St Maximillian Kolbe teaches; given this unity, it makes eminent sense that in the creation of the World, as seen in Proverbs 8:22, both the Holy Spirit and Mary can be understood as "Wisdom," since the Holy Spirit in His Person is so united to Mary as to be her Spouse. Again, while Mary had not yet been created in time at the time of the creation of the cosmos, she was from eternity in the mind of God as His Beloved.
11. St. Alphonsus later points out the words of St. Bonaventure to Mary, "The world which thou with God didst form from the beginning continues to exist at thy will, O most holy Virgin,"
12. St. Alphonsus, *The Glories of Mary*, p. 288
13. ibid, p. 368
14. ibid 676
15. Part Two, Chapter 3, "Mary's Heart, the Sun." He goes on in Part II to speak of Mary in relation to the heavens, the center of the earth,

a fountain, the sea, and the Garden of Eden.

16. Cf. *Redemptoris Mater*, par. 8: "In the mystery of Christ she is present even "before the creation of the world," as the one whom the Father "has chosen" as "Mother of his Son in the Incarnation."
17. Proverbs 8:32-36
18. Wisdom 6:19-21
19. ibid 7:25,26
20. Ecclesiasticus 24:24-26

Chapter Four
Lady Wisdom, Divinely Charming

There is an interesting verse in Jeremiah, specifically 20:7: "Thou hast deceived me, O Lord, and I am deceived." The root word used here for "deceive" also means "seduce," since *pathah*, can mean "allure or persuade"[1] as well. But the tone of this passage and the depth of meaning related to the word *pathah* hint at a deeper meaning than mere deception. However, we can understand a seduction as a species of deception, as deception can be implicit in the word "seduce": for example, a person could be seduced into counterfeiting money when such a life is portrayed in enticing terms: wealth, power, pleasure! But alas—it is a deceit, and in reality this is a life of crime. So we can say in this passage that *pathah* is "deceit" and "seduce," though seduce adds a depth that is already implicit in the word "deceit." Now that that is clear as mud, why belabor the point at all?

Well, in our times, people usually use the word "seduce" as "induce someone to do evil." But here it means something quite different—it means "to induce toward good." God shows His beauty and goodness, He sweeps us away with His sweetness and mercy, and we go to Him. He allures us. He speaks this way in Hosea 2:14 as well to unfaithful Israel; "Therefore, behold I will allure her, and will lead her into the wilderness: and I will speak to her heart." Likewise, Lady Wisdom. Recall that women's beauty is meant to "allure" man to God. It's not wrong to be the temptress in itself, and women are made to be so. It is the *object* of the temptation that makes the tempting good or bad: she can tempt to good, or to evil. Eve allured Adam to sin, Lady Wisdom allures us to goodness, to God, to life. A woman is able, by her beauty, wit, and charm to say to the man she knows, "Have you been to Mass today? Come with me, let's go to Mass, then we'll pray the Rosary." And the man, despite his desire to just watch sports and drink beer, is overcome, perhaps instantly, and he thus spends his time in a much better way. Mary is a sort of incarnation of God's beauty, sweetness and charm: "For she is the brightness of eternal light, and the unspotted mirror of God's majesty, and the image of his goodness."[2]

In other words, what we find Lady Wisdom doing in Proverbs chapters 1-8, and other passages in the Wisdom literature of the Bible, is encouraging the reader to cleave to her, to live life with her, to develop an intimate, personal relationship with her, and so she is speaking of her beauteous charms. The relationship she is alluring us to is a particularly intimate one, bearing on life and death, Heaven or Hell, and thus she wants us to know well who she is before she actually extends the invitation. Only by knowing our options can we make an informed, thus valid, decision.

There is, however, another reason she tells us about herself, and that reason is to give a warning. There is an enemy, another lady, and along the way she also will tempt us, not to God but to sin. The innate desire for intimacy and union with the beautiful that we all have can be worked to our destruction, and here we encounter not "alluring," but true deceit. Along with telling us about Wisdom, we learn too of this other option, one that appears just like Lady Wisdom at first, like a weed growing next to a good plant. "Therefore I am come out to meet thee, desirous to see thee, and I have found thee. I have woven my bed with cords, I have covered it with painted tapestry, brought from Egypt. I have perfumed my bed with myrrh, aloes, and cinnamon."[3] Lady Wisdom. The bride of *Song of Songs*. Wrong. Same kind of language. But when she comes out to meet us we notice that she has an "impudent face" and "flattereth."[4] At first glance, this woman, who is adulterous and known as Lady Folly, looks beautiful, but her face does not possess the purity that shines in Lady Wisdom. And so it's not simply the mere setting we need to look at: same kind of bed, same spices… We need to look at the face, and examine the words that follow: "let us enjoy the desired embraces, till the day appear. For my husband is not at home, he is gone on a very long journey. He took with him a bag of money: he will return home the day of the full moon. She entangled him with many words, and drew him away with the flattery of her lips."

We have to look not only at outer beauty and the desire of union with beauty. It can't simply be "she *looks* attractive…" Character—that needs to be well known, because the devil will lay traps throughout life such that the unwary will fall into the pit. The whole picture is the beauty we *see* and the beauty we don't see but that in various ways betrays itself: in the face, in the words, in the circumstances. Lady Wisdom is such a treasure that the enemy will attempt ruses, don disguises, plan plots in order to kill any who might venture off to Lady Wisdom's house—because to be with her is to be with God, and that is the last thing the enemy wants to happen.

Lady Wisdom's Character

One cannot "compare her unto any precious stone: for all gold in comparison of her, is as a little sand, and silver in respect to her shall be counted as clay."[5] She is loveable "above health and beauty," and it is better to choose "her instead of light: for her light cannot be put out."[6] "All good things" come to one "together with her, and innumerable riches through her hands…[7] For she is an infinite treasure to men! which they that use, become the friends of God…"[8]

> For in her is the spirit of understanding: holy, one, manifold, subtile, eloquent, active, undefiled, sure, sweet, loving that which is good, quick, which nothing hindereth, beneficent, Gentle, kind, steadfast, assured, secure, having all power, overseeing all things, and containing all spirits, intelligible, pure, subtile. For wisdom is more active than all active things: and reacheth everywhere by reason of her purity. For she is a vapour of the power of God, and a certain pure emanation of the glory of the almighty God: and therefore no defiled thing cometh into her.
>
> For she is the brightness of eternal light, and the unspotted mirror of God's majesty, and the image of his goodness. And being but one, she can do all things:

> and remaining in herself the same, she reneweth all things, and through nations conveyeth herself into holy souls, she maketh the friends of God and prophets. For God loveth none but him that dwelleth with wisdom. For she is more beautiful than the sun, and above all the order of the stars: being compared with the light, she is found before it. For after this cometh night, but no evil can overcome wisdom.[9]
>
> She reacheth therefore from end to end mightily, and ordereth all things sweetly.[10]
>
> She glorifieth her nobility by being conversant with God: yea and the Lord of all things hath loved her. For it is she that teacheth the knowledge of God, and is the chooser of his works. And if riches be desired in life, what is richer than wisdom, which maketh all things?
>
> And if sense do work: who is a more artful worker than she of those things that are? And if a man love justice: her labours have great virtues; for she teacheth temperance, and prudence, and justice, and fortitude, which are such things as men can have nothing more profitable in life. And if a man desire much knowledge: she knoweth things past, and judgeth of things to come: she knoweth the subtilties of speeches, and the solutions of arguments: she knoweth signs and wonders before they be done, and the events of times and ages.[11]

After reading this, the initial reaction might be, "Wait…*who are you*, exactly?" Because what she is saying is that, essentially, she is God's beloved daughter, not a Divine Person, but yet she is somehow brought into the divine intimacy. Moving from the end to the beginning of this passage, the details bear this out:

She "glorifieth her nobility by being conversant with God; yea the Lord of all things hath loved her." Who has been "conversant with God" since the time that Adam and Eve walked in the Garden with Him?

"She reacheth therefore from end to end mightily, and ordereth all things sweetly." She is Queen of the entirety of God's creation.

"...she is the brightness of eternal light, and the unspotted mirror of God' s majesty, and the image of his goodness." She is a *theophany* of God. To see her, is to see the very goodness of God, and to see God's majesty in her.

Not only that, she is the "brightness of eternal light" and a "vapor," that is a "breath," of the *power of God.* That is like saying, "See the light of the sun? I am in such union with the sun that, while I am not the sun nor its light, I am its brightness." We begin to see here an inkling of Mary's phrase, "I am the Immaculate Conception," which is tantamount to saying, "I am not only white, I am whiteness itself; I am not only pure, I am purity itself." Likewise, we can say that as Mary is *the* Virgin, she is virginity itself. Mary=Virgin, and Virgin=Mary. The one who would be pure will find purity with Lady Wisdom.

She is perfectly spotless, immaculate: there is nothing defiled that enters this "garden enclosed, a fountain sealed up."[12] But who is *not* defiled? Who can enter? Only God. God is undefiled, and this Garden, a creation of God, is undefiled, and she will remain so. Those made white in the Blood of the Lamb become undefiled, and they too enter this Paradise, and no one else.

This next passage is lengthy, but striking, as it is a sort of summary of Lady Wisdom and all that has been said of her. It describes her royal dignity, beauty and power.

> Wisdom shall praise her own self, and shall be honoured in God, and shall glory in the midst of her people, And shall open her mouth in the churches of the most High, and shall glorify herself in the sight of his power, And in the midst of her own people she shall be exalted, and shall be admired in the holy assembly. And in the multitude of the elect she shall have praise, and among the blessed she shall be blessed, saying: I came out of the mouth of the most High, the firstborn before all creatures:
>
> I made that in the heavens there should rise light that never faileth, and as a cloud I covered all the earth: I dwelt in the highest places, and my throne is in a pillar of a cloud. I alone have compassed the circuit of heaven, and have penetrated into the bottom of the deep, and have walked in the waves of the sea, And have stood in all the earth: and in every people, And in every nation I have had the chief rule:
>
> And by my power I have trodden under my feet the hearts of all the high and low: and in all these I sought rest, and I shall abide in the inheritance of the Lord. Then the creator of all things commanded, and said to me: and he that made me, rested in my tabernacle, And he said to me: Let thy dwelling be in Jacob, and thy inheritance in Israel, and take root in my elect. From the beginning, and before the world, was I creat-

> ed, and unto the world to come I shall not cease to be, and in the holy dwelling place I have ministered before him. And so was I established in Sion, and in the holy city likewise I rested, and my power was in Jerusalem.
>
> And I took root in an honourable people, and in the portion of my God his inheritance, and my abode is in the full assembly of saints. I was exalted like a cedar in Libanus, and as a cypress tree on mount Sion. I was exalted like a palm tree in Cades, and as a rose plant in Jericho: As a fair olive tree in the plains, and as a plane tree by the water in the streets, was I exalted. I gave a sweet smell like cinnamon. and aromatical balm: I yielded a sweet odour like the best myrrh:
>
> And I perfumed my dwelling as storax, and galbanum, and onyx, and aloes, and as the frankincense not cut, and my odour is as the purest balm. I have stretched out my branches as the turpentine tree, and my branches are of honour and grace. As the vine I have brought forth a pleasant odour: and my flowers are the fruit of honour and riches.
>
> I am the mother of fair love, and of fear, and of knowledge, and of holy hope. In me is all grace of the way and of the truth, in me is all hope of life and of virtue.[13]

"And in the multitude of the elect she shall have praise, and among the blessed she shall be blessed, saying: I came out of the mouth of the most High, the firstborn before all creatures." All generations call Mary blessed… She is not the first creature God made, but she is the first creature in God's thought; perhaps better said, the first creature of His Heart.

"And by my power I have trodden under my feet the hearts of all the high and low: and in all these I sought rest, and I shall abide in the inheritance of the Lord. Then the creator of all things commanded, and said to me: and he that made me, rested in my tabernacle..." That is, she has ravished hearts, stolen them, won them, charmed them, made them all hers and delivered them to God! Never has defeat been so victorious nor sweet—to be conquered by her is to be more than a victor. She has power to win hearts and make them fall in love with her in an absolutely pure way that is a path to God.

"I gave a sweet smell like cinnamon. and aromatical balm: I yielded a sweet odour like the best myrrh: And I perfumed my dwelling as storax, and galbanum, and onyx, and aloes, and as the frankincense not cut, and my odour is as the purest balm. I have stretched out my branches as the turpentine tree, and my branches are of honour and grace." She sweetens everything with which—and everyone with whom—she comes into contact. No one leaves her except that they are better than they were before she gently allured their hearts.

This is the bride of the *Song of Songs*. It is this woman with a love-sickness so strong that she will suffer at the Cross with her Son, and for each of us suffer pain of an almost infinite sort. Loveliness itself, who has the scent of every beautiful flower and tree, who is—how familiar sounding—blessed among all the blessed, sweet of voice and gentle of speech, calls to you, and to me.

All we have learned of Lady Wisdom thus far is meant to *lead somewhere*: specifically, to a falling in love with Lady Wisdom and a special, intimately personal relationship with her. She is God's beloved, and she is our beloved, given to us by God as a sort of sweet bait…or better said, as a sweet tie that binds us to God. That's why we learn so much about her. It's not a scriptural beauty contest, wherein one looks but does not love, where we see many beautiful women and then one who surpasses them all and vote her as "the winner." Rebecca, Judith, Esther, they were all historical people, but they all point to one Woman, and the reason for displaying the loveliness of body and soul of these women is to draw us to Lady Wisdom—to Mary—so that we cleave to her: not temporarily, not as a passing fad, but as one's very life, sweetness and hope. This is not hyperbole, nor mere rhetoric, and Lady Wisdom could not be any more clear: she is here for all who desire her and who want eternal life, and she paints a portrait of herself that is so holily tempting, so purely seductive, no one in their right mind would want to say "no" to her! And it is easy to be hers: "I love them that love me," she says. We need to know this because we are much more apt to cling to true beauty when we realize that beside that only real source of loveliness is its opposite—which seems at first glance to be desireable, but by comparison to Lady Wisdom is a ditch full of thorns and muck. Why settle for less than Lady Wisdom? Not everyone will love her, however; there is that other choice, and the weakness we all have due to original sin. We must be careful.

—Notes—

1. *Strong's Hebrew* 6601
2. 7:26
3. Proverbs 7:15-17

4. ibid 7:13
5. Wisdom 7:9
6. ibid 7:10
7. ibid 7:11
8. ibid 7:14
9. ibid 7:22-30
10. ibid 8:1
11. ibid 8:3-8
12. *Song of Songs* 4:12
13. Sirach 24:1-25

Chapter Five
Lady Wisdom or Lady Folly, the Princess or the Witch?

"You shall no more be termed Forsaken, and your land shall no more be termed Desolate; but you shall be called My delight is in her, and your land Married; for the LORD delights in you, and your land shall be married. For as a young man marries a virgin, so shall your sons marry you, and as the bridegroom rejoices over the bride, so shall your God rejoice over you." [1] A mysterious and enigmatic passage if ever there was one. It's about salvation coming, one day, to Israel. But there is deeper meaning here as well. Who is God's ultimate delight amongst all creatures? Who is the concretized personification of Israel? Mary, aka Lady Wisdom. She is God's "delight." That she is God's delight is already clear; we saw this in the *Song of Songs*. The really mysterious part of the above passage is this: "For as a young man marries a virgin, so shall your sons marry you." How is that possible? What does it mean? On a natural level, it makes no sense. But what is spoken of here, like so many things in Scripture, does not take place on the natural level, but on the spiritual level. On the natural level, the arena of flesh and blood, Mary is the natural Mother of Jesus, the Incarnate Son of God. He is flesh of her flesh and blood of her blood. On the spiritual level, however, she is His spouse: the New Eve with the New Adam. But notice that Scripture uses the plural: "so shall your sons marry you." Plural. Here the supernatural plot thickens.

Marriage to Lady Wisdom

What Solomon wants to do he makes abundantly clear…

I preferred her before kingdoms and thrones, and esteemed riches nothing in comparison of her. Neither did I compare unto her any precious stone: for all gold in comparison of her, is as a little sand, and silver in respect to her shall be counted as clay. I loved her above health and beauty, and chose to have her instead of light: for her light cannot be put out.[2]

"Her have I loved, and have sought her out from my youth, and have desired to take her for my spouse, and I became a lover of her beauty."[3]

"I purposed therefore to take her to me to live with me: knowing that she will communicate to me of her good things, and will be a comfort in my cares and grief. For her sake I shall have glory among the multitude, and honour with the ancients, though I be young…"[4]

"I went about seeking, that I might take her to myself."[5] (Wisdom 8:16-18)

"Send her out of thy holy heaven, and from the

> throne of thy majesty, that she may be with me, and may labour with me, that I may know what is acceptable with thee: For she knoweth and understandeth all things, and shall lead me soberly in my works, and shall preserve me by her power."[6]

This is a big step! He's not saying, "I want to be friends with her," or "She became like a sister to me." Instead, it is *marriage* he intends—the most intimate of unions. He wants to live a life of total intimacy and unity with her, one life. Of course, Solomon is not speaking about marriage in an earthly sense, and this marriage is certainly not to be understood in a carnal way. People of our days automatically equate marriage with sexual relations, but physical intimacy is not the foundation of marriage; rather, there is a union of hearts, a deep intercommunion of souls, two faces not merely side by side, but each gazing at the other, two people living one life together. While the distinction of the two individuals is not lost, yet there is a fusion of the two persons. Physical intimacy is an outer expression of this inner reality, and one that is not necessary for this unitive bond to exist.

The question remains, however: how is this union effected? What does Solomon do? Indeed, what is he telling you and I that we have to do? We are implicated in the plural of "sons" as well. First, one has to profess love truly and then find her, and second one has to enter into this union with her.

Profession of love and finding her

This step is not hard at all, though the decision needs to be taken seriously. It can't be a half-hearted, "Sure, I guess I'll marry you? I think? Yeah…I suppose so?" One must provide a distinct "yes." You may not be worthy (no one is but God); you may not be successful in life or handsome. Smart? That doesn't matter either. Lady Wisdom points out two special qualifications: A free choice to love her, and then that one go to her…

1) *A free choice to love her*. "I love them that love me…"[7] The Latin for this phrase is vitally important: *Ego diligentes me diligo*. In particular, the word *diligo* is crucial, and also consoling. The sacred author here does not use the word *amare*. Why not? Because *amare* means all kinds of loves; it's a sort of common word that can mean, "I like toast," "I love bacon," "I am in love with Theresa," or it can even speak of a tendency, as in "I love to get up early in the mornings, I'm a morning sort of person." If *amare* were used here we would not know exactly what to make of Lady Wisdom's intentions, which would be odd, because she is quite clear about them everywhere else. *Diligo*, on the other hand, as noted in the fine book, *The Love of Mary*, means "…she not only loves them, but she *cherishes* them with the partiality and the tenderness of a mother and spouse…*diligere* signifies a very strong, special, and most partial love, and distinguishes and selects the one loved, and prefers him to all others."[8] And it's not one sided! She also does not say, *Ego amantes me diligo*. That would mean the love is not the same on either side; one can't "sort of like" Lady Wisdom, one has to love her in a special way, as she loves us. Notice too that while *amare* refers to more frivolous and changing things (love of toast, or the emotions associated with falling in love), *diligo* is deep,

serious, unchanging, love that by its nature is a self-gift of irrevocable totality.

2) *Go to her.* "…and they that in the morning early watch for me, shall find me,"[9] Lady Wisdom tells us. She's not hard to find! She is at "the gates of the city"—that is, she is obvious, out in public, one can't miss her, not if you are looking for her. From this conspicuous place, she calls out, "Come over to me, all ye that desire me, and be filled with my fruits. For my spirit is sweet above honey, and my inheritance above honey and the honeycomb. My memory is unto everlasting generations."[10]

Union with her; the marriage is made…unless…

But prior to the longed for union with Lady Wisdom, there is a trial. Walking with jaunty step to Lady Wisdom, one is accosted by Lady Folly, and never has the old joke been so utterly true as for those who embrace her:

"Who was that lady I saw you with?"

"That's no lady, that's my wife."

Lady Folly is not a woman you want to be your wife, yet most people in the world take her as one. After all, there are only two choices presented: Lady Wisdom and Lady Folly. We know that nothing evil, nothing defiled, no sin, gains entrance into the locked garden that is Lady Wisdom, and we also know that much of the world embraces even serious sin as some sort of fun pastime. They have not taken as their spouse Lady Wisdom, but Lady Folly, who has enticed them. Again, women are by nature the temptress, tempting to good (Lady Wisdom) or evil (Lady Folly). In the Old Testament we have the warning of Scripture to avoid the pseudo-lady, and we also have conscience, and it is clear from the warnings we find that people cannot accidentally get caught up with Lady Folly—they choose her. Like Eve they let themselves listen and they are beguiled…

> …keep thee from the woman that is not thine, and from the stranger who sweeteneth her words.
>
> For I look out of the window of my house through the lattice, And I see little ones, I behold a foolish young man, Who passeth through the street by the corner, and goeth nigh the way of her house. In the dark, when it grows late, in the darkness and obscurity of the night, And behold a woman meeteth him in harlot's attire prepared to deceive souls; talkative and wandering, Not bearing to be quiet, not able to abide still at home, Now abroad, now in the streets, now lying in wait near the corners. And catching the young man, she kisseth him, and with an impudent face, flattereth, saying: I vowed victims for prosperity, this day I have paid my vows. Therefore I am come out to meet thee, desirous to see thee, and I have found thee…[11]
>
> …She entangled him with many words, and drew him away with the flattery of her lips. Immediately he followeth her as an ox led to be a victim, and as a lamb playing the wanton, and not knowing that he is drawn like a fool to bonds, Till the arrow pierce his liver: as if a bird should make haste to the snare, and knoweth not that his life is in danger. Now therefore, my son, hear me, and attend to the words of my mouth. Let not thy mind be drawn away in her ways: neither be thou deceived with her paths.[12]

The final line to this pericope, the *coup de grâce*, is stunningly stark; warnings are rarely more vivid than this one: "For she hath cast down many wounded, and the strongest have been slain by her. Her house is the way to hell, reaching even to the inner chambers of death."[13] This is what the mere semblance of a conversation with the devil leads to: evil is dressed up by the deceiver, it sounds good, it flatters, it promises intimacy and union, but walking too close to Lady Folly—a witch, the devil in disguise—leads to a very bad end: arrows piercing livers and birds ensnared does not a pleasant time sound.

In chapter 9 of Proverbs, we come to a final decision for intimacy with either Lady Wisdom or Lady Folly. Each offer a meal. Even on a natural level, a meal is an intimate affair, but in this case the meal stands for an exclusive union with one of two personages. Here we find the making of the marriage, the consummation, the final "yes." This is what Lady Wisdom has desired for us: total union with her, because a total union with her means a total union with God. But here, right at the door of Lady Wisdom, Lady Folly tries one more time. She calls out to those passing by, "He that is a little one, let him turn to me. And to the fool she said: Stolen waters are sweeter, and hidden bread is more pleasant. And he did not know that giants are there, and that her guests are in the depths of hell."[14] Here the mask is completely off! First, what's the actual meal here, which is a symbol of union? *Stolen* water and *hidden* bread; the *RSVCE* says "bread eaten in secret." That's a wretched meal: Water—stolen water at that, from who knows where—and bread, probably aged and unpleasant. It's the sort of meal one would want to keep secret. In other words, this intimate unity is hidden, not proclaimed. No justly married couple desires to keep their union a secret, only adulterers do. And here is the worst part. Not only is the meal both paltry and immoral, there are "giants" in Lady Folly's house. Notice that one does not see them until one passes into her house (everything looks well on the outside). More to the point, all of Lady Folly's guests are *dead*. She brings her victims to giants and the victims are tossed into "the depths of Hell." When tempted to think, "sin isn't so bad," look at the Crucifix, look at Mary, and remember where Lady Folly's co-sinners end up. It's not like they weren't warned, everyone has been. Some hold their eyes shut and pretend it's not so bad, a trick that works until the giants grab you.

If we heed the warnings given, and if we let ourselves fall in love with Lady Wisdom, and if we love her with *diligere* love and go to her house, we will find a meal that is quite different than that of Lady Folly. Again, Lady Folly has made her meal similar in some respects, but the differences are immense.

> Wisdom hath built herself a house, she hath hewn her out seven pillars. She hath slain her victims, mingled her wine, and set forth her table. She hath sent her maids to invite to the tower, and to the walls of the city: Whosoever is a little one, let him come to me. And to the unwise she said: Come, eat my bread, and drink the wine which I have mingled for you.[15]

There are astonishing words and phrases in this passage:

1) "..she hath hewn her out seven pillars." A house with "seven pillars," i.e. the Catholic Church and her seven Sacraments, the place where we are baptized and brought into union with

Christ to live His own divine life.

2) "She hath slain her victims [*RSVCE* has 'beasts,' which makes 'victims' a bit more clear], mingled her wine..." This is a much better meal than Lady Folly's meager and deadly fare that is bait for a giant's snare. Here we have meat and wine! While Lady Folly's meal goes from bad to the worst, this meal gets better and better...
3) "Come, eat my bread, and drink the wine which I have mingled for you." Again, the *RSVCE* sheds some light here, in particular on the word "mingled": "drink of the wine I have mixed." Bread and wine—mixed wine. Recall the wine from the *Song of Songs*. What Lady Wisdom is offering is nothing less than the Eucharist.[16] In her womb she mixes her wine—Jesus Who is true God *and* true man. His flesh and blood is from the flesh and blood of Mary, so this really *is* her bread and wine, her meal, one that she prepared with her *fiat* and in her womb. Lady Wisdom in reality does give us divine life, immortality. And the intimacy of union is the most intimate that can be had: in the reception of Holy Communion a person becomes one with Jesus and thus one with Mary, because those two cannot be separated. Jesus' flesh and blood is hers, she clothes Him with herself, and thus the Word of God comes to us as milk from Mary. There is then a certain presence of Mary in regard to the Eucharist, since the Eucharist is the Incarnate Word:

> It is in the Eucharist, and especially in Holy Communion, that our union with the Madonna becomes a full and loving conformity with her. We receive her devoted care and protection along with the Blessed Sacra-

ment. Her tender attentions overlook nothing as Christ is united to each of us, her children, moving her to pour out all her motherly love on our souls and bodies... It cannot be otherwise...there is no bond so close and so sweet with the Madonna, as the one realized in receiving the Holy Eucharist. Jesus and Mary "always go together," as St. Bernadette said.[17]

Who is it that we have just consented to live our life with?

...The queen stood on thy right hand, in gilded clothing; surrounded with variety.

Hearken, O daughter, and see, and incline thy ear: and forget thy people and thy father's house. And the king shall greatly desire thy beauty; for he is the Lord thy God, and him they shall adore. And the daughters of Tyre with gifts, yea, all the rich among the people, shall entreat thy countenance. All the glory of the king's daughter is within in golden borders, Clothed round about with varieties. After her shall virgins be brought to the king: her neighbours shall be brought to thee.

They shall be brought with gladness and rejoicing: they shall be brought into the temple of the king. Instead of thy fathers, sons are born to thee: thou shalt make them princes over all the earth. They shall remember thy name throughout all generations. Therefore shall people praise thee for ever; yea, for ever and ever.[18]

The Queen!—and as her chosen love, what is there to worry about? Proverbs has an answer for that as well, because Solomon describes how Lady Wisdom treats us after we unite ourselves to her. In Proverbs 31 he does not mention her by name, but since he has clearly repeated that one should marry Lady Wisdom and in so doing come to live with God, then the wife he speaks of here as "perfect" could only be Lady Wisdom; and various phrases certainly speak of Mary…

> Who shall find a valiant woman? far and from the uttermost coasts is the price of her.
>
> The heart of her husband trusteth in her, and he shall have no need of spoils. She will render him good, and not evil, all the days of her life. She hath sought wool and flax, and hath wrought by the counsel of her hands. She is like the merchant' s ship, she bringeth her bread from afar. And she hath risen in the night, and given a prey to her household, and victuals to her maidens.
>
> She hath considered a field, and bought it: with the fruit of her hands she hath planted a vineyard. She hath girded her loins with strength, and hath strengthened her arm. She hath tasted and seen that her traffic is good: her lamp shall not be put out in the night. She hath put out her hand to strong things, and her fingers have taken hold of the spindle. She hath opened her hand to the needy, and stretched out her hands to the poor.
>
> She shall not fear for her house in the cold of snow: for all her domestics are clothed with double garments. She hath made for herself clothing of tapestry: fine linen, and purple is her covering. Her husband is honour-

> able in the gates, when he sitteth among the senators of the land. She made fine linen, and sold it, and delivered a girdle to the Chanaanite. Strength and beauty are her clothing, and she shall laugh in the latter day.
>
> She hath opened her mouth to wisdom, and the law of clemency is on her tongue. She hath looked well to the paths of her house, and hath not eaten her bread idle. Her children rose up, and called her blessed: her husband, and he praised her. Many daughters have gathered together riches: thou hast surpassed them all. Favour is deceitful, and beauty is vain: the woman that feareth the Lord, she shall be praised.
>
> Give her of the fruit of her hands: and let her works praise her in the gates.[19]

Lady Wisdom handles *all* the details of life! She arranges everything, as queen, Mother, spouse, with the utmost humility and care, as she humbly remains in the background while her husband is "honourable in the gates," because his Lady Wisdom has made him successful.

So, our hearts can trust her totally with everything. After that is established, we find that she brings her bread from afar to feed her household. This is a link to Proverbs 9: what Lady Wisdom hath wrought with her hands is that she clothes the Word in her flesh; she is like a Merchant ship, because she brings bread from afar—the Bread from Heaven; and then in the night that is this life, where we walk in the shadow of death, she distributes the Word enfleshed with her flesh to her household. First things first: we have to be alive! No Bread of Life equals no life. So she first feeds her household with He Who is true food and true drink.

It is only after she established her trustworthiness and feeds those who belong to her with this Bread from Heaven that she sets to work in regard to other matters. Not only does she take care of all her household, she also gives to the poor—to those who are not yet hers (she is ever trying to charm people to her and encourage them to marry her, rather than that they commit adultery with Lady Folly, the world, the flesh and the devil, and die). These gifts to the poor we could see as actual graces that move souls to repentance and conversion, setting them on the road to the sanctifying grace found in her seven-pillared house.

But what are we to make of this: "She shall not fear for her house in the cold of snow: for all her domestics are clothed with double garments"? St. Louis de Montfort explains it this way:

> She bestows a new perfume and a new grace upon their garments and adornments, in communicating to them her own garments, merits, and virtues, which she bequeathed to them by her testament, when she died... Thus all her domestics, faithful servants and slaves, are doubly clad in the garments of her Son and in her own... It is on this account that they have nothing to fear from the cold of Jesus Christ, who is white as snow...[20]

As for Lady Wisdom's garments, they are, significantly, purple. Purple was an expensive color, and worn by royalty. Lady Wisdom is a queen, of course. According to St. Louis, we are dressed in her garments and those of her Son—we are wearing purple as well, as princes of the Kingdom of Heaven, which is why the one who belongs to Mary is honorable and spends time "among the senators of the land."

We also learn that she is clement, that "the law of clemency is on her tongue." She is all mercy. If we are honest, we will admit that logically she must be, because to offer *us* a life of union with *her* is a true "beauty and the beast" scenario: she is all pure, holy, beauteous, royal, humble, filled with every grace, while we are, of ourselves, despicable, vile creatures who have sinned against God and man. We are like a filthy, destitute beggar sitting outside the gates of the palace…and miracle of miracles, blessing of blessings, Lady Wisdom calls to me and to you, and if we are not too proud to give her our hand, she will make something royal of us, and she will make every single detail of our lives work out marvelously, and even unite us to her Heart. It is no wonder that in the next line we read that "Her children rose up, and called her blessed: her husband, and he praised her," and this we see over and over in relation to Marian types, as we read in Psalm 44: "They shall remember thy name throughout all generations. Therefore shall people praise thee for ever; yea, for ever and ever," and in Judith, "…Blessed art thou, O daughter, by the Lord the most high God, above all women upon the earth[21]...and therefore thou shalt be blessed for ever. And all the people said: So be it, so be it.[22]"

Solomon ends Proverbs with these fitting phrases, calling again to mind the singular lovely goodness of this Woman: "Many daughters have gathered together riches: thou hast surpassed them all. Favour is deceitful, and beauty is vain: the woman that feareth the Lord, she shall be praised. Give her of the fruit of her hands: and let her works praise her in the gates."

Now the phrase "Favour is deceitful, and beauty is vain" might throw some off, because it sounds like Solomon is taking a step back from the beauty department. But what he means is that without fear of the Lord, all the favour one receives and the beauty one possesses is useless; one would ultimately become a sort of image of Lady Folly. It is love of God, and fearing to offend Him because of that love, that leads one to be justly praised. And the praise Lady Wisdom receives comes from her works—we are her works, the ones she fashions into the image of her Son so that we inherit an eternal kingdom.

> Now all good things came to me together with her, and innumerable riches through her hands, And I rejoiced in all these: for this wisdom went before me, and I knew not that she was the mother of them all. Which I have learned without guile, and communicate without envy, and her riches I hide not. For she is an infinite treasure to men![23]
>
> When I go into my house, I shall repose myself with her: for her conversation hath no bitterness, nor her company any tediousness, but joy and gladness. Thinking these things with myself, and pondering them in my heart, that to be allied to wisdom is immortality, And that there is great delight in her friendship, and inexhaustible riches in the works of her hands, and in the exercise of conference with her, wisdom, and glory in the communication of her words: I went about seeking, that I might take her to myself.[24]
>
> Forsake her not, and she shall keep thee: love her, and she shall preserve thee. The beginning of wisdom, get wisdom, and with all thy possession purchase prudence. Take hold on her, and she shall exalt thee: thou shalt be glorified by her, when thou shalt embrace her.

> She shall give to thy head increase of graces, and protect thee with a noble crown.[25]

Finally it is absolutely key to keep in mind that the unitive bond with Lady Wisdom is presented as the meal of bread and wine. The Eucharist is the focus, because this requires a consistent and deliberate choice to live with her in a union of life. Yes, we have been baptized, but every Eucharist received is a sort of wedding that unites us to Christ *through* Mary and to Christ *with* Mary by physically receiving the glorified flesh of Jesus. Only a person who is one with Jesus can be one with Mary, and to live the life of union with Mary as another of her sons is, as a fundamental aspect, to receive the Eucharist.

There is no union of "two in one flesh" so close as Jesus and Mary: Jesus gets His flesh and blood only from Mary! To receive the Eucharist is to participate in Jesus' union with Mary, and in Mary's union with Jesus. The meal of Lady Wisdom is the consummation of a soul saying "yes" to the bride of the *Song of Songs*, and it is a "yes" that brings immortality.

—Notes—

1. *RSVCE* Isaiah 62:4, 5. The *Douay-Rheims* has, "For the young man shall dwell with the virgin, and thy children shall dwell in thee." The word translated in the *Douay-Rheims* as "dwell" means "marry"—"dwell" is taken in that sense.
2. Wisdom 7:8-10
3. ibid 8:2
4. ibid 8:9,10
5. ibid 8:16-18

6. ibid 9:10,11
7. Proverbs 8:17
8. D. Roberto, p. 153
9. ibid
10. Ecclesiasticus (Sirach) 24:26-28
11. Proverbs 7:5-15
12. ibid 7:21-25
13. ibid 7:26,27
14. ibid 9:16-18
15. ibid 9:1-5
16. As Fr. Manelli writes in his book, *Jesus Our Eucharistic Love*, chapter 6, "The Bread That Our Heavenly Mother Gives Us": "Thus it is quite natural that the great as well as the lesser Marian shrines always foster devotion to the Holy Eucharist, so much so that they can also be called Eucharistic shrines. Lourdes, Fatima, Loretto, Pompei, come to mind, where crowds approach the altar in almost endless lines to receive Mary's blessed Fruit. It cannot be otherwise; for there is no bond so close and so sweet with the Madonna, as the one realized in receiving the Holy Eucharist."
17. Fr. Manelli, *Jesus Our Eucharistic Love*, chapter 6, "The Bread That Our Heavenly Mother Gives Us."
18. Psalm 44:10-18
19. Proverbs 31:10-31
20. *True Devotion*, n. 206
21. Judith 13:23
22. Judith 15:11,12
23. Wisdom 7:11-14
24. ibid 8:16-18
25. Proverbs 4:6-9

—SECTION TWO—

The New Testament

The Sketch is Colored

Chapter One
Sketch to Portrait, Sketch with Portrait

Quae est ista?

"Who is she that goeth up by the desert, as a pillar of smoke of aromatical spices, of myrrh, and frankincense, and of all the powders of the perfumer?"[1]

"Who is she that cometh forth as the morning rising, fair as the moon, bright as the sun, terrible as an army set in array?"[2]

"Who is this that cometh up from the desert, flowing with delights…?"[3]

At Mary's conception this must have been the cry of the angels, who sung to one another,"Who is she?" and who each replied overjoyed, "Mary!" It's similar to spending a tough night, having experienced a terrifying nightmare, and the darkness holds no cure, only more phantoms. One must simply sit it out and try to sleep. But when the sun begins to rise, the heart exclaims, and sometimes the voice too, "At last, the dawn! The sun is coming, finally, and the horrible night is over." How much more so did the holy angels see the Immaculate one and exclaim, "Finally, the dawn of grace, the night of sin and death is at an end!"

All that we learn of Mary in the Old Testament is both a preparation for, and an element of, Mary living in the New Testament. The Old Testament is a sort of commentary on the New: it fills in some fine details. When we read of Mary at the Annunciation, the Visitation, Cana, the Cross, Revelation, we should have in mind the Mary we come to know in the Old Testament; vice versa, when we read the Old Testament we should have Mary in mind as we read of her in the New Testament. These are not two portraits of Mary! True, in the Old Testament we also need to consider the history involved: for example, Esther. She was a real person, who by her intercession as queen really saved the Jews from destruction. At the same time, this concrete historical individual is also a type of Mary. We might consider this as analogous to marriage. The Sacrament of marriage points to the reality of the union of Christ and His Church, but that does not mean the concrete marriage that is a sort of concretized view of the union between Christ and His Church is *only* an example—it is a marriage in its own right that points to still deeper realities.

In the Old Testament we find the foundational outlines and measurements, the contours and shapes, the essential proportions and dimensions that form the underlayment of the portrait of Mary. Just as these are not put aside but filled in with color and shading and detail in an oil painting, so here they cannot be set aside. In fact, the Old Testament provides much more detail for the New Testament completion of Mary's portrait than any underlayment for an oil painting. What we have learned of Eve, Rebecca, Rachel, Judith, Esther, Bathsheba, the Ark, the Bride and Lady Wisdom is both *present* and *surpassed* in concrete form in Mary. None of the essential details of those types has been set aside, they have only been augmented, as a charcoal underlying sketch is augmented by the colors and details of the oil paint. Mary is the "brightness of eternal light, and the unspotted mirror of God's majesty, and the image of his goodness"[4] with "lips…as a scarlet lace and thy speech sweet,"[5] who "is more beautiful than the sun, and above all the order of the stars"[6] who says at the Annunciation, "Behold the handmaid of the Lord…"

But let's begin this section of the New Testament with a contemporary account of Mary's beauty—Lady Wisdom in person—by way of moving from sketch to painting, from shadow to colorful reality. Certainly some people must have visited Mary after Jesus' Ascension into Heaven and prior to her passing and Assumption into Heaven. Saint Dionysius the Areopagite, friend of St. Paul, was one such person (though this fact is disputed—*nota bene* the endnote concerning this). In a letter to St. Paul[7], attributed to St. Dionysius, we read of this encounter:

> I confess before God, my master, that that which I have seen not only with my mental but even my bodily eyes, surpasses the conception of men; for I beheld the Godlike, excelling the angels in sanctity, the Mother of Our Lord Jesus Christ, whom the goodness of God, and clemency of the Savior and the glory of the Divine majesty has deigned to show me; for when by John, the prince of the prophets and the evangelists, who, dwell-

ing in the flesh, shines as a sun in the heavens, I was conducted to the Godlike presence of the Holy Virgin, so divine a splendor shone around without me, and more fully illuminated me within; such fragrance of all perfumes abounded, that neither my unhappy body, nor my spirit, could bear the weight of so great and entire happiness. My mind was lost; my spirit failed me, overcome by the glory of such majesty. I call to witness that God who was present in the Virgin, that had not what I had learnt from you taught me otherwise, I should have believed her to be the true God; for it would seem that the blessed could possess no greater glory, than that happiness which I, now unhappy, but then most happy, tasted.[8]

—Notes—

1. *Song of Songs* 3:6
2. ibid 6:9
3. ibid 8:5
4. Wisdom 7:26
5. *Song of Songs* 4:3
6. Wisdom 7:29
7. The debate on whether or not this, and other letters, of St. Dionysius are authentic seems not to be totally resolved. Much apparently depends on the dating of the Assumption of Mary and whether that dating fits into the known years of St. Dionysisus' life. Nevertheless, this description is included here, not as a certainty of authenticity that St. Dionysius really did visit Mary and truly wrote this letter, but rather as, at the very least, a wonderful description

of what it might have been like to visit her prior to her Assumption into Heaven. Authentic or not, this description imparts something of the reality of Mary's sweet heavenly beauty.

8. D. Roberto, *The Love of Mary*, pp. 96-97

Chapter Two
Espousal of St. Joseph to Mary

The marriage of Mary and St. Joseph took place prior to the Annunciation, and their espousal is a critical element of this book's premise: that Mary is the Beloved of God and of each of us. St. Joseph—as will become more clear in the section on consecration to Mary—is, after Jesus, the *exemplar* of one's relationship to Mary.

Mary was truly the spouse of St. Joseph and their marriage was a virginal one, and a legal one. But, St. Joseph's espousal to Mary was a *participation* in the reality of God as spouse of Mary. She is first and foremost the spouse of the Father, the Son, and the Holy Spirit. St. Peter Chrysologus (380-450) is the first Saint, of the Latin Fathers at least, to write about Mary as "God's Spouse."[1] Of course we often hear of Mary as spouse of the Holy Spirit, and this is true. But the reality of Mary as spouse of God is not limited to the Holy Spirit; she is entirely God's. Our union with her is based upon one's union with Christ as He shares His divine life with us. We are not her natural children (only Jesus is), though we are her children more surely than any natural mother-child relationship. She truly brought *spiritual* life to us and suffered to do so, and the life we receive is the life of God, the life that Mary lives by. And so we *participate* in God's relationship with Mary, as St. Joseph's relationship with Mary was by participation:

> Mary is…the virginal, real spouse of God the *Father*, who willed her to be the Mother, according to His human nature, of His only-begotten Son (Gal 4:4); the spouse of God the *Son*, the Redeemer, who intimately associated her with Himself in His redemptive work, as the New Eve beside the "New Adam" [cf. Rom 5:12ff. 1 Cor 15:21-26, 54-57; see also Jn 2:1-11]; the spouse of God the *Holy Spirit*, who, overshadowing her, enabled her to conceive Jesus (Lk 1:35).[2]

Father Mathias Scheeben delved into the fact of Mary as spouse of God in an amazing way in his book, *Mariology*. He considers Mary's relationship to the Father, the Son, and the Holy Spirit.[3]

1) *Mother and Spouse of God the Son.* That Mary and Jesus have a spousal unity is perhaps more clear than Mary's union with the Father and the Holy Spirit, inasmuch as Jesus and Mary are the New Adam and the New Eve. As Scheeben points out, it is only Mary, of all creatures, that gives something to God that God takes to Himself, indeed clothing Himself for all eternity with what Mary gives to Him. And she shares in the dignity of her Son, Who is a Divine Person—no higher dignity can be imagined. In fact, "Mary cooperates with the proper spiritual activity of God the Father, through which He produces the same Son in her bosom…"[4] Mary's relationship to Jesus, the

God-Man, is also a relationship of both blood and affinity—that is, a relationship with God in Himself!

> It is a spiritual affinity to God, something like a family relationship… Affinity is a relationship which a person has to another person through the marriage of a blood relation with the latter…this relationship to God into which Mary enters through the hypostatic marriage of the humanity related to her by blood with the Logos, is not only an equally true affinity but also a much more perfect and closer one than that which can take place among men.[5]

What he is building up to is this: there is a spiritual marriage taking place:

> Mary is as much anointed and made the Mother of God as the flesh, taken from her, is made the flesh of God, for the Logos is so taken up in her that she herself is taken up in Him in an analogous way as the flesh taken from her. Consequently the relation of the mother to the divine Son appears as a marriage with His divine person.[6]

Scheeben concludes that "no other name may be given to the mother than 'bride of God,' which of itself expresses a purely spiritual relation."[7] At the natural level, there is a blood relation between Mary and Jesus; on the spiritual level we can speak of her as God's bride. So deep and fundamental is Mary's union with God that Scheeben speaks of an "absolute community of possession and life" between them. We are adopted children of God; Mary's life in God goes beyond this, to a "most perfect and substantial admission into the family of God." And as the moon reflects beautifully and sweetly—we could say, "magically"—the light of the sun, so Mary has been made by God to be both the mirror of God and even an image of God. Scheeben points out that this likeness of God is similar to what St. Paul speaks of in I Corinthians 11:7,[8] in that she is the likeness and glory of God as "woman is the likeness and glory of the man."[9]

2) *Daughter and Spouse of God the Father*. Mary is often considered as the daughter of God the Father since she is related to His Son in the sense of a blood relation and as spiritual marriage. After Jesus, Scheeben notes, she is, outside of God, the most perfect image of the Father. As we are all in Christ made "sons in the Son," so Mary does this perfectly and, as already discussed, in the most superior manner. She is as a woman the daughter of God in a way that makes her "the most perfect image of the sonship of the eternal Son."[10] She can also be called "bride of the Father" since she possesses Jesus as Son with the Father in a joint manner, not by strict necessity, but by God's will. Jesus is Son of the Father *and* the Son of Mary. The Father begets Jesus eternally, Mary begets Jesus in time.
3) *Spouse of the Holy Spirit*. This is the most frequent way that Mary is understood as Spouse of God. She is the temple of the Holy Spirit and lives in such a close union

with Him that "Spouse" hardly gives an idea of the reality. The Holy Spirit forms Jesus in her womb. Scheeben thus speaks of the Holy Ghost "as the representative of the entire Trinity in its marriage with Mary…the bringing into prominence of the person of the Holy Ghost in the principle and the term of the marriage causes the union of Mary with God to appear, not as specifically limited to the person of her Son, and still less to that of the Father, but as extending to the entire Trinity."[11] St. Maximillian Kolbe will bring out the reality of Mary's union with the Holy Spirit *in particular* and in a still more specific manner, but Scheeben here speaks of the Holy Spirit's relation to Mary as spouse in regard to the Holy Trinity.

Mary then is the true "Spouse of the Triune God." Properly speaking, Mary cannot be the spouse of a human person in the sense of exclusivity—e.g., as if only St. Joseph *or* God could be the spouse of Mary. Her relationship with God is so intimate, unique and total that every other substantial relationship with her is truly a participation in living the life of God. Given this, St. Joseph is Mary's spouse by a God-willed participation in God's relationship with her.

In St. Joseph's marriage to Mary he loved her in a way that was truly exclusive: to her alone he gave his heart and his affections, shared his emotional life and his difficulties, manifested his deepest thoughts and shared his whole life, caring for her as his true wife. Their earthly marital union was a true union of mind and heart, and totally virginal. Theirs was a true communion of the domestic life, a family, the *Holy Family*, with Jesus as central.

Crucially for St. Joseph, and us, it is Mary who brings him into union with Jesus. Jesus only comes from her, and without intimacy with her, St. Joseph would never have been so intimate with Him. It is Mary that put the baby Jesus in St. Joseph's arms, and it is to Mary that Jesus returned when he was hungry, or wanted to sleep, or wanted to snuggle with His Beloved. It was upon her lap that Jesus would pray while St. Joseph was at work, and from her that He would run to him when he came home at night. It is no less for us: it is Mary who hands the infant Jesus to us in Holy Communion, and after He unites our hearts to His He goes back to her, bringing us with Him.

—Notes—

1. Luigi Gambero, *Mary and the Fathers of the Church*, p. 296
2. Fr. Manelli, FI, *All Generations Shall Call Me Blessed*, p. 418
3. For a fuller understanding, there is no substitute to reading Scheeben's book; often enough quotes can be taken and a work analyzed and that might suffice for a very thorough understanding of the author's intent, but in the case of Scheeben's book, there can be no substitute whatsoever—a treatment of Scheeben in this book truly embellishes in an important way the ideas here dealt with, but is like dipping one's hand into the deep end of a swimming pool—to really get everything out of Scheeben, one must simply jump in.
4. Scheeben, *Mariology*, p. 160
5. ibid, p. 161
6. ibid, p. 162
7. ibid, p. 163
8. "The man indeed ought not to cover his head, because he is the image and glory of God; but the woman is the glory of the man."
9. Scheeben, *Mariology*, p. 168
10. ibid, p. 174
11. ibid, p.177

Chapter Three
The Annunciation

"...and he that made me, rested in my tabernacle"[1]

The King, the Bridegroom, sends a message to the Queen, His Beloved. Consider: a holy angel, and one of the highest, is *saluting* a *human being*: an angel venerates Mary! This is not the normal way of things. Angels may talk to humans, relating God's commands and delivering blessings and punishments, but never have we seen an angel bow before a human being. Why not? Because human beings are a) sinners, and b) of a lower nature. Angels are superior both in nature and in grace. For an angel to act like St. Gabriel is with Mary means that this human person is a) not a sinner, and b) is exalted over all the angels. With Zacharias the angel commands and punishes; with God's Beloved the angel defers, ravished by love and respect, because he is before the Woman, she who is his Queen, and I dare say, like us, she is every angel's sweetheart as well. Here is the whole passage:

> And in the sixth month, the angel Gabriel was sent from God into a city of Galilee, called Nazareth, To a virgin espoused to a man whose name was Joseph, of

> the house of David; and the virgin' s name was Mary. And the angel being come in, said unto her: Hail, full of grace, the Lord is with thee: blessed art thou among women. Who having heard, was troubled at his saying, and thought with herself what manner of salutation this should be. And the angel said to her: Fear not, Mary, for thou hast found grace with God.
>
> Behold thou shalt conceive in thy womb, and shalt bring forth a son; and thou shalt call his name Jesus. He shall be great, and shall be called the Son of the most High; and the Lord God shall give unto him the throne of David his father; and he shall reign in the house of Jacob for ever. And of his kingdom there shall be no end. And Mary said to the angel: How shall this be done, because I know not man? And the angel answering, said to her: The Holy Ghost shall come upon thee, and the power of the most High shall overshadow thee. And therefore also the Holy which shall be born of thee shall be called the Son of God.
>
> And behold thy cousin Elizabeth, she also hath conceived a son in her old age; and this is the sixth month with her that is called barren: Because no word shall be impossible with God. And Mary said: Behold the handmaid of the Lord; be it done to me according to thy word. And the angel departed from her.[2]

So, first, the angel comes—and note this well—he comes to a "virgin espoused." Mary was not—let's get this right—*not* an "unwed" mother. We cannot look at "espousal" or sometimes rendered "engagement" anachronistically and, further, by foisting our own culture upon it. In the times when the Annunciation took place, Jewish marriage had two stages. The first was espousal, and this was a true marriage; this is when the essential matter of marriage took place. Should the husband want to leave her at that point, he would have to seek a divorce. After this first stage the spouses lived apart for some period of time, from weeks up to a year at most, and then the bride would come to live with her husband. Children born in this time were considered legitimate. But in plain, simple common sense, we could ask: would God allow His Beloved to be an unwed mother? St. John Paul II points out that the answer is most certainly "no," in paragraph 18 of his Apostolic Exhortation, *Redemptoris Custos*:

> Above all, the "just" man of Nazareth possesses the clear characteristics of a husband. Luke refers to Mary as "a virgin betrothed to a man whose name was Joseph" (Lk 1:27). Even before the "mystery hidden for ages" (Eph 3:9) began to be fulfilled, the Gospels set before us the image of husband and wife. According to Jewish custom, marriage took place in two stages: first, the legal, or true marriage was celebrated, and then, only after a certain period of time, the husband brought the wife into his own house. Thus, before he lived with Mary, Joseph was already her "husband."

The emphasis in the Annunciation, however, is also on "virgin." She is "*the virgin*." A young lady of Mary's age would be generally considered a virgin. So why the emphasis? For one, it would be no miracle if a woman who is married is soon with child. That is the normal course of things. This, however, would be extraordinary: a virgin shall be a mother! But there is more—this emphasis on "virgin" regards not only something that has not happened (marital relations), it is emphasized because, more importantly, this is Mary's very character; it speaks to *who she is* in the depths of her person: she is virginal as part of her very being.[3] She is "a garden enclosed, a fountain sealed"[4] in the depths of her soul and that is reflected bodily.

This reality is emphasized still more in the next words: "Hail, full of grace, the Lord is with thee." Here we see a rare biblical name change—however, this is not so much a name change as it is the *revealing* of Mary's identity. The angel does not call her "Mary" but "Full of Grace," which is best capitalized since it is a name, and it describes the reality of Mary. The word for "Full of Grace" is the Greek *kecharitomene*. Grammatically, *kecharitomene* is the feminine perfect passive aorist participle of the Greek verb "charitoo."[5] This Greek tense means that Mary had been transformed prior to the Annunciation, and that this transformation was a perduring state. As Dr. Machen points out in his book, *New Testament Greek for Beginners*, "The Greek perfect tense denotes the present state resultant upon a past action."[6] More specifically, "the past perfect participle form of the verb, 'charitoo' present in *kecharitomene*, is causative, indicating a change or transformation in the recipient, prior to the grace of maternity."[7] Dr. Scott Hahn writes of the word *kecharitomene*,

> It comes from charis, the Greek word for "grace" and basically means "made full of grace" or "transformed by grace."
>
> This is how the word is used in Paul's letter to the Ephesians[8], where he describes how God "granted"

> His grace to all of us in Jesus (see Ephesians 1:6-7). This sheds light on what the angel means—Mary has been "transformed by God's grace."[9]

It must also be stated that this distinct word is important for another reason: others are said to be "filled with the Holy Spirit," "full of the Holy Spirit" or "full of grace" as well. Yet the Greek for those situations is not *kecharitomene*, but the common *pletho*, Greek for "filled" (as in the lives of John the Baptist, Elizabeth and Zechariah). This indicates that Mary was not only sanctified before birth, as was John the Baptist, but that something still more unique happened to Mary; otherwise why stress the past action and perduring state with a new word, why not relate that she was "filled with the Holy Spirit" using the word "*pletho,*" as with John the Baptist? But this is not all. Connected to this phrase, yet before Mary's *fiat* to becoming the Mother of God, St. Gabriel says "…the Lord is with thee." The Archangel says this *before* Mary's *fiat*, thus before Jesus was incarnate within her…yet the Lord is already with her. Thus the phrase "full of grace" (*kecharitomene*) comes to be seen in a still more brilliant light, and leads to a few conclusions: 1) logically, no one could be "*full of grace*" if there were any trace of sin whatsoever, nor if there were any other blocks to grace such as faults, even the slightest; 2) this happened *in the past*, signified by *kecharitomene*; 3) the Lord is with her *prior* to her "yes" to being the Mother of God; 4) and she belongs to God so completely that He can "overshadow" her in a radically transformative way such that God's own Son is Incarnate within her (in this regard, common sense asks, "Would God assume a human nature from a *sinful* human being?" The heart rebels at such a thought!).

Scheebben speaks to this reality when he writes,

> ...the sanctifying grace bestowed on her surpasses incomparably that of all other creatures. Her grace is particularly distinguished from that of other mortals as a *gratia perpetua; perpetua a parte post*, i.e., never ceasing, as contrasted with the first couple; *perpetua a parte ante*, i.e., beginning with her origin as contrasted with the descendants of our first parents. However, the specific character of Mary's divine relationship as child of God is inexhaustible; in it sanctifying grace must be pictured as based on, borne, and animated by her special relation to God.[10]

Indeed, "the Fathers call Mary the 'only beloved' and 'only begotten' child or daughter of God."[11] In regard to Mary we are not speaking merely of a sinless woman—Eve, too, was sinless at first. Mary, however, is both Immaculate and "full of grace," brought into a unique relationship with God immediately upon her conception that made it possible for her to become the Mother of God. What kind of woman would a woman have to be to clothe God and raise Him as her own Son? She would in essence have to be made as close to God and as like God as possible for a creature to be.

At the Annunciation, Mary is transformed still more as the Holy Spirit "overshadows" her, and God the Son is Incarnate within her; she is transfigured by the Holy Spirit into the *Mother of God*. The specific language used by Luke to describe the Holy Spirit's transforming power at the Annunciation is intriguing, and he uses the same language when describing the cloud of the Transfiguration, out of which God the Father speaks to Peter, James and

John. In both instances, Luke uses the word *episkiazo* for "overshadow," a rich word with a specific history. This word "seems to have been drawn from the familiar OT idea of a cloud as symbolizing the immediate presence and power of God."[12] More specifically, "The expression used by the angel is the same used in the Greek version of Ex. 40:35 to describe how Yahweh 'overshadowed' the Tabernacle, making it his dwelling place in Israel."[13] *Episkiazo* thus does not have a salvation-historical reference to a meaning such as a "haze" or something like, "to impose a shadow upon something or someone." Rather, *espiskiazo* means "to *invest* with preternatural influence."[14] Specifically relating to Mary, this word is, "Used of the Holy Spirit exerting creative energy upon the womb of the Virgin Mary…"[15] But perhaps Venerable Fulton Sheen provides some of the best commentary on the word, "overshadow"[16]:

> God had told Moses, "Make a tabernacle that I may dwell with my people." Tabernacles were of stone and gold until an angel came to the Blessed Mother and asked her if she would become the mother of our Lord. She said, "I am a virgin. I do not know man."
>
> And God said: "In the older tabernacles there was the Shekinah, 'the cloud of my presence,' that overshadowed the temple. Now my Holy Spirit will overshadow you, and he that will be born of you will be called the Son of the Most High God."[17]

Between God and Mary we also see the whispering of a secret; it is an intimate secret, and God first shares it with Mary prior to revealing it to any other person on earth:

> And Mary said to the angel: How shall this be done, because I know not man? And the angel answering, said to her: The Holy Ghost shall come upon thee, and the power of the most High shall overshadow thee. And therefore also the Holy which shall be born of thee shall be called the Son of God.

This secret could hardly be more intimate! God, through the angel, has just revealed Himself in His inner life; He is Three Persons yet one God, a Trinity of Love: "the Holy Ghost" "the most High," "the Son"; and the Son—the *Heart of the Father*, we could say—is given to Mary. Prior to this, as St. Gregory of Nazianzus points out,[18] only the Father, and to a lesser extent the Son, had been revealed in the Old Testament. Thus the first instance of the transformation of mankind's knowledge of God as Holy Trinity is given at the Annunciation to Mary. God gives Mary His Heart, and at this Mary's reaction must have been a sort of fulfilment of this phrase from the *Song of Songs*: "My soul melted when he spoke."[19] And in her utter abasement, her ocean of humility, Full of Grace calls herself only—though truly—"Handmaid of the Lord." With her *fiat* the Heart of God becomes man within her, and God and humanity are married, and the first part of the Proverbs 9 meal with Lady Wisdom is fulfilled: "she has mixed her wine…"[20]

Thus for the first time, a human being totally and completely belongs to God.[21] This is a new thing in creation! Opposed to Eve's "no" to God is Mary's "yes" to God. As St. Maximillian Kolbe wrote, "In the Holy Spirit's union with Mary we observe more than the love of two beings; in one there is all the love of the Blessed Trinity; in the other, all of creation's love… So it is that in this union heaven and earth are joined; all of heaven with all the earth."[22] This is the first time, and due to the Holy Spirit's transforming power, that "all of creation" has loved God perfectly.

This also puts to rest a question sometimes asked: Did Mary know her Son is God? Yes. The angel made this clear by calling him "Son of God" in context with the Trinitarian nature of God, and by proclaiming that her Son would be King "forever"—something that surpasses the bounds of time and space; this would be no mere human/temporal kingship. As Fr. Manelli writes, "By the presence and operation of the Holy Spirit in the virginal womb of Mary, the new conception will not only be miraculous but 'divine'…The two terms *'holy'* and *'Son of God'* are an even more explicit reaffirmation of the divinity of Christ."[23] There is also the important aspect of her consent at issue here: to give her full and perfect consent she had to know what was being asked of her. Fr. Manelli speaks to this as well, citing the work of Fr. Harrington, who writes that absent an understanding of the heart of the message, Mary could not have given consent to God via the angel or made an act of faith; this act of faith includes the matter of the divinity of Christ, though there is a certain "darkness that is a necessary feature of faith."[24] To be confused about or lacking in essential knowledge of what God was asking her would imply some defect in her consent.

Also note the length of the conversation with the angel; it's short! We learn something of Mary in this, too. From her incessant union with God, uninterrupted prayer and her studies of Scripture, she who is Lady Wisdom did not need to interrupt the conversation to look things up, consult with someone, or ask for a few days to think about what God was asking. She had only one question, concerning her virginity—which was a total and exclusive gift of self to God and thus she rightly had to inquire about this aspect—and the answer from God via the angel she immediately and humbly accepted. This is the fruit of her incessant prayer, absolute unity with God, and her study and pondering of Scripture; the astounding speed with which she was able to grasp and consent to all the angel said leads to that conclusion. She is able to perceive with an extreme clarity the mysteries of God. And at the time of the Annunciation she was a fourteen or fifteen-year-old Jewish girl of her time and culture, when prayer and study were expected and practiced, and so she did (though it must have been obvious to some degree that Mary was not usual in this regard. If it strikes us in our own lives to see a young person who is on fire for love of God and is truly holy, to see Mary would have been fascinatingly wondrous).

And we too are implicated in the Annunciation, more than one would think at first glance, just as we are implicated in regard to Lady Wisdom. True, we are implicated in the general sense that Jesus is our Redeemer and in that without Mary's "yes" we would be without Him. Yet our inclusion here is more specific and more intimate: we are each present at the Annunciation, and in the most intense way imaginable for we are mere human creatures: we are each, individually, present in Mary's womb with the Eternal Word at the moment Mary says "yes." Let that sink in for a moment. It is incredible to think that a very few people in the realm of history actually have their names recorded in the Bible, in the written Word of God (some to their glory, some to their shame). And we are as well (and this will become clearer at the Cross). Pope St. Pius X explains:

> Wherefore in the same holy bosom of his most chaste Mother, Christ took to Himself flesh, and united to Himself the spiritual body formed by those who were to believe in Him. Hence Mary, carrying the Savior within her, may be said to have also carried all those whose life was contained in the life of the Savior. Therefore all we who are united to Christ, and as the Apostle says are members of His body, of His flesh, and of His bones (Ephes. v., 30), have issued from the womb of Mary like a body united to its head.[25]

In a mystical but *true* way, you and I were carried in Mary's Immaculate Heart and Body with Jesus.[26] From eternity we were meant to be one with Christ—we were made for this—and it is Mary's "yes" that made us His brethren. This reality exists on a level we cannot fathom, but it is true nonetheless. She knew that saying "yes" to God's Incarnation was saying "yes" to you and me. Now in regard to Jesus, she and He knew each other and communicated with each other, though Mary's communication with God has taken on an added dimension; we need only consider the biological facts of the amazing bond physical and otherwise between mother and baby in the womb. As for us, while she knew she carried us as well, and although in a mystical fashion, this aspect was much like any other motherhood, where the mother knows there is a baby, but the knowledge of that specific, new little individual is darkened until the baby is born and they see each other face to face and she can hold him in her arms close to her heart. And as with such mothers, Mary loved us while we were in the womb too, spiritually as yet unborn.

—Notes—

1. Sirach 24:12
2. Luke 1:26-38
3. With the dogma of the Immaculate Conception and St. Maximilian Kolbe's insights, this reality of Mary as Virgin, such that "Mary" and "Virgin" are synonymous, will become more clear, and will be covered in another chapter.
4. *Song of Songs*
5. Paul Haffner, *The Mystery of Mary*, p. 74
6. p. 187
7. Paul Haffner, *The Mystery of* Mary, p. 74
8. For a more in-depth treatment of Paul's use of *kecharitomene* see page 74 of *The Mystery of Mary* by Paul Haffner.
9. Hahn, "The Angel and Mary"
10. Scheeben, *Mariology*, pp. 169-170
11. ibid, p. 169
12. *Strong's Greek* 1982
13. Scott Hahn, *Ignatius Catholic Study Bible*, p. 105
14. *Strong's Greek* 1982
15. *Thayer's Greek Lexicon*. Also see the *New Jerome Biblical Commentary*, page 681, #35 for another gloss on this fact of the Holy Spirit's transformative action, as well as CCC 497 and 723.
16. See these works as well, which also contain a study of the words "Shekinah" and "overshadow" in regard to Mary: "Mary, the Ark of the New Covenant," by Steve Ray; "The sign of the Temple," by Danielou; and "Jesus, the New Temple, and the New Priesthood" by Brant Pitre.
17. From, "Mary, Tabernacle of the Lord"
18. CCC 684 quotes St. Gregory at greater length concerning the revelation of the Holy Trinity.
19. *Song of Songs*, 5:6
20. Proverbs 9:2
21. Cf. *Redemptoris Mater*:, par. 8: "And, what is more, together with

the Father, the Son has chosen her, entrusting her eternally to the Spirit of holiness. In an entirely special and exceptional way Mary is united to Christ, and similarly she is eternally loved in this 'be-loved Son,' this Son who is of one being with the Father, in whom is concentrated all the 'glory of grace.'"

22. Manteau-Bonamy, p. 5
23. Manelli, *All Generations Shall Call Me Blessed*, pp. 174-175
24. p. 176
25. *Ad Diem Illum*, par. 10
26. St. Louis de Montfort speaks of this as well, writing in his book *True Devotion*, "God the Father has communicated to Mary His fruitfulness, as far as a mere creature was capable of it, in order that He might give her the power to produce His Son, and all the members of His mystical body" n. 17.

Chapter Four
The Visitation

> The admirable Heart of Mary is the Heaven of Heaven...who would dare contradict St. Bernardine of Siena, who tells us that the Most Blessed Virgin Mary, like a good mother, carries all her children in her Heart? Who will contradict me if I add that Our Lady will forever carry all the inhabitants of heaven in her inmost Heart, which becomes the Heaven of Heaven, and a true Paradise of the elect, in which they find delight and joy, due to the inconceivable love for each soul which consumes her maternal Heart?...O Heaven, enclosing Him whom the heaven of heavens cannot contain... wherein the King of Heaven reigns more completely than in all other heavens![1]

One day in the hill country of Juda, God's Beloved came, she who is the true Ark of God's presence: Lady Wisdom carries Wisdom Incarnate! We could say that she who is a new Heaven and the new Earth, from which springs the New Adam, has encountered the old earth and the old Adam, and the new has completely eclipsed the old. "Who is this that cometh up from the desert, flowing with delights, leaning upon her beloved?"[2] The first earth, says St. John Eudes, was given to Adam and to mankind, and is now a place that is corrupt and dark, full of weeds, a place of death; the new earth, he writes, is full of grace and sweetness, light and life and is Mary, while the first earth is "only an imperfect image and sketch" of the new earth.[3] Yes, delights flow from her, and Elizabeth and her child in the womb experience them.

> And Mary rising up in those days, went into the hill country with haste into a city of Juda. And she entered into the house of Zachary, and saluted Elizabeth.
>
> And it came to pass, that when Elizabeth heard the salutation of Mary, the infant leaped in her womb. And Elizabeth was filled with the Holy Ghost: And she cried out with a loud voice, and said: Blessed art thou among women, and blessed is the fruit of thy womb. And whence is this to me, that the mother of my Lord should come to me? For behold as soon as the voice of thy salutation sounded in my ears, the infant in my womb leaped for joy. And blessed art thou that hast believed, because those things shall be accomplished that were spoken to thee by the Lord.[4]

Mary, the Ark

Mary goes "with haste"—not because she doubted the angel, but rather she went in haste to do something charitable.[5] This is not a sudden change in Mary, as if she had never gone to another in haste before. Rather, "with haste" describes *who she is, what she is like*. This is an aspect of her personality. Had we known her then as friend or family, we would have seen her do this kind of thing other times as well. She always went in haste, and does still now in a more perfect manner, anytime she was needed. At Cana, too, she will hasten to help the married couple. And so she goes in haste, to the "hill country," and stays there for three months, in a clear reference to 2 Samuel 6:11,12, where the Ark stays with Obededom for three months in the Hill country: "And the ark of the Lord abode in the house of Obededom the Gethite three months: and the Lord blessed Obededom, and all his household. And it was told king David, that the Lord had blessed Obededom, and all that he had, because of the ark of God." Luke, and God through Him, is telling us in no uncertain terms that Mary is in fact the *new Ark*. He doesn't end there either, he goes on: just as in 2 Samuel 6:14-16 we read that,

> "David danced with all his might before the Lord: and David was girded with a linen ephod. And David and all the house of Israel brought the ark of the covenant of the Lord with joyful shouting, and with sound of trumpet. And when the ark of the Lord was come into the city of David, Michol the daughter of Saul, looking out through a window, saw king David leaping and dancing before the Lord."

So here in Luke, as the fourteen or fifteen-year-old Mother of God comes to St. Elizabeth and the enwombed St. John, we find it is said of Elizabeth that "the infant leaped in her womb. And St. Elizabeth was filled with the Holy Ghost: And she cried out with a loud voice, and said: Blessed art thou among women, and blessed is the fruit of thy womb." David leaps, and John leaps; Israel shouts with joy over the first Ark, and St. Elizabeth, representing Israel, shouts with joy at the new and perfect Ark.

There is one more parallel here to be noted. Just prior to David bringing the Ark to Obededom, Oza takes it upon himself, "rashly" Scripture says, to touch the Ark, and he is killed by the Lord on the spot, right before the Ark.[6] Living close to the Ark of God's presence calls for the utmost respect that is borne out of the utmost love. St. Joseph surely knew this Scripture passage, and now he finds himself in constant and close proximity—in the most intimate bonds!—with the new Ark, an Ark that far surpasses the ark of old, carrying the presence of God in a way superior to the ark of old. This couldn't have been lost on St. Joseph. The difference, however, is love. St. Joseph would never have presumed to touch Mary in any way except the most purely virginal, as he had what Oza did not—an incomprehensible love for God and Mary, far beyond our own, and a mission far beyond our own since he would be the father of Jesus on earth, representing the Father (it is no mere hyperbole to call him "good St. Joseph").[7] A presumptuous touch of the new Ark is something that would be totally out of his character, as an act of presumption in this regard would have been truly lacking in that respect borne out of love.

Motherly-Queenly Mediation

It can initially be deduced, by considering the visits of St. Gabriel to Zechariah and Mary, that in Luke 1:41-45 St. Elizabeth experiences a transformation of her understanding via the Holy

Spirit. Indeed she is flooded with grace; according to Luke, while Mary was told that St. Elizabeth was with child, St. Elizabeth did not know about Mary being with child, nor what St. Gabriel told Mary. Yet we read that,

> ...when Elizabeth heard the salutation of Mary, the infant leapt in her womb. And Elizabeth was filled with the Holy Ghost: And she cried out in a loud voice, and said: Blessed art thou among women, and blessed is the fruit of thy womb. And whence is this to me, that the mother of my Lord should come to me? For behold as soon as the voice of thy salutation sounded in my ears, the infant in my womb leapt for joy. And blessed art thou that hast believed, because those things shall be accomplished that were spoken to thee by the Lord.

There is only one way that St. Elizabeth could have come to any of these conclusions: "And Elizabeth was filled with the Holy Ghost..." In the three canticles (Mary's, Zachariah's, Simeon's) we see that before the canticle is presented the person proclaiming the canticle is specifically noted by Luke to be influenced by the Holy Spirit. As in the case of St. Elizabeth's son, we find here the Greek *pletho*, which means to "*imbue, influence, supply*"[8]; St. Elizabeth's understanding is thus *supernaturalized* by the Holy Spirit, and this is manifested in her words to Mary.

A striking instance of St. Elizabeth's supernaturalized insight in verses 41-45 is the phrase "mother of my Lord." "This title reveals the twin mysteries of Jesus' divinity and Mary's divine maternity (CCC 449, 495). Note that every occurrence of the word *Lord* in the immediate (1:45) and surrounding context refers to

God (1:28, 32, 38, 46, 58, 68)."[9] More to the point, as Scott Hahn points out in his book *Hail, Holy Queen*, the queen in the Davidic kingdom was the *mother* of the king, not his wife; the king often had many wives—which then would be the queen? The title of this woman was *Gebirah*, or "Great Lady," which was no empty title, but told of the immense authority of the Queen Mother.[10] Without the dynamic, transforming influence of the Holy Spirit, St. Elizabeth could not have known that Mary's child is the heir of the Davidic Throne, God Himself Incarnate, and thus Mary the Queen and Mother of "the Lord."

Mary's Canticle

> And Mary said: My soul doth magnify the Lord. And my spirit hath rejoiced in God my Saviour. Because he hath regarded the humility of his handmaid; for behold from henceforth all generations shall call me blessed. Because he that is mighty, hath done great things to me; and holy is his name. And his mercy is from generation unto generations, to them that fear him. He hath shewed might in his arm: he hath scattered the proud in the conceit of their heart. He hath put down the mighty from their seat, and hath exalted the humble. He hath filled the hungry with good things; and the rich he hath sent empty away. He hath received Israel his servant, being mindful of his mercy: As he spoke to our fathers, to Abraham and to his seed for ever.[11]

In this canticle we again find, as we did in the account of

the Annunciation, an instance of Mary's own words. They have, in fact, the feminine touch of a devout teenaged Jewish girl of the time, and we know this because the various holy women of the Jewish people in Scripture is something they would have particularly studied. Mary knew better than any the Scriptures and the canticles therein: she knew Proverbs, she knew about Judith, Esther, Hannah and other women of Jewish history[12] who were model examples of women, and of course she speaks of God as understood by a devout Jew at that time. Fathers Hoffman and Cole in their study, "The Canticles of Luke: Arguments for Authenticity," note that "...a woman would be attracted to the exemplary women of the Old Testament, especially those as worthy of imitation as Hannah," and they go on to show that Mary uses the canticle of Hannah[13] as a sort of basic form for the Magnificat (she would have known these various passages by heart from study and memorizing), but Mary turns it into something brilliant; indeed, the two Fathers point out that "The speaker [Mary] is humble and at the same time intelligent and self-possessed. Unlike some men and women on great occasions she is not overly emotional. These ten verses are, in short, the literary masterpiece that Hannah's is not." And of course it is no coincidence that Mary uses similar language, taking phrases that in fact pertain to her, perhaps most obviously the phrase, "All generations shall call me blessed," which are spoken by Judith and reiterated in Proverbs 31. Here we find not a conceited or prideful boasting, but Mary's humble acknowledgement of what *God* has done in her, she who thinks of herself in her utter humility as "the handmaid," while she is in fact also the Mother of God, God Who is King of Kings, thus making her Queens of Queens. Words, however, are never enough: she not only names herself "handmaid," she lives it—she went to Elizabeth not to be served, but to serve.

The Holy Spirt and Mary's Canticle

It is noteworthy that the canticle of Mary is the only one of the three canticles in Luke that does *not* begin with a statement that the person proclaiming the canticle is undergoing some type of transformative experience of the Holy Spirit. Both Elizabeth (although her words do not constitute a canticle) and Zechariah (as we will see) are "filled," *pletho*, with the Holy Spirit, and their minds are illumined with divine insight, while Simeon (Luke 2:25) is "inspired" or led ("came by the Spirit"), *en o pneuma*, and speaks by the light of the Holy Spirit. The silence concerning the Holy Spirit immediately prior to Mary's canticle, however, is the sort of silence that speaks volumes, and is essentially no silence at all. There are two points in regard to this: 1) Luke knew perfectly well what he meant when he wrote *kecharitomene*. Again, this word "indicates that God has already 'graced' Mary previous to this point, making her a vessel who 'has been' and 'is now' filled with divine life"[14]; 2) The Holy Spirit "overshadowed" Mary at the Annunciation; *espiskiazo* means "to *invest* with preternatural influence,"[15] and it is clear from St. Gabriel's words that the child she was carrying in her womb is Himself divine. There is thus no cause to reiterate prior to her canticle that Mary was "filled" with the Holy Spirit, since this was manifestly the truth. Mary's canticle too, then, is borne out of the prevenient transformation of Mary by the Holy Spirit in her Immaculate Conception. Luke's silence on this point just prior to Mary's canticle thus implicitly emphasizes both her immaculate nature from her conception and her divine motherhood.

—Notes—

1. St. John Eudes, *The Admirable Heart of Mary*, chapter 11 "Mary's Heart, the Heavens"
2. *Song of Songs* 8:5
3. *The Admirable Heart of Mary*, chapter IV, "Mary's Heart, the Center of the Earth"
4. Luke 1:39-45
5. Bastero, *Mary, Mother of the Redeemer*, p. 113
6. See 2 Samuel 6:6-10
7. The question may arise, "But what of St. Catherine Laboure, who knelt right by Mary with her hands folded on Mary's lap for two hours?" Neither are we Oza, any more than St. Joseph was; we are truly her children, and as Jesus no doubt prayed by kneeling with His hands on her lap, so do we share His intimacy with her—indeed, we share His sonship, His Father becomes Our Father, and thus His Mother our Mother.
8. *Strong's Greek* 4128
9. Hahn, *The Ignatius Catholic Study Bible, New Testament*, p. 106
10. Pages 78-82. Hahn also points to 1 Kings 2:19 as a striking example of the power structure in Israel, as well as chapter 31 of Proverbs.
11. Luke 2:46-51
12. Concrete connections are something that we need as human beings. One aspect of holy relics is that they make solidly real various facets of salvation history and lives of Saints. The relic of the Cross is the actual wood touched by Jesus and seen—and no doubt touched as well—by Mary. They read the same Old Testament books. And on earth they saw the same moon and sun that we do.

13. 1 Samuel 2:1-10
14. Hahn, *The Ignatius Catholic Study Bible, New Testament*, p.105
15. *Strong's Greek* 1982

Chapter Five
The Nativity through Cana

Here we find another fulfillment of Proverbs 9—*Lady Wisdom's meal is set out.* The Bread from Heaven, born in Bethlehem—"Bethlehem" means "House of Bread"—is placed by Mary in the manger, which is a feeding trough for animals. We became like animals when Adam fell into sin, and now God comes down to our level as heavenly food to lift us up from our lowly estate to His Divine Life. The wine has been mixed, and now the Bread is ready. At the Last Supper, the first Mass—that is, Calvary, since the Mass makes the Sacrifice of Jesus on the Cross present—we will (and today still do) find the final fulfillment of Lady Wisdom's meal in Proverbs 9: "And entering into the house, they found the child with Mary his mother."[1] This is what the wise do: they enter Lady Wisdom's house. And when you find Lady Wisdom, you find the Child. In Lady Wisdom's house of seven pillars (the Catholic Church) we find, under sacramental form, "the child with Mary his mother." Here in Bethlehem, we find unveiled in history "the child and his mother." Proverbs 9 then points to our times—we encounter Lady Wisdom in the Church of seven pillars/seven Sacraments and find the Child, the heavenly meal of the Mother, at the altar under the appearance of bread and wine.

Indeed, the phrase "the child and his mother" must be important since Matthew uses it several times, in verses 11, 13, 14, 20 and 21. He never says of St Joseph in these verses, "take your wife and child." The focus is on a) the child and b) his mother. Those two particularly are together and form one unit. If you want one, you get the other. When the wise men come to adore Christ, Mary isn't ushered out of the room. They adore God Incarnate, and they do this in Mary's presence. Immediately after the wise men leave, Matthew continues with the phrase "the child and his mother." Similarly, if you go to a married friend's house, you get both husband and wife—one does not leave simply because a friend of one or the other arrived. Here the union of Jesus and Mary is still greater, and to adore Christ is also to honor His Mother, and honoring His Mother means adoring Christ. Certainly it pleased Mary to no end, with raptures of joy, to present her Son to the world for loving adoration. And there is no doubt that it made Jesus very happy that when the wise men adored Him Mary was not excluded. Again, "they found the child with Mary his mother, and falling down they adored him," and from this we see that they entered and Jesus and Mary were together, and that *immediately* they adored Jesus who was in the arms of His Mother. Mary leads to Jesus, and to find Jesus is also to find Mary. They weren't shy about kneeling down before Jesus and Mary both, *adoring* Jesus in their hearts while *honoring* Mary in their hearts at the same time and in the same place. Jesus, after all, made His own Mother and had her in mind from eternity; to adore Jesus and ask Mary, in effect, to leave in the meantime would have been, and still is today, an awful offense against God and His Mother.

St. Joseph, of course, was the first one to enter the abode of Lady Wisdom and her Heavenly Bread, and the phrase above continues with St. Joseph, who takes not once, but three times, the "child and his mother." He took them to Bethlehem, then to Egypt, then out of Egypt and to Nazareth. In fact, we see two manners of life here. The life of the wise men was wise; we could say they visit the child and his mother on the biggest occasions (Sunday Mass and holy days of obligation). This is indeed wisdom! But then there is the life of St. Joseph: he lived with the child and his mother, daily, and later died in their arms. Both are available, but that the latter mode of life is open to us is beyond astonishing. One type adores Christ and honors Mary, the other does as well, but goes further, as that soul takes Mary as beloved and her Jesus becomes, for that soul and Mary, "our Jesus," as they live together *one life*. Luke seems to emphasize this as well, in a different way, writing, "And they [the shepherds] came with haste; and they found Mary and Joseph, and the infant lying in the manger." Here we find a unity stressed between Mary and Joseph, a unity that is *based on* Jesus, the Bread from Heaven, as central. In some way, we all step into St Joseph's place, also sharing in this participatory union with Mary as he does. When someone comes to us we could ask, do they too find "[Name], Mary and the infant Jesus"? Every Catholic in the world that we come across should, spiritually, be a finding of that individual, Mary and Jesus together. To put it in a concrete phrase, you meet your friend Rachel, and you find "Rachel, Mary and the infant Jesus." We likely won't see this with our physical eyes (though it's not impossible[2]), but the spiritual reality is present.

Loss of Jesus

After all the phrases of "the child and his mother" (Matthew's Gospel), it is jarring to then read that the child is lost to his mother (Luke's Gospel). Luke here continues his theme of "Mary and Joseph" and Jesus as central to them as a couple (rather than Matthew's "the child and his mother" and then mentioning Joseph). Jesus is the Heart of Mary's Heart, and to lose Him would have been a hellish experience—the loss of Jesus is the loss of all, and for Mary God is all, her life *in toto*, her every good. It was a dark night for her beyond what any Saint has or ever will experience when God seems to have forsaken a person; it's a rupture of the highest magnitude. Joseph, too, experiences this terrifying and saddening loss, albeit to a degree much less than Mary. And so upon the fear and terror of the loss of a child on the natural level there was also the sense of supernatural loss. This loss was much greater than her other sufferings in one particular way: in this suffering she had no idea where Jesus was! What could the reason be? It was all darkness without consolation. Mary feels the thrust of the sword of which Simeon had spoken, a first thrust of the sword. Abandoned by God. Her Heart and soul are expanded by indescribably heroic acts of love, faith, and hope. Joseph is brought into this experience because he lives one life with Mary, the two espoused, and when Jesus is found again He is found by Joseph *with Mary*. St. Alphonsus points to several phrases from the Old Testament that are connected to this experience[3], and they can be chained together to form one whole lament:

> I sought him, and found him not. I will rise, and will go about the city: in the streets and the broad ways I

> will seek him whom my soul loveth: I sought him, and I found him not.[4] The boy doth not appear and whither shall I go?[5] As the hart panteth after the fountains of water; so my soul panteth after thee, O God. My soul hath thirsted after the strong living God; when shall I come and appear before the face of God? My tears have been my bread day and night, whilst it is said to me daily: Where is thy God?[6] Shew me, O thou whom my soul loveth, where thou feedest, where thou liest in the midday.[7] My heart is troubled, my strength hath left me, and the light of my eyes itself is not with me.[8]

Although she and Joseph know that Jesus is Divine, this loss of Jesus was not entirely understood. It was something for Mary to ponder in her Heart. Jesus knows how to play with souls, to form them, to expand their hearts, and in all of Mary's sufferings we find an expansion of love, virtues and further inundation of grace. At the Annunciation she is "full of grace," and with each passing sword she swells to a veritable infinity of overflowing graces.

And in her sufferings she grows ever closer to us as well. She endears herself to us more and more: she knows the blackness where there seems to be no God, she knows what it is like to not comprehend trials, she knows what it is to love and lose, she knows what it is to experience the most vexing and heart-rending of tragedies as sword after sword pierces her Heart—a Heart that has no sin. That suffering is compounded unimaginably since she perceives more deeply even than all the angels the infinite love and goodness of God, and this infinitely precious love is hers: what she experiences by His loss and later suffering and death is, then, an almost, or *quasi*, infinite torment. She will later hear her most Beloved—her God, her Son, her Father, her Spouse—utter the most haunting words; imagine hearing this of your own child (think two-year-old) innocent, tortured and nailed to a cross: "My God, my God, why have you abandoned me?" She knows suffering.[9] There is no heart from atheist to pagan to sinner to Saint who cannot find comfort in Mary. She is the Queen of all Hearts, her Heart encompasses and understands all other hearts. She is also the "Queen of Gentleness": there is no rebuke when she says to Jesus, "Son, why hast thou done so to us? behold thy father and I have sought thee sorrowing."[10] It is a complaint of trusting love, filled with grief of loss giving way to joy. Nevertheless…it is a mystery, something to ponder within one's heart.

Cana

Cana—or rather, the road to Cana—really begins at John 1:1, not John 2:1. John 1:1 begins as Genesis did: "In the beginning…" John's Gospel begins in eternity, with God, and then enters time at verse 6 and the details of this first day come at verse 19 when the priests and Levites come to John the Baptist. We also know this is "day one," because day two begins at verse 29 with the words, "The next day, John saw Jesus coming to him…" Thus this is day two. Then in verse 35 we find this: "The next day again John stood, and two of his disciples." This is day three. In 1:43 we find Jesus gathering his disciples, and that is a new day too: "On the following day, he would go forth into Galilee…" So we are now at day four. Chapter two simply continues where chapter 1 left off (originally there were no chapter and verse separations in Scripture, such as we have now): "And the third day, there was a marriage in Cana…" This isn't a reversion to day three, of course—rather, three more days have been added to the first four: the wedding takes place on the seventh day, as in Genesis. What is happening here, John is telling us, is a new creation. Now, although the wedding at Cana is on the natural level the earthly marriage of a particular couple, a wedding to which Mary and Jesus were invited, there is no mention of any names except those of Jesus and Mary, who quickly become the focus of the wedding. And so on this seventh day of the new creation, what we find are two specific people known by name: Jesus and Mary, the New Adam and the New Eve.[11] Jesus makes this more apparent by calling Mary "Woman," a connection to the prophecy of Genesis 3:15—Mary is the New Eve, who with her seed crushes the devil's head. And once Jesus reveals Himself by a miracle that only God could work, Mary will no longer be simply "the Mother of Jesus," but the time of her birthing of *us* will commence, her birth pains will begin, she will be the Woman, and our Mother too. The specific verse pertaining to this commencement of Jesus' public ministry and road to the Cross is, "And the wine failing, the mother of Jesus saith to him: They have no wine. And Jesus saith to her: Woman, what is that to me and to thee? my hour is not yet come. His mother saith to the waiters: Whatsoever he shall say to you, do ye."[12] So Jesus calling Mary "Woman" was not a rebuke. In fact, not only does it refer to Mary as the promised Woman of Genesis, it was a term of honor that is best translated as "Lady."[13] And Jesus knows that Mary's words are the words of the Holy Spirit, and here the Holy Spirit in union with Mary is leading Jesus on to His public ministry, as the Holy Spirit led Jesus into the desert.[14] This is mentioned in Matthew and Luke. But there is another detail here as well, because the verse before this adds to the next. In whole it reads, "And there came a voice from heaven: Thou art my beloved Son; in thee I am well pleased. And immediately the Spirit drove him out into the desert."[15] Only Mary beside God the Father can call Jesus, "my beloved son; in thee I am well pleased." This seems to be the situation at Cana; Mary is well pleased in her Son, and she in union with the Spirit send Him to His public ministry, just as the Holy Spirit sent Jesus into the desert after the Father expressed His pleasure in Jesus. So Jesus is not saying "You're wrong, it's not my hour." If that were the case, logically Jesus would not have performed the miracle of the wine! But as He would not become incarnate without Mary's presence and consent, He won't begin His public ministry without her presence and consent, and neither will He die without her presence and consent.

In this we also see Mary as the Beloved, and the New Adam allowing Himself to be moved at the request of His Spouse. The *Song of Songs* also comes into play here with a fulfillment of the verse, "O my sister, my spouse, I have gathered my myrrh, with my aromatical spices: I have eaten the honeycomb with my honey, I have drunk my wine with my milk: eat, O friends, and drink, and be inebriated, my dearly beloved." The *RSVCE* phrases that last portion of that verse, "Eat, O friends, and drink: drink deeply, O lovers!" The lovers of course are especially the New Adam and Eve, and "be inebriated" or else "drink deeply, O lovers!" certainly seems connected to the massive amount of wine that Jesus created: "Now there were set there six waterpots of stone, according to the manner of the purifying of the Jews, containing two or three measures apiece."[16] Each water pot of that type was known to contain around twenty or more gallons; so at least 120 gallons of the best wine, if not more. Later the New Adam will turn wine into Blood, again with the consent of the New Eve,[17] and there we find perhaps an application of these verses from the *Song of Songs*: "For your love is better than wine, your anointing oils are fragrant, your name is oil poured out; therefore the maidens love you. Draw me after you, let us make haste. The king has brought me into his chambers. We will exult and rejoice in you; we will extol your love more than wine; rightly do they love you."[18] Better than wine indeed is the Blood of Christ.

And so, as she does every step of the way, Mary here makes a sacrifice of Christ for us. She will no longer simply be the Mother of Jesus, she will more actively step into her role as the Mother of the new humanity! She immediately sacrifices Jesus when He is born, placing Him in the manger. She does it here at Cana, too, sending Him on to His public ministry and death on the Cross. They both know this is what will happen when He manifests His divinity by the miracle of turning water into wine. But this is not the first time that she has made this sacrifice. Let's do a sort of flashback here...

The Presentation and Her Sorrowful Heart

Thirty years or so earlier she had brought Jesus to the Temple[19] when He was eight days old. This is a sort of pre-Sacrifice, or Jesus' Sacrifice in miniature. At the Visitation, we saw that Mary saw something of herself in Hannah, and in Hannah a sort of model to follow. Hannah could have no children, "because the LORD had closed her womb."[20] But He hears her lament and gives her a baby boy, and then Hannah presents her little one to Eli the priest, a presentation that has clear parallels to Mary's:

> So the woman remained and nursed her son, until she weaned him. And when she had weaned him, she took him up with her, along with a three-year-old bull, an ephah of flour, and a skin of wine; and she brought him to the house of the LORD at Shiloh; and the child was young. Then they slew the bull, and they brought the child to Eli. And she said, "Oh, my lord! As you live, my lord, I am the woman who was standing here in your presence, praying to the LORD. For this child I prayed; and the LORD has granted me my petition which I made to him. Therefore I have lent him to the LORD; as long as he lives, he is lent to the LORD."[21]

As soon as He is eight days old He is offered to God in the Temple as Mary's offering of Jesus to the Father in the form of a preliminary rite, one that will take vivid form on the Cross. Mary gives up her Beloved as a sacrifice several times in fact: at the Nativity, the Presentation, Cana and the Cross. She always does what God wants, even at the cost of tremendous pain in the face of humanly baffling circumstances. Mary trusts God with absolute confidence, never wavering. Her faith far exceeds that of Abraham, who was asked to believe that he and his wife, both quite old, would have children. Mary has to believe she who is a virgin will have a child without the help of a man. She has to believe the little boy she sees, in flesh and bone, is God incarnate. She has to believe that this Son, seemingly stricken to utter defeat on the Cross, has by this Cross vanquished the enemy and saved souls from the devil and sin. She has to believe that God has a plan that is good, while at the same time knowing the Messiah would suffer, as she gave Him flesh in order that He may be the Sacrifice. Simeon tells Mary in particular, "Behold this child is set for the fall, and for the resurrection of many in Israel, and for a sign which shall be contradicted; And thy own soul a sword shall pierce, that, out of many hearts, thoughts may be revealed."[22] Mary will be struck with her Son—imagine conceiving, bearing, and raising your beloved child for the purpose of your child being sacrificed! That's a daily, moment by moment sword in the heart. But St. Joseph is not mentioned. More sorrow, he would not be there with them when this happens! It's important to note that Mary already knew from Isaiah's prophecy that the Messiah would suffer torture of mind, body and soul. Imagine reading this, knowing it is the fate of your innocent child, as Mary did:

> And he shall grow up as a tender plant before him, and as a root out of a thirsty ground: there is no beauty in him, nor comeliness: and we have seen him, and there was no sightliness, that we should be desirous of him: Despised, and the most abject of men, a man of sorrows, and acquainted with infirmity: and his look was as it were hidden and despised, whereupon we esteemed him not. Surely he hath borne our infirmities and carried our sorrows: and we have thought him as it were a leper, and as one struck by God and afflicted. But he was wounded for our iniquities, he was bruised for our sins: the chastisement of our peace was upon him, and by his bruises we are healed.

> All we like sheep have gone astray, every one hath turned aside into his own way: and the Lord hath laid on him the iniquity of us all. He was offered because it was his own will, and he opened not his mouth: he shall be led as a sheep to the slaughter, and shall be dumb as a lamb before his shearer, and he shall not open his mouth. He was taken away from distress, and from judgment: who shall declare his generation? because he is cut off out of the land of the living: for the wickedness of my people have I struck him. And he shall give the ungodly for his burial, and the rich for his death: because he hath done no iniquity, neither was there deceit in his mouth. And the Lord was pleased to bruise him in infirmity: if he shall lay down his life for sin, he shall see a long-lived seed, and the will of the Lord shall be prosperous in his hand.

She probably also knew of Psalm 22 (the version below is the *RSVCE*; 21 in Douay Rheims):

> My God, my God, why hast thou forsaken me? Why art thou so far from helping me, from the words of my groaning? O my God, I cry by day, but thou dost not answer; and by night, but find no rest. Yet thou art holy, enthroned on the praises of Israel. In thee our fathers trusted; they trusted, and thou didst deliver them. To thee they cried, and were saved; in thee they trusted, and were not disappointed. But I am a worm, and no man; scorned by men, and despised by the people. All who see me mock at me, they make mouths at me,

> they wag their heads; "He committed his cause to the LORD; let him deliver him, let him rescue him, for he delights in him!" Yet thou art he who took me from the womb; thou didst keep me safe upon my mother's breasts. Upon thee was I cast from my birth, and since my mother bore me thou hast been my God. Be not far from me, for trouble is near and there is none to help. Many bulls encompass me, strong bulls of Bashan surround me; they open wide their mouths at me, like a ravening and roaring lion. I am poured out like water, and all my bones are out of joint; my heart is like wax, it is melted within my breast; my strength is dried up like a potsherd, and my tongue cleaves to my jaws; thou dost lay me in the dust of death. Yea, dogs are round about me; a company of evildoers encircle me; they have pierced my hands and feet—I can count all my bones—they stare and gloat over me; they divide my garments among them, and for my raiment they cast lots.

Most of us do not know—thank God—what is in store. If we did, we would be crippled. But Mary knows in great detail, while not knowing every detail. But Psalm 22, as well, is very clear for Jews of that time concerning what sort of death includes piercing of hands and feet; the Romans were known masters of this sort of death. When Mary read the Psalms, it is more than likely that she saw this as pertaining to the Messiah since it is in perfect accord with Isaiah. The passage of Psalms 22 in question is as follows:

> I am poured out like water, and all my bones are out

> of joint; my heart is like wax, it is melted within my breast; my strength is dried up like a potsherd, and my tongue cleaves to my jaws; thou dost lay me in the dust of death. Yea, dogs are round about me; a company of evildoers encircle me; they have pierced my hands and feet—I can count all my bones—they stare and gloat over me; they divide my garments among them, and for my raiment they cast lots.[23]

These are prophecies. At the Temple, Mary is now holding the beautiful baby in flesh and blood. And so when Simeon says, "And thy own soul a sword shall pierce," he brings those prophecies before Mary's eyes in a concrete way, a new and solid way. It's not anymore a future prophecy, but pertains *now*, to *this* Child of her own substance, Her own Child Who is also Her God, Who is literally an adorable baby. This is perhaps akin, for example, to St. Thomas More, or any other martyr awaiting death. He knew it was coming, but until the guard opened the door and said, "It's time to walk over to put your head on the chopping block" it was still distant to some degree; there is some separation, some respite. But once led out of prison and toward the scaffold, reality hits. It is no longer "tomorrow." And so the sorrow one felt at the knowing the night before has now become acute—now the goodbye actually happens. For Mary, this goodbye, this sorrow, was renewed every moment of her life with Jesus.

When she said "yes" to becoming God's Mother, she said "yes" to the Messianic prophecies that she well knew. Thus she becomes Mother of God and Sorrowful Mother at once… Yet… due to her love of God and knowing that the Messiah would suffer, her Heart was no doubt Immaculate *and* Sorrowful prior to becoming the Mother of God. There is no sorrow like her sorrow in degree, depth, or duration, excepting that of her Son.

This is the sword of which Simeon speaks. The Greek word for this sword is *rhomphaia*, a large, curved-blade sword that was used for both cutting and piercing in battle against armored soldiers. Here the sword is not aimed at an armored soldier, but at a lovely, delicate young Lady. What such an attack on this young lady would look like physically is what will happen spiritually. Again, it's not a small knife, it's a lethal, deadly weapon of war. A great sword will pierce your heart, Mary—it will not give you a bit of a wound, a cut, or a scar—it will slice through your Heart, into the depths of your being. A physical heart driven through by a *rhomphaia* is simply not going to live; Jesus is spiritually and mystically the Heart of Mary, and when He is pierced, in a way spiritual but real, Mary, too, is pierced. By some miracle she did not physically die at Calvary, yet she suffered the agony and pains of torture and death more than all the martyrs put together from the beginning to the end of the world. This spiritual suffering spilled over into her physical being as well, just as her immaculate nature shown perfectly in her physical aspect. But this is all to come, the martyrdom of Calvary is not yet. The Presentation is a revelation of what will happen in the ultimate way with the Crucifixion.

—Notes—

1. Matthew 2:11
2. Fr. Trochu, in his book, *The Cure D'Ars*, records on pp. 531-532 that a lady named Étiennette Durié once came to visit Fr. Vianney and heard him talking to a young lady as she waited just outside

Fr. Vianney's door, which was slightly open. The woman in question heard a woman say in a "very gentle tone of voice: 'What do you ask?'" After mentioning several things, firstly that of the conversion of sinners, Fr. Vianney mentions a sick woman who either wanted to be healed or to die. Mary says she will get well in the not too distant future. Étiennette Durié, not knowing who Fr. Vianney was talking to but realizing the conversation pertained to her, opened the door all the way and relates this: "What was my astonishment on beholding, standing in front of the fire-place, a lady of ordinary stature, clad in a robe of dazzling whiteness, on which were scattered golden roses. Her shoes appeared to be as white as snow. On her fingers shone the brightest of diamonds, and around her head was a wreath of stars which flashed like the sun…" A conversation between Mary and Étiennette Durié then ensues, and then Mary simply disappears. Fr. Vianney came to himself, and confirmed that the lady was truly Our Lady. In fact, she was not the only one to actually see Fr. Vianney talking to Mary, there were more—sometimes Mary was dressed in white, sometimes pale blue (p. 535). Is it likely any of us will see Mary in this life with our waking eyes? Probably not…but it does happen.

3. *The Glories of Mary*, "The Dolors of Mary—III. Loss of Jesus in the Temple"
4. *Song of Songs* 3:1, 2
5. Genesis 37:30
6. Psalm 41:2-4
7. *Song of Songs* 1:6
8. Psalm 37:11
9. Yet Jesus does not let Mary experience this suffering alone—He will experience it to a degree that only God Incarnate could.
10. Luke 2:48
11. For a masterful presentation of this at a fuller level, see Dr. John Bergsma's *New Testament Basics for Catholics*, Part IV, chapter 6 "Gospel of John."

12. John 2:2-5
13. Bastero, *Mary, Mother of the Redeemer*, p. 141
14. Matthew 4:1, Luke 4:1, Mark 1:12
15. Mark 1:11, 12; Matthew also records the Father's voice at the end of chapter 3.
16. John 2:6
17. At the Cross, that is, where Mary consents to Jesus' Sacrifice, and this Sacrifice Mary consents to is present at every Mass, when the priest turns the bread and wine into the Body and Blood of Christ—the sacrifice of Christ is made truly present.
18. *RSVCE Song of Songs* 1:2-4
19. Luke 2:21-40
20. 1 Samuel 1:5
21. 1 Samuel 1:23-28
22. Luke 2:34
23. Verses 14-18

Chapter Six
The Cross

"And being with child, she cried travailing in birth, and was in pain to be delivered."[1]

Lady Wisdom's meal of Proverbs 9 is fulfilled at the Cross. At the Last Supper, the Mass, which makes present the very Sacrifice of Jesus, the Lamb of God, the Eucharist: this is the terminus, to *eat* the meal of Lady Wisdom, and in so doing, one experiences true union both with her and God such that only marital terms can come at all close to explaining this heavenly union. A mother naturally gives of her own substance to feed her child, since she feeds him with her own milk. Here we go beyond the natural self-giving of mother-to-child to supernatural self-giving of Mother-to-child; Mary's *natural* milk is *for* Jesus, and Mary's *supernatural* milk *is* Jesus. She gives Jesus physical life and nourishes it; she gives us supernatural life and nourishes it. At Mass Mary gives of her substance, and Mary, by God's will an essential aspect of His sacrifice, is also present at the Mass, where Jesus says to us, "Behold your Mother." This is something to ponder frequently—who does not want to truly spend time with Mary? Who would not want to hold her Adorable Baby against their heart? If these realities were pondered and allowed to take root, daily Mass would begin to fill; our greatest goal to strive after in this life would become being present at Mass every day.

> When I go into my house, I shall repose myself with her: for her conversation hath no bitterness, nor her company any tediousness, but joy and gladness. Thinking these things with myself, and pondering them in my heart, that to be allied to wisdom is immortality, And that there is great delight in her friendship, and inexhaustible riches in the works of her hands, and in the exercise of conference with her, wisdom, and glory in the communication of her words: I went about seeking, that I might take her to myself.[2]

St. Pope John Paul II writes some amazing things in this regard, as in paragraph 57 of his encyclical, *Ecclesia De Eucharistia*:

> In the "memorial" of Calvary all that Christ accomplished by his passion and his death is present. Consequently *all that Christ did with regard to his Mother* for our sake is also present. To her he gave the beloved disciple and, in him, each of us: "Behold, your Son!" To each of us he also says: "Behold your mother!" (cf. Jn 19:26-27)
>
> Experiencing the memorial of Christ's death in the Eucharist also means continually receiving this gift. It means accepting—like John—the one who is given to us anew as our Mother. It also means taking

> on a commitment to be conformed to Christ, putting ourselves at the school of his Mother and allowing her to accompany us. Mary is present, with the Church and as the Mother of the Church, at each of our celebrations of the Eucharist. If the Church and the Eucharist are inseparably united, the same ought to be said of Mary and the Eucharist. This is one reason why, since ancient times, the commemoration of Mary has always been part of the Eucharistic celebrations of the Churches of East and West.

Mary is an inseparable part of Jesus' Sacrifice, which is made truly present at the Mass. Given this, it's imperative to understand better what she did at the Cross. We know the obvious, what we can see with our eyes, so to speak: Mary standing (not falling over—everyone else was leaning on her) at the Cross, offering her Son for our salvation. She has carried us mystically in her womb, and here she gives spiritual birth to us. But what was that birth like? Prior to the birth of her children, when Jesus presents each of us to Mary and Mary to each of us, Mary undergoes something beyond our ability to imagine, a suffering that is second only to that of her Son's. It is coredemptive suffering, a suffering only she could endure. She is our true Mother—more than most realize. She's not just Mother to us in that she suffers along with her Son, but in *how* she suffers; that is, she suffers in every respect that a Mother does to bring her child into the world, but to a mind-numbing degree. That is, she suffers with *full knowledge concerning for whom and for what reason she suffers*. She is not in a daze and not left in the dark, as if she were a mother who gives birth while unconscious or semi-conscious. This means she suffered with total consciousness both in body and in soul. It's crucial to point that out, though it may seem obvious. It's not uncommon to hear people say, "She had no physical suffering when she gave birth to Jesus, she doesn't understand," or "I had tremendous pain giving birth, and she didn't; I can't relate to her as one mother to another." But both of those opinions are as far from the truth as the north is from the south.

Physical Suffering

Venerable Fulton Sheen points out that Mary experienced physically all the pains of Jesus; he writes,

> As in the Annunciation when she conceived—unlike human love—the ecstasy was first in the soul and then in her body; so now in her compassion, the pains of martyrdom are first in her soul and only then in her sympathetic flesh, which echoed to every scourge that fell on her Son's back or pierced His hands and feet.[3]

What He suffers, she suffers! She is "crucified spiritually with her crucified Son," said St. John Paul II,[4] and this echoes in perfect harmony with Sheen's words that Mary felt in "her sympathetic flesh" what Jesus did, though this suffering first enters her soul, then afflicts her bodily. When Jesus was struck and wounded, so was she, albeit in a way invisible to human eyes. Of course we, too, suffer when we see someone we love suffering. This suffering enters our hearts, our souls, our minds; it afflicts our memories as something we could never forget. We know that great mental suffering has a direct effect on our bodies, too; great sadness, depression, emotional pain can make us physically sick. But this is at the level of persons who are not fully integrated—there is a disconnect between body and soul due to the wound of original sin. When we are baptized, we don't regain the original total integration of body and soul. But Mary had this. When she suffered—with a Heart far more sensitive than ours—the outrageous treatment of God, Who is on the cross truly her Son, she suffered like us in her soul, her mind. A giant battle sword has struck her in the Heart. But this then echoes in her body as well and in a way that is far more keen than the merely long-term, mildly deleterious effects such suffering would have on you and me. The physical pains of Jesus were felt in her body, too. There is no blood—for one reason, seeing Mary bleeding as Jesus was—a tremendous amount—would have resulted in a crowd of shocked and confused people, and taken away from the focus of Jesus as the Lamb of God without Whom we cannot be saved. For a second reason, nails were not physically driven into her hands. Nevertheless, the physical pain was true: every physical pain of Jesus she felt as well. Thus Mary is "crucified spiritually with her crucified Son," and this echoes in her body as true pains of scourging and crucifixion. She isn't the Queen of Martyrs simply because she witnessed the sacrifice of Jesus; she experienced it spiritually and physically.

This is certainly reminiscent of the portrait of Mary that we find in the *Song of Songs*:

> I opened the bolt of my door to my beloved: but he had turned aside, and was gone. My soul melted when he spoke: I sought him, and found him not: I called, and he did not answer me. The keepers that go about the

> city found me: they struck me: and wounded me: the keepers of the walls took away my veil from me.[5]

Her Heart burns with love for both Jesus and each of us; we are worth to her the infinite value of her Son, and she goes to the extremest length of suffering to save each of us from destruction; all of this is implied in the above verses as she looks for us but cannot find us because we, her beloveds, are dead in sin. She called and we did not answer. As she goes about to find us, she suffers at the hands of evil people, who nail her Son to the Cross and mock Him cruelly before her eyes. You and I are Mary's beloved as well in that passage, and here we find an intersection of those verses and the Crucifixion, with you and I deeply involved. This is how…

Eventually the bride in the *Song of Songs* does find the one she loves, and prior to that she gives a description of what this person looks like. First the bride asks the "daughters of Jerusalem" to keep an eye out for her beloved, and they ask the bride what he looks like, and she replies:

> I adjure you, O daughters of Jerusalem, if you find my beloved, that you tell him that I languish with love. What manner of one is thy beloved of the beloved, O thou most beautiful among women? what manner of one is thy beloved of the beloved, that thou hast so adjured us? My beloved is white and ruddy, chosen out of thousands.

First, the thing that colors everything else, is the fact that the bride "languishes with love." "Languish" in the sense used here is to desire someone out of intense love such that one suffers. It is a yearning, pining, *love sickness*. The bride here experiences the intense selfless love that longs to give of oneself and to obtain the best for the beloved. The line, "My beloved is white and ruddy, chosen out of thousands" is important here for a few reasons. Again, this first applies to Jesus (as implied in "chosen out of thousands," which can mean "of incalculable worth"). But this also applies to each soul. We are each "chosen out of thousands" of souls, of worth so great that God would become Incarnate and die for them. Second, the soul beloved by her is both "white and ruddy." The word for "white" is *tsach*, which means "white," "clear," and "dazzling,"[6] and the word for "ruddy" is *adom*, which means "red."[7] How can the beloved soul be white and red at the same time? This certainly applies to Jesus Who is "clear/pure," and Who is covered in His own Blood. Of course this could, on a natural level, mean something as simple as white skin and rosy cheeks too, but there is another meaning here: "These are they who are come out of great tribulation, and have washed their robes, and have made them white in the blood of the Lamb."[8] Those souls who are washed in Jesus' Blood are the object of this Lady's special love; they are each her "white and ruddy" beloved, for whom she offers her Son and herself, to win us: "to each of us, she is a personal romance."

Suffering...for Each

Applying the fact of Mary's perfection to the reality that she spiritually gives birth to us at the Cross, we must then say that just as any mother gives birth to her children one at a time, and just as any mother seeing and holding each child begins to know each one on an individual basis, that Mary does this perfectly at the Cross. She not only witnessed, inconsolably, her Son's torture and death on the Cross; there were other sons too that she saw in her mind and Heart. Mary, "…as it were con-crucified with her Redeemer Son, begot each of the Redeemed, knowing each singly and suffering for each singly."[9] This is a jaw-dropping reality. How is this possible? "Mary Most Holy, specially at the foot of the Cross received an infused knowledge of the sins of all those for whose salvation She had cooperated in a singular and generous manner as Coredemptress of mankind, suffering and interceding for each human person."[10] As Bertrand de Margerie points out, several Saints, such as Aquinas, Bonaventure, de Sales and Blessed John Henry Newman held this.[11] Mary is thus not a blind Beloved; she knew us better than we know ourselves 2,000 years ago! People become beloved to each other as they come to know each other, and Mary's love, being far superior to ours, is a beloved in the finest sense of that word. "She knows me" we can each say, "she is the first human person ever to know me." But what did she see when she knew us at the Cross?

At the Cross then, she perceived each person and truly knew them and saw all the sins of each individual person. This immediately produces simply shocking realities. For example, supposing the amount of individuals she knew—knowing each person and their sins—is only one million. This spiritual but true birthing of each individual took place from the time Jesus was nailed to the Cross until He said, "Woman, behold thy son…" That is the moment when the child is born, and Jesus can thus say to Mary, "See, here is your child!" This takes about three hours of chronological time. On a purely natural level it would be impossible for Mary to know each individual intimately. It would take a finite but impossibly long time for any human person, without divine assistance, to do this. But God is the master of time, and although Mary is a human person, her soul is so expansive, her union with God so deep and perfect, that she is able to receive this infused knowledge. To understand this a little better, we might consider the experience people in a near-death situation have of seeing their entire lives, in detail, flash before them. It happens in the blink of an eye. There is nothing stopping God from allowing Mary to see the "blink of an eye" life-reviews of every single person in three hours. But for Mary, these life-reviews would have been detailed beyond what you and I would see so that when she offered the Blood of her Son for an individual she did this with full knowledge and consent, knowing each person and all of their sins. But it wasn't one million people. It was billions.

There is still more to consider, however, because to better understand what Mary did in our regard, we need to know what sin does to us. Sin has a disintegrating effect on the soul. It is like cutting into one's skin with a knife; the skin that should be covering that spot is no longer integrated, and what is left is a privation of health that should be present (as Thomas would say), but the privation is not simply an absence of everything, it doesn't result in total non-being—it is an absence of something that should be there, and the result, rather than non-existence plain and simple, is the existence of a person who is *bleeding from a wound*, perhaps from a cut so bad that the muscle is visible. Or maybe there is a skull fracture such that the brain is exposed. The spiritual effect of sin is akin to this, but far worse. Seeing a soul with all its attendant sins would be like seeing her child devoured by acid, sliced open with knives, covered with infected abscesses, and stinking of decaying flesh. We might simply consider the wounds left after being hit by a train. *Sin is devastating*, the worst thing in the world, something we all too easily forget (assuming we already realize this). Whatever happens to the body it is on the level of the flesh only, it is temporary, and there is no disintegration of the *person*. But with sin, the wounds affect the *person*, and untended lead not to physical demise of the body, but to eternal demise of the soul. Now, imagine seeing your little child in the physical condition described, and realizing that the spiritual is like this but worse, and realize that Mary saw not her one child, but her billions of children, many souls being in a simply horrific state, others with more minor wounds, but each a soul she is deeply in love with and each a soul that is suffering some sickening trauma. A mother (or father) would be loath to see just one small infected abscess on her child, much less see her child effectively hit by a train. Given this, merely reviewing *one* person's sins would be a sorrowful horror. She saw the pitiful, heart-wrenching state of each of us; she saw what our *souls* look like, one person at a time.

On the natural level, a mother giving birth to such a child would imagine death was the outcome; at the Cross, the Blood of Christ offered for each made those lives not despaired of, but potentially healed and fully alive. And now, as Mediatrix of all Grace, she obtains the grace of Baptism for us, plunging us into Jesus' healing Blood: "I am come that they may have life, and may have it more abundantly. I am the good shepherd. The good shepherd giveth his life for his sheep,"[12] Jesus tells us, and now, before Jesus returns, Mary rushes to each soul, striving with incredible activity and strength—she is the Woman of Proverbs 31, after all—to sign each soul with the Blood of the Lamb.

This is what it took for Mary to give us life. Only *after* this will Jesus say, "Woman, behold your son." We would weep at seeing a fallen, though holy and beautiful young lady, suffer as she beholds her child bleeding mortally; none of us have considered well enough a) how deeply well Immaculate Mary has known each of us, *most intimately*, on a totally individual level, these 2,000 years past, and b) how much she has suffered for each of us, again on a totally individual level, so that we might live in Heaven forever and not be lost in Hell. Wonder no more why Mary weeps in her apparitions to see her children being lost forever on a daily basis. To suffer what she and her Son did, and then to lose forever the child who cost her so much—that is the heartbreak of heartbreaks. It is no surprise then that Venerable Mary of Agreda, in a vision of Mary's love for us, tells us that,

> There is another special favor, which the most holy Mary received for the benefit of the mortals on the third day and in that vision of the Divinity; for during this vision God manifested to Her in a special way the desire of his divine love to come to the aid of men and to raise them up from all their miseries. In accordance with the knowledge of his infinite mercy and the object for which it was conceded, the Most High gave to Mary a certain kind of participation of his own attributes, in order that afterwards, as the Mother and Advocate of sinners, She might intercede for them. This participation of the most holy Mary in the love of God and in his inclination to help Her, was so heavenly and powerful

> that if from that time on the strength of the Lord had not come to her aid, She would not have been able to bear the impetuosity of her desire to assist and save mankind. Filled with this love and charity, She would, if necessary or feasible, have delivered Herself an infinite number of times to the flames, to the sword and to the most exquisite torments of death for their salvation. All the torments, sorrows, tribulations, pains, infirmities She would have accepted and suffered; and She would have considered them a great delight for the salvation of sinners. Whatever all men have suffered from the beginning of the world till this hour, and whatever they will suffer till the end, would have been a small matter for the love of this most merciful Mother. Let therefore mortals and sinners understand what they owe to most holy Mary.[13]

Spiritual Birth

"Woman, behold thy son." As is the case in any natural birth, the baby is first presented to the mother, and filled with joy, the husband (or doctor), handing the newly born babe to the mother, says much the same: "Here he is, your son! Look, he has your hair, your nose, your eyes, your ears…" Here Fr. Manelli cites de La Potterie, who points out that John's "primary task is not to go and preach the gospel; but to become the son of Mary…to be a child of Mary and of Mother Church is the first and most essential aspect of the life of a Christian."[14] Everything flows from this: belonging to Mary. So for Jesus, so for us. It is because He gives

Himself wholly over to her that He is able to put on her flesh and vanquish the devil and sin. In the Gospels, we move from slave to friend, and from friend to brethren of Christ. Being one with Christ=being a child of Mary. The primary task, in other words, is to be a child of Mary because that makes us an *alter Christus*, and because without her there is no Christ and no *alter Christus*, and because if we are one with Jesus we live His life, which is a life lived with Mary.

This gift of Jesus is, after Himself, the greatest gift He gives. Mary is not an afterthought! When a person is dying, and is uttering the last words that he or she will ever speak in mortal flesh, those words tell us something. This is Jesus' last gift to us, His greatest gift, to present Mary with her children and entrust them to her (they are, after Him, hers by right of Motherhood), and to give her to us. This tells us of the preciousness of the Gift, that He saved it for last. Jesus understands human nature; He created it. He knows that the last words of a sentence, the last words of a paragraph, the last words of a husband to his wife as he goes out the door to work in the morning, the last words of a coach to his team before the game starts, are most important because they reveal what is in the heart; but further, He knows that what is last said is best remembered. There is a definite emphasis to the last word or words. Giving Mary to us in this way thus emphasizes the gift He has given and the value of it.

A Wedding Completed

The New Adam and Eve. Spiritual children birthed at the Cross. Indeed we find at Calvary three instances of nuptials, all integrated:

1) Jesus and Mary, the New Adam and the New Eve. They together obtain our salvation, and together they bring forth spiritual children. This is a reiteration, a fulfillment, in the concrete, of the mystical wedding of the New Adam and the New Eve at Cana: at Cana we see them as mystical bride and groom; at the Cross we see that brought to completion with spiritual children proceeding.[15]
2) Jesus and the Church (including each of us, members of the Church, the Bride of Christ), as the Church proceeds from His pierced side, as Eve proceeded from the first Adam out of his pierced side.
3) Mary and each soul. The first two elements, above, for the purposes of this book, take less explanation than this third element, partly due to the focus of the book, and partly due to the fact that we have heard explained the first two before in some way. But this third element is little treated. "Woman, behold thy son. After that, he saith to the disciple: Behold thy mother. And from that hour, the disciple took her to his own."[16] At this point, we are not merely friends of Jesus, we are now His *brethren*, we are of the same flesh and blood, and that flesh and blood is from Mary. As we are one with Him, we are one with her, "two in one flesh," in a mystical manner. We could also say that she *won* us. In any merely earthly romance, the man and woman each attempt to win the other. The man does his best to become a good man, an attractive man, a strong man, the man she both needs and desires, and that means being a sort of knight. But a woman, too, strives to win; if she shows lack of interest, lack of kindness, lack of

gentleness, lack of beauty, lack of decorum, lack of wisdom, then the man will look elsewhere. Often enough, at one point either the woman or the man strives more. It can take a while before one or the other realizes the treasure before his or her eyes. In the case of us and Mary, we are simply incapable of winning Mary's Heart in the sense of making ourselves truly pure, good, holy; we are lazy, our eyes are easily turned to Lady Folly, we are covered in the sores of sin. Mary's love is greater than our love though, and not only does she love us in spite of our failings, she *wins* us by going as far to win souls as is possible for any creature. God could not make a creature who could allure her beloved to her with greater fervor or charm than Mary.

"The disciple took her to his own"

St. John immediately embraces the new and sweet horizon of reality that Jesus has opened up for him. "...he saith to his mother: Woman, behold thy son. After that, he saith to the disciple: Behold thy mother. And from that hour, the disciple took her to his own."[17] No sooner does Jesus give John to Mary and Mary to John than John "took her to his own." But what does that mean? It is often thought to mean that Jesus is simply entrusting John to Mary's care. There are several elements that show us it is not so simple. *First*, Jesus would not be so remiss as to wait until the moment He is literally about to expire to make temporal arrangements for his Mother. *Second*, John is the one entrusted to Mary—that is the main point! If she were given over to John, John would have come first. Again, we are here at a spiritual birth, and like a natural birth, the first words are direct to the mother: "Here is your baby! His hair is like yours!" Then it is to the baby, "Here is your mother!" This also speaks to Mary's mission—to form us into Christ. Jesus gives us to her especially for this. *Third*, John's name is not used. It should be read like this, as is clear from the absence of any sort of name or appellation: "[insert name here], behold thy Mother." It is not "John," because not all of us are men, and it is not John because not all of us are priests, and it is not John because none of us are one of the twelve Apostles. Only "disciple" is mentioned. There is no narrowing the giving down to a man or woman, nor to a person in this or that state of life. The only narrowing down is when Jesus refers to Mary as "Woman," a clear link to Genesis 3:15; here we have *the Woman* of Genesis, the New Eve, the new Mother of a new, theandric humanity!

There is more to this phrase, "the disciple took her to his own," however. The Greek used here, *eis ta idia*, does not translate as John taking her into his house or household in order to look after her, as mentioned above. Rather, "these words describe the spiritual space in which the disciples live, a space constituted by his communion with Jesus…the mother of Jesus is taken by the disciple into an interior space already made for him by his relationship with Jesus."[18] Whatever belongs to the disciple, to the very depths of his being, is given over to Mary. He belongs to her, and she to him. Indeed, "her physical motherhood with respect to Jesus is extended in a spiritual motherhood towards believer and towards the Church."[19] This is not a "you can live in my house and I will provide for you" sort of thing only, which would restrict the gift to the material and only to John; rather, any physical care for Mary, such as John bringing her into his home, would be an outward manifestation of the inner reality of an intimate oneness that exists between the disciple and Mary. In Jesus, we truly belong to her as "flesh of her flesh."

—Notes—

1. Revelation 12:2
2. Wisdom 8:16-18
3. *The World's First Love*, p. 247
4. *Guayaquil (Ecuador)—Thursday, January 31, 1985* Wednesday general audience, the 33rd installment in a series on Mary.
5. *Songs of Songs* 5:6, 7
6. *Strong's Hebrew* 6703
7. *Strong's Hebrew* 122
8. Revelation 7:14
9. Fr. Manelli, FI, *All Generations Shall Call Me Blessed*, p 378
10. ibid, p. 379
11. ibid, p. 379
12. John 10:10
13. Venerable Mary of Agreda, *The City of God*, Second Part, Book III, par. 32
14. ibid, p. 378
15. Sheen, video: "The Blessed Virgin Mary—The Woman I Love"
16. John 19:26, 27
17. John 19:26, 27
18. Juan Bastero, *Mary, Mother of the Redeemer*, p. 148
19. ibid, p. 149

Chapter Seven
Revelation

The Golden Thread that begins the Bible runs through to the end—and at the end we find a revelation of Heaven. At this point in history, the Ark of the Covenant has been missing since about the 6th century B.C., and it was the Ark where the presence of God on earth had resided, like the King on His throne amongst His people. So when John speaks of the Ark reappearing it is an eschatological occurrence, a revelation pointing to the end toward which history is moving: to God being present again amongst us and lifting us up to Himself. Luke showed in his Gospel that the true Ark has indeed come, and now John lifts the veil of reality still more:

> And the nations were angry, and thy wrath is come, and the time of the dead, that they should be judged, and that thou shouldest render reward to thy servants the prophets and the saints, and to them that fear thy name, little and great, and shouldest destroy them who have corrupted the earth. And the temple of God was opened in heaven: and the ark of his testament was seen in his

> temple, and there were lightnings, and voices, and an earthquake, and great hail.
>
> And a great sign appeared in heaven: A woman clothed with the sun, and the moon under her feet, and on her head a crown of twelve stars: And being with child, she cried travailing in birth, and was in pain to be delivered. And there was seen another sign in heaven: and behold a great red dragon, having seven heads, and ten horns: and on his head seven diadems: And his tail drew the third part of the stars of heaven, and cast them to the earth: and the dragon stood before the woman who was ready to be delivered; that, when she should be delivered, he might devour her son. And she brought forth a man child, who was to rule all nations with an iron rod: and her son was taken up to God, and to his throne.[1]

After this a great battle takes place in which St. Michael and the good angels defeat the devil, whom John links to the serpent in Genesis, calling him, "that old serpent, who is called the devil and Satan." He goes on to write, "And the dragon was angry against the woman: and went to make war with the rest of her seed, who keep the commandments of God, and have the testimony of Jesus Christ."

The woman of this passage can indeed apply to the Church, but it also applies to Mary, the very person who is the Ark in the flesh. When she comes, she crushes the devil. In fact, she is clothed—*clothed*—with the sun! The moon is beneath her feet. That is, everything "under the sun" is beneath her, and the phrase "under the sun" is precisely the phrase used in Ecclesiasticus for all things earthly and materialistic, all of which without God are useless, and all of which are inexplicable without the gift of faith:

> And I proposed in my mind to seek and search out wisely concerning all things that are done under the sun. This painful occupation hath God given to the children of men, to be exercised therein. I have seen all things that are done under the sun, and behold all is vanity, and vexation of spirit.[2]
>
> The eyes of a wise man are in his head: the fool walketh in darkness: and I learned that they were to die both alike. And I said in my heart: If the death of the fool and mine shall be one, what doth it avail me, that I have applied myself more to the study of wisdom? And speaking with my own mind, I perceived that this also was vanity.
>
> For there shall be no remembrance of the wise no more than of the fool for ever, and the times to come shall cover all things together with oblivion: the learned dieth in like manner as the unlearned. And therefore I was weary of my life, when I saw that all things under the sun are evil, and all vanity and vexation of spirit.[3]

Mary is not "under the sun": she is clothed with the sun as with a cloak! At Fatima, she will play with the sun like a little daughter playing with a ball given to her by her Father. And if the moon is under her, the earth is under her. The sun is the light of God, the moon beneath reflecting His light, and the earth is below the heavens... If Mary is clothed with the sun, she is clothed with God, and if the moon is beneath her feet, the devil and his demons who have been thrown down to earth are completely crushed by her.

That this Woman of Revelation "cried travailing in birth, and was in pain to be delivered" also tells us something of the earth—specifically about us, and it makes more sense when considered in light of this verse: "And the dragon was angry against the woman: and went to make war with the rest of her seed..." Mary had no pain in the birth of Jesus; pain in childbirth is a punishment meted out to Eve due to sin. But Jesus and Mary, sinless, take on the curses of Adam and Eve: Jesus suffers, toiling in a Garden, sweating blood, and later he is crowned with thorns: "...cursed is the earth in thy work; with labour and toil shalt thou eat thereof all the days of thy life. Thorns and thistles shall it bring forth to thee; and thou shalt eat the herbs of the earth. In the sweat of thy face shalt thou eat bread till thou return to the earth."[4] Mary's pain at the Cross in giving spiritual birth to us ("the rest of her seed"), after having carried us mystically in her womb with Jesus, is sorrowfully painful beyond any human calculations: "I will multiply thy sorrows, and thy conceptions: in sorrow shalt thou bring forth children."[5]

But finally this is a most consoling reality! Yes, there is the angry devil...but there is the Woman who is above him in a way more superior than the sky's distance to the ground, and we are "the rest of her seed." This means being an *alter Christus*—she forms us each into Jesus; and this means some degree of suffering...but she makes it to be sweet, of short duration, and lead to eternal life where there will be no more pain, and forever there will be joy in Mary, in whom we are truly in God's tabernacle, and thus in the presence of God:

> Behold the tabernacle of God with men, and he will dwell with them. And they shall be his people; and God himself with them shall be their God. And God shall wipe away all tears from their eyes: and death shall be no more, nor mourning, nor crying, nor sorrow shall be any more, for the former things are passed away. And he that sat on the throne, said: Behold, I make all things new. And he said to me: Write, for these words are most faithful and true. And he said to me: It is done. I am Alpha and Omega; the beginning and the end. To him that thirsteth, I will give of the fountain of the water of life, freely. He that shall overcome shall possess these things, and I will be his God; and he shall be my son.[6]

There is one final point here (for now—Revelation will be looked at again in the dogma of the Assumption of Mary into Heaven): at just about the end of the Bible we read, "There shall not enter into it [the New Jerusalem, which John says looks like, 'a bride adorned for her husband'[7]] anything defiled, or that worketh abomination or maketh a lie, but they that are written in the book of life of the Lamb."[8] Mary is the new Jerusalem *personified*—recall Lady Wisdom, of whom it is written, "For she is a vapour of the power of God, and a certain pure emanation of the glory of the almighty God: and therefore no defiled thing cometh into her." In some way, we can say that Mary is "the book of life of the Lamb." To be written upon Mary's Heart is to be written in the book of life, it is to be brought by her to her Son, there to be purified in the Blood of the Lamb and made worthy to enter where "no defiled thing cometh."

—Notes—

1. 11:18-12:5
2. Ecclesiastes 1:13, 14
3. ibid, 2:14-17
4. Genesis 3:17-19
5. ibid, 3:16
6. Revelation 21:5-7
7. ibid, 21:2
8. ibid, 21:7

—Section Three—

Four Dogmas and a Doctrine

Chapter One
The Immaculate Conception, the Virgin

> The Fathers, from this point of view, speak of Mary as...agna Dei (the little ewe-lamb of God), and as the only-beloved and only-begotten daughter of God.[1]

> "To become the mother of the Savior, Mary 'was enriched by God with gifts appropriate to such a role'... the Fathers of the Eastern tradition call the Mother of God 'the All-Holy' (Panagia), and celebrate her as 'free from any stain of sin, as though fashioned by the Holy Spirit and formed as a new creature.'"[2]

A key element found in the Wisdom literature is that Lady Wisdom appears as deeply united to God, and to such a degree that the word *ruah* is used both for the Holy Spirit and for her; indeed she was present in the mind of God as the Spirit moved over the waters in Genesis. And at Lourdes, Mary tells us who she is in a remarkable way. St. Maximilian Kolbe realized this, and began to bring out the amazing reality: Mary reveals her special secret in her self-revelatory phrase, "I am the Immaculate Conception."

From eternity, the Holy Spirit is the "Uncreated Immaculate Conception"; Mary is the "created Immaculate Conception."[3] The implications are immense.

Of course it must first be understood what it means that Mary was conceived immaculately. She is God's Daughter, and she says of herself in Ecclesiasticus 24:5, "I came out of the mouth of the most High, the firstborn before all creatures." She will be the Mother of God, and because of this she will be the Immaculate Conception; that is, she was never, for the slightest moment, at enmity with God. She was never in the devil's camp, never separated from God by lack of sanctifying grace in her soul, thus she was never a spiritual enemy or traitor in regard to her own Son. As St. Cyril pithily and correctly says, "Who ever heard of an architect who built himself a temple, and yielded up the first possession of it to his greatest enemy?"[4] People could then have rightly said that the Mother of the Messiah is a sinner.[5] And people would wonder if God could not make for Himself a clean dwelling.[6] And how could she, who is the dawn and brings forth the Savior, she who is the very Ark of the Incarnate God, have at any moment have been the object of His displeasure?

It is because she would be the Mother of God that she was endowed with much more than Eve, who was also immaculate but not destined to be the Mother of God. St. Alphonsus writes that, "the sovereign architect, who destined Mary to be the Mother of his own Son, adorned her soul with all the most precious gifts."[7] Fr. Matthias Scheeben lays out the details a bit more specifically:

> …in Mary, even during her life, and in Mary alone of mankind, could there be found that complete immunity from sin and that perfection of justice which is real-

> ized in other members of the Church only after death or after resurrection. On earth it can be pursued merely as an ultimate aim to be achieved only later. Likewise, Mary possessed in her earthly body the same perfection of purity and justice, as that of which the angels are capable on account of their purely spiritual nature. Further, because the inward grace that shielded her from all sin was higher than that of the angels, and also because the grace of her motherhood made sin utterly impossible, Mary possessed a higher degree of purity from sin than did the angels.[8]

Pope Pius IX put it this way in *Ineffabilis Deus*, the document in which he declares the Immaculate Conception a dogma:

> And indeed it was wholly fitting that so wonderful a mother should be ever resplendent with the glory of most sublime holiness and so completely free from all taint of original sin that she would triumph utterly over the ancient serpent. To her did the Father will to give his only-begotten Son—the Son whom, equal to the Father and begotten by him, the Father loves from his heart—and to give this Son in such a way that he would be the one and the same common Son of God the Father and of the Blessed Virgin Mary.

The Pope goes on to say that Mary,

> ...was resplendent with such an abundance of heavenly gifts, with such a fullness of grace and with such inno-

> cence, that she is an unspeakable miracle of God—indeed, the crown of all miracles and truly the Mother of God; that she approaches as near to God himself as is possible for a created being; and that she is above all men and angels in glory.

This next description of Mary by Pope Pius IX is also pertinent, and leads into the next section. He writes that Mary is,

> ...innocent, and verily most innocent; spotless, and entirely spotless; holy and removed from every stain of sin; all pure, all stainless, the very model of purity and innocence; more beautiful than beauty, more lovely than loveliness; more holy than holiness, singularly holy and most pure in soul and body; the one who surpassed all integrity and virginity; the only one who has become the dwelling place of all the graces of the most Holy Spirit. God alone excepted, Mary is more excellent than all, and by nature fair and beautiful, and more holy than the Cherubim and Seraphim. To praise her all the tongues of heaven and earth do not suffice.

How can someone be "more beautiful than beauty, more lovely than loveliness, more holy than holiness"? She would have to *be those things in themselves*, they bespeak a quality that is essentially absolute as the very essence of that person. Someone may possess beauty—but this can be lost. But if someone *is beauty*, this cannot be lost, and it is beyond merely possessing beauty as an accidental quality. To be beauty itself would mean that such a person is not accidentally "beautiful"and thus does not possess beauty as a quality, but rather the very nature of that person *is beauty*:

> The Mother of our Lord Jesus Christ had not said: "I am Mary immaculate." She had said, "I am the Immaculate Conception," as if to mark the absolute character, the substantial character in some sort, of the divine privilege which she alone had had since Adam and Eve were created by God. It is as if she had said, not "I am pure," but, "I am purity itself;" not "I am a Virgin," but "I am Virginity living and Incarnate;" not "I am spotless," but "Spotlessness itself." A thing that is white may cease to be so, but whiteness is always white; it is its essence, not its quality.[9]

Mary, then, is somehow an incarnation, not of God, but of God's beauty, loveliness, purity, and holiness; we could also say a sort of incarnation of His maternal qualities, such as His gentleness and desire to nurture His creation; all of these are elements that do not simply *adorn* this Woman who is a human person, but *constitute who she is in her very being*. It is because of this unutterably radical holiness, purity, beauty and so on that she is suited to be Full of Grace, "adorned…with all the most precious gifts," and the Spouse of the Holy Spirit, a reality that is intimately linked with Mary's definition of herself at Lourdes: "I am the Immaculate Conception." To wit, we could say she is a created version of the Holy Spirit, not the Holy Spirit incarnate, but as Kolbe will say, she is in such union with and so like the Holy Spirit that we could say she is the Holy Spirit *quasi-incarntus*: *living so utterly one life with the Holy Spirit and so like to the Holy Spirit—Who is the very Person of Love and Who possesses the name "Love" as a proper name—that it is "as if" the Holy Spirit is incarnate in her.* It is to this reality of Mary—one that leads us still deeper into the knowledge of who she is—that we now turn…

Mary and the Holy Spirit

In his audiences on the Holy Spirit, St. John Paul II shares many and varied insights concerning the characteristics and mission of the Holy Spirit. However disparate these points may at first appear, the truth exists in unity such that the connection between one reality and another intersect in mutual complementarity. This intersection often reveals new insights into these supernatural realities. Two such intersecting insights from the audiences of John Paul II involve the *characteristics of the Holy Spirit* (as found in his audience, "I Believe in the Holy Spirit") and *Mary's union with the Holy Spirit* (as found in his audience, "Mary's Motherhood is Linked to the Spirit").

The union of Mary and the Holy Spirit is a mystery that, to this day, has been little explored; it is a wide-open field, a barely plumbed gold mine. Until the early 20th century, this gold mine extended, in a sense, approximately as far as the reality that Mary is the Spouse of the Holy Spirit. In the 1930s, however, St. Maximilian Kolbe, after many years of pondering Mary's description of herself as "the Immaculate Conception," came to some astonishing conclusions. He pointed out that the word "spouse," while conveying the reality of the relationship between the Holy Spirit and Mary to some degree, is a term inadequate to the task of conveying the true depth of the union between Mary and the Holy

Spirit. Kolbe was here given profound light: Mary is Spouse of the Spirit indeed, but so deep is their union that Mary can rightly be described as a "quasi-incarnation" of the Holy Spirit.[10] This, along with his idea that Mary is a sort of "personification" of the Holy Spirit,[11] was like locating a great vein of gold in the mine. These insights of Kolbe coincide with the thought of John Paul II, as together their theology reveals a unique coalescence of Persons in regard to the Holy Spirit and Mary, a coalescing that becomes visible in two ways: the first way involves the level of *characteristics*; the second way demonstrates that the unity between the Holy Spirit and Mary is so deep that, while incomprehensible to the human mind, is visible in the *face* of Mary, the Beloved.

The Character of the Holy Spirit, the Character of Mary

A study of the *characteristics* of Mary and the Holy Spirit will set up crucial scaffolding against which the personalism of the face will be more clearly seen. Indeed, characteristics to some degree make visible the person in terms of action and even dictate a person's appearance, as what is done to the body affects the soul and vice versa. Thus a young woman who is well-adjusted and embraces her femininity and intrinsic call to motherhood (spiritual and/or physical) will often be noticeably soft, warm and approachable in mannerisms and in physical appearance, while a woman who is selfish, embraces her "rights," and the idea that a woman may kill her own children, will often be noticeably cold, rigid and unapproachable in mannerisms and physical appearance.

Of course, it goes without saying that to know a person, one must look to *character*, which, again, is visible in terms of action. Personal characteristics are outer behaviors born of an interior life, and although one may attempt to deceive others as to one's true character, inevitably the truth becomes clear. Nevertheless, here we speak of characters who are wholly true.

Further, various characteristics can be extremely similar, and for those who live a life of deep union, each person's particular characteristics tend to become something shared. Concerning the Holy Spirit and Mary, it is to these outer actions we first turn our attention, and three short descriptive phrases will, so to speak, start us upon the path.

- Mary is made for the Holy Spirit.
- The Holy Spirit is Person Gift-Love.[12]
- Mary is given to us as person Gift-Love.[13]

These three phrases form a sort of foundation for discerning the character of the Holy Spirit and Mary, and in these phrases we begin to see a confluence of personal characteristics between them, and these distinct and unique characteristics of the Holy Spirit and Mary coincide in essential ways in regard to these three phrases about their persons.

1) *Mary is made for the Holy Spirit.* It is because she is made to be the Mother of the Son that she is the Immaculate Conception.[14] Further, it is specifically the Person of the Holy Spirit *with* the person of Mary who *together* bring about the Incarnation of the Son.[15] This specific facet of their relationship becomes still more pronounced when we take into account Kolbe's insight that Mary is the created "Immaculate Conception" as the Holy Spirit is the "Uncreated eternal Conception."[16] Thus between the Holy Spirit and Mary we find a shared reality of *a)* being

Immaculate and *b)* acting to bring about the Incarnation.[17] These coinciding facets are absolutely unique to the Spirit and Mary; or perhaps more to the point, only Mary shares these characteristics of the Spirit's very Person in her own person. As Fr. Rene Laurentin writes, "But Mary is the most beautiful reflection of the Holy Spirit in a mere human creature; she is also the supreme feminine expression of the Spirit. She manifests visibly the Spirit's invisible fecundity. She does so by her divine and spiritual maternity."[18]

2) *The Holy Spirit is Person Love-Gift.* The Holy Spirit, as Thomas explains, is both Love and Gift. These are not merely "aspects" of the Holy Spirit, rather these are *proper names* of the Spirit, and they tell us something of Who He is in Himself. How is He Gift? Thomas explains: "Now a divine person is said to belong to another, either by origin, as the Son belongs to the Father; or as possessed by another. But we are said to possess what we can freely use or enjoy as we please: and in this way a divine person cannot be possessed, except by a rational creature united to God."[19] He goes on to say that, "Gift as a personal name in God does not imply subjection, but only origin, as regards the giver; but as regards the one to whom it is given, it implies a free use, or enjoyment, as above explained."[20] The Love of God Who is God is poured out into us, a Gift, the Love of God Who is Himself Love.

3) *Mary is given to us as person Love-Gift.* At the level of creatures, no one is given to a person quite like a person's mother.[21] In a distinct way, to the baby the mother *is* "love," and indeed is "life." She is the gift without which one would not come to live in this world. This is so for Jesus as well. Mary,

as our spiritual Mother, is also given to us by God to be a true Mother to us. In fact, the words Thomas uses for the Holy Spirit as Gift, above, could also apply to Mary with a few changes to the wording: "Gift as a personal name for Mary does not imply subjection, but only origin, as regards the giver, and the One Who gives Mary to us as our Mother is God Himself and with Mary's consent; but as regards the one to whom the gift is given (her children), it implies a free use, or enjoyment, as above explained." As the Spirit is Love and Gift, so the Mother is love and gift; as the Spirit makes us alive with God's own life, so the Mother feeds us (mediates grace) to make us alive with God's life, and indeed feeds us with God Himself.[22]

This also explains the double gift of both the Holy Spirit and His masterpiece, Mary, given from the Cross: at the conclusion of St. John's telling of the Passion,

> Jesus begins by entrusting his Mother to his disciple (Jn 19, 25-27); then, immediately afterward, he gives us his Spirit by dying for us and "yielding up his Spirit." (Jn 19, 28-30)…These two gifts made by Jesus: that of his own mother and that of the Holy Spirit, are intimately connected, inseparable from each other; the Spirit is present wherever the action of the Most Blessed Virgin takes place.[23]

The similarities here are notable: Jesus sends us the Spirit to be our Advocate and Consoler once He is gone; Jesus gives Mary to John "the disciple" (and each of us individually in him) to be advocate and consoler (as is proper to mothers) once He is gone. His final gift of love is a *double gift* that is essentially linked (though not by absolute necessity): *the gift of Mary and the Holy Spirit*. Indeed we can say that as the Holy Spirit is "uncreated Love-Gift,"[24] Mary is "created love-gift," just as Kolbe says that the Holy Spirit is the "eternal Immaculate Conception" and Mary is the "human Immaculate Conception."[25]

This confluence of *personality characteristics* and *mission* between the Holy Spirit and Mary signified by the above three phrases becomes quite evident when read in the light of John Paul II's audience, "I Believe in the Holy Spirit." In this audience, he points out certain specific characteristics of the Holy Spirit's personality, action and mission:

> He teaches all things and reminds us of what Jesus said (Jn 14:26).
>
> He bears witness to Jesus (Jn 15:26).
>
> He guides us into all truth (Jn 16:13).
>
> He glorifies Christ (cf. Jn 16:14).
>
> He convinces the world of sin (Jn 16:8).
>
> He gives His gifts "to each one individually as he wills" (1 Cor 12:11).
>
> "He intercedes for the saints" (Rom 8:27).

Mary shares in a manner both particular and complementary these characteristics of the Holy Spirit: Mary reminds us of what Jesus said; Mary bears witness to Jesus and offers her Son on the Cross (we see her martyrdom—her witness—at the Cross: the sorrowful Mother as Coredemptrix); Mary continually teaches us the truth (we see this in her apparitions[26]); Mary glorifies her Son; Mary convicts the world of sin;[27] Mary imparts grace as Mediatrix, as a Mother nourishing her children, giving grace as she will and to whom she will;[28] Mary is our Advocate, "interceding for the saints." It is no coincidence that in these similarities we find the doctrine of Mary as *Coredemptrix*, *Mediatrix* and *Advocate* as a parallel to the Holy Spirit's mission and activity!

In regard to Mary as Coredemptrix, we begin to move from shared characteristic actions between her and the Holy Spirit, to Mary making the Spirit, in some mysterious way, physically visible to our eyes. How so? Certainly we *see* her intense suffering at Calvary, and in her person (soul and body) she helps make visible the reality of sin as she is "crucified spiritually with her crucified Son."[29] Of course, we see the effect of sin in looking at the crucified Savior, but as the Spirit and Christ work together in the mission of salvation as sent from the Father, so Mary and Christ work together, and the tears of Mary, His Mother and ours, fall upon our hearts and like a potent nectar open our eyes and "convince us of sin."[30] She is the one left behind, in union with the Spirit, and it is her still-living face that looks at us, piercing us with her gaze, and this gaze says to us, "See what sin does, and see the love of God for you." Thus in Mary there is a physical, tangible, concrete representation of the mission of the Spirit to "convince the world of sin."[31] Indeed it is in the person of the Sorrowful Mother, and she *with her crucified Son*, that the Spirit, in a concrete, visible way, "convinces the world of sin." The *Stabat Mater Dolorosa* captures this reality:

> Is there one who would not weep,
> whelmed in miseries so deep,
> Christ's dear Mother to behold?
>
> ***
>
> Holy Mother! pierce me through,
> in my heart each wound renew
> of my Savior crucified...[32]

The Face, Where the Person is Revealed

It is clear that there is a union of characteristics and mission between the Holy Spirit and Mary, but the reality of their union goes *beyond* this confluence of characteristics and mission. As explored above, the Holy Spirit in some way makes Himself *visible* in the Sorrowful Mother, and in doing so He visibly "convinces the world of sin." Fr. Rene Laurentin puts it this way:

> The best answer, perhaps, is that Mary is the *transparency* of the Holy Spirit...a transparency is, precisely, a print of a picture illuminated from behind (within); and Mary is, precisely, the most perfect visible image or expression of the Holy Spirit in this world, illuminated as she is by the Spirit from within... She enjoys the most intimate union with, as well as the most perfect *resemblance* to, love. The affinity is perfect, in fact.[33]

In other words, beyond shared characteristics and roles, in some mysterious way she makes the invisible Holy Spirit *physically visible*.

When considering a coalescing of characteristics, which concerns outer behavior as well as a union of hearts and wills, there is nevertheless a certain distance. Two such persons do not necessarily, nor ordinarily, come to such a union that while remaining two distinct persons one is *literally seen* in the other. We might pick up a certain spirit as our own by spending much time voluntarily with someone, and we may also pick up certain mannerisms and modes of thought and speaking from that person... but in this it is never said, "I cannot tell where you begin and the other one ends...to see you is to see the other person." Yet in Mary and the Holy Spirit this *is* in a real sense what we find. As Fr. Manteau-Bonamy writes,

> At Cana, the Holy Spirit through Mary provoked the response of Jesus when she said: "They have no more wine"; for Jesus knows full well that everything his mother says and does is inspired by the Spirit of truth and love. So when Mary told the servants, "Do whatever he tells you," Jesus obeyed the Spirit which thus launched him definitely on the mission which would lead him to Calvary.[34]

How can Fr. Manteau-Bonamy make such a claim? Because so deep is the union between Mary and the Holy Spirit that while they are *two distinct persons*, without any mixing or confusion, they share, as Kolbe says, "one sole life,"[35] such that we can truthfully say, "Mary spoke at Cana" and just as truthfully say, "the

Holy Spirit spoke at Cana." Fr. Manteau-Bonamy also notes that the union of the Holy Spirit and Mary is "...above all an interior union, a union of her essence with the 'essence' of the Holy Spirit."[36] And here we must ask: where do we primarily *see* the "revelation" of a human person, their essence? True, in the *character* we see the person revealed in action. There is at times a coalescing union of characters that is seen in people's behavior, such that one can say, "I can tell you have been spending time with *x*." Between the Holy Spirit and Mary, however, such unity goes fundamentally deeper, such that to *see her* is to *see the Spirit,*[37] since we find amongst them not only a unity of characteristics and mission, but a unity of essence,[38] "one sole life."[39] Yet greater specificity is called for in the question posed above: in what feature of a human person do we see their personal essence?

In his audience, "Mary's Motherhood is Linked to the Spirit," John Paul II writes: "From the Cross the Savior wished to pour out upon humanity rivers of living water (cf. Jn 7:38), that is, the abundance of the Holy Spirit. But he wanted this outpouring of grace to be linked to a mother's face, his Mother's."[40] Fr. George Montague, S.M., explores this same theme and (inadvertently) expands upon it (as he demolishes the heretical idea that God could ever be truly called or considered a "divine mother"):

> Jesus, whose mother was Mary, called God "Abba," and it was Mary, not God whom he called "Imma."... Those who think this "less perfect" would do well to reflect on this: Jesus gave us the title Abba to express both the transcendence and intimacy of God. For the maternal face of God[41] he did not leave us a title. He left us instead a living symbol, a human person, a human mother.[42]

Still more specifically, in his book, *Crossing the Threshold of Hope*, John Paul II writes,

> God, who is the supreme Legislator, forcefully enjoined on Sinai the commandment "Thou shalt not kill," as an absolute moral imperative. Levinas, who, like his coreligionists, deeply experienced the tragedy of the Holocaust, offers a remarkable formulation of this fundamental commandment of the Decalogue—for him, the face reveals the person. This philosophy of the face is also found in the Old Testament: in the Psalms, and in the writings of the Prophets, there are frequent references to "seeking God's face" (Ps. 26[27]:8). It is through his face that man speaks...[43]

Thus in the face, more than anywhere else, the *person* is seen: directly, immediately, concretely. "The face reveals the person," as John Paul II notes.[44] Thus if the "maternal face" of God is seen in a living symbol, if the Spirit is linked to the maternal face of Mary, and if as Fr. Manteau-Bonamy writes of Kolbe's theology, "By saying 'I am the Immaculate Conception,' Mary clearly showed that she is intimately united with the third Person of the Trinity whose privileged sanctuary, whose *image* she is; we can truly say that her life is the very life of the Spirit in her" and "…the Holy Spirit…made her the obvious sign of his personal presence in the world"[45] then what we see in Mary's face is not simply the characteristics of a Person who influences her, but rather we actually see in Mary's face, in some mysterious way, not only Mary but the Person of the Holy Spirit[46] (as Mary says of herself, "My soul doth magnify the Lord"[47]): there is between them a union of essence, and indeed Mary "has no life except in her relationship with God."[48] This transparency of Mary, along with her union with the Spirit, is so intrinsic to her being that while we see Mary, she yet disappears and "magnifies the Lord." S. C. Biela, in his masterful book, *In the Arms of Mary*, makes this same point: "There should be in each one of us the desire of Mary—that of remaining hidden and unnoticed… When you perform an important function in professional or social life, you should try, as much as possible, to 'disappear' like Mary."[49]

Again, there are *two* persons involved here, not one; the Holy Spirit is merely "quasi-incarnate"[50] in Mary. He does not assume Mary to His Person as the Word assumes a human nature to His Person. Fr. Mathias Scheeben uses a particular word to describe this union of the Holy Spirit and Mary that complements Kolbe's "quasi-incarnate": "Ectype." This word comes from the Greek ἐκ and τύπος. Since ἐκ is a preposition that denotes origin (out of, from), and τύπος is something that is struck, like a die, or is something that is in the style/resemblance/model of an original—that is, a reproduction[51] —calling Mary the "ectype of the Holy Ghost" is tantamount to Kolbe saying that "...the Immaculata is, in a certain sense, the 'incarnation of the Holy Spirit,'"[52] and provides yet another nuance, strengthening our understanding of this union; that is, she is a created version of the Holy Spirit, her own distinct person, but such that her life is His, and such that she perfectly reveals Him (as much as a creature is able) as He shines through her in unimaginable union as His beauty, purity, gentleness and love is concretized in Mary.

Thus we can say: "When we see the face of Mary, we see Mary; when we see the face of Mary, we see the Holy Spirit revealed in Mary's face."[53] This is similar to the reality that when we see Jesus we see the Father,[54] except that Mary is a created person. To use the words of Kolbe and phrase this reality as an analogy (keeping in mind the necessary distinctions and differences between a created person's union with God as opposed to the circumincession of the three Persons of the Trinity): *to see the created Immaculate Conception (Mary) is to see the Uncreated Immaculate Conception (the Holy Spirit), as to see the Incarnate Word is to see the Father.* This is a bold analogy, and again, the proper qualifications are absolutely necessary; it should also be borne in mind that an analogy, by definition, is to show how two *different* things are *similar*, not to show or claim they are the same, and clearly in this case we do not speak of "sameness," but only of a certain similarity. To make the reality of this analogy clearer still, we might phrase the reality of the union between Mary and the Holy Spirit in Nestorian terms. Concerning Jesus, Nestorius is absolutely in error, but applied to Mary, his theory, in some regard, fits: between Mary and the Spirit there is no hypostatic union, and there are two distinct persons in this union, one human, one Divine, and yet they live "one sole life"[55] in an unimaginable union, to the point where it can be said that Mary is "the gift of God outside of God."[56]

To understand the reality of Mary's face still more, a brief phenomenology of the human face is indispensable. First, physical beauty of the face itself does not directly concern us here. As Dietrich von Hildebrand writes, "This beauty of the visible and audible tells us nothing about the personality. For it is an aesthetic value which attaches directly to the visible, in this case, to the face. It is not grounded in other values."[57] Yet, the face is where we *see* the person: "In the face, however, there is always an expression of the personality; if it were devoid of all expression, it would be a mask."[58] This is why in a wedding the bride's face is at first hidden: to reveal her *face* is to reveal *this particular person*, indeed, this person as *gift*; the face, with all its expressions, in fact reveals the person's inner life. "The face needs expression,"[59] writes Von Hildebrand, and "Although the beauty expressed in the face is dependent in its visible manifestation on purely visible factors, it is itself the beauty of a human person, and hence a metaphysical beauty."[60] This is a reality that we can understand by human reason. But we also know from Divine Revelation, as mentioned above, that a divine Person, too, can reveal His "metaphysical beauty" in a human face.

Given the fact of unity between the Holy Spirit and Mary, this phenomenology of the face is enlightening. Consider this passage in light of the above insights of Von Hildebrand:

> Scheeben also taught that the Holy Spirit animates and in a certain sense "informs" Mary, so that she forms a moral person (one identity) with him and he so-to-say sets the signature upon her personality. Christ cannot be united to his Mother without giving her in a particular way, his Spirit, which he always gives—which is always proceeding from him. If he gives his Spirit to the Church, then how much more to his Mother, who is not only the image (Abbild) of the Church, but also its (Urbild) original unique image.[61]

"The face reveals the person."[62] Applied to the Holy Spirit and Mary, who together form "a moral person (one identity)," it becomes clear that to see Mary's face is to see Mary, and to see Mary's face is to see the Holy Spirit, and that in this there is no contradiction. To paraphrase Von Hildebrand, Mary's face "is itself the beauty of both a human person and a Divine Person, the Divine revealed in the human as 'one identity,' and hence a metaphysical beauty."

One Face

Is it possible to see *two* persons in one face? On the level of divinity—and this includes Mary (and in regard to created beings, only Mary)[63]—the answer is "yes." Of course in Jesus we see Jesus *and* the Father. Given this, these two Persons of the Holy Trinity are truly revealed to us in the one face of Jesus, Who is the Person of the Son and the perfect image of the Father. It is by the face that we, as human beings, recognize persons, and in the face of Christ we see the face of the Father and the Son (albeit in a rather limited way—i.e., for a person wayfaring on earth to have seen Jesus before or after His Resurrection is not yet to experience the Beatific Vision). There is, in regard to Jesus, a *human face*, that of the Word and also the Father, a face that we can see, touch and kiss.[64] Given the unity of Persons in the Trinity, it is reasonable to ask: would the Holy Spirit, like the Father and the Son, not *also* desire to become visible—we could say "accessible"—to us in a human face? Clearly the answer is yes, He does, and He did; not to the point of becoming incarnate—and certainly not to the level of union found in the mutual immanence of the Persons of the Trinity, since Mary is a mere creature—but nevertheless, in the face of Mary we see a true theophany of the Holy Spirit.[65] The face of Mary allows her children to see, touch and kiss her, and, in some mysterious way, to also *see, touch and kiss the Holy Spirit,* Who, while not incarnate in her, yet reveals Himself in her lovely face. This makes complete sense in light of Jesus' words that what is done to His Body is done to Him, and this while our union with Him is as yet imperfect; Mary's union with the Holy Spirit is as perfect as can be had by any creature, and since their union is so deep and complete, in some remarkable way—and pertaining only to Mary—to experience her is to experience the Holy Spirit, and this experience includes her loving caresses to us, and ours to her. In Mary we are loved by God's love, and when we love her we love the very Love of God and Who is God and quasi-incarnate in Mary as a theophany of the Holy Spirit. To live one life with Mary is to live one life with the Holy Spirit. Both, as distinct persons and as a unity of "one sole life" are the Beloved of the soul.[66]

In this particular way then, to be one with Mary is to be one with the Holy Spirit. Mary forms us into members of Christs—indeed other Christs—just as she did with Jesus, but does she do this alone? Rather, she does this with the Holy Spirit, and loves the Son of God with God's own Love, the Person of the Holy Spirit. And so we read this in St. Gemma Galgani's[67] last letter, written to Mary:

> Dear Mother, I am not at all well, as you know: my life is consumed. And as to my soul?... Oh, God, I am tormented by wicked and impure thoughts, but Jesus tells me to turn to you, Mother, saying, "Daughter, commend yourself daily to her; she will make you beautiful, gentle, amiable, because she can win souls and save them; she will make you tranquil and at peace." How my celestial Mother loves me! She says

> often to me: "Gemma, long for me; I too, am sighing for you. As many times as you have offended me, just so many times have I blessed you! Do you think that I say this to shame you? No, I say it to enflame in you love for Me."[68]

How can Mary tell Gemma to "long for her"? Why does Jesus send us to her? Can't He Himself make Gemma beautiful, gentle, etc.? Of course He can. He is God. But He has chosen from eternity to do this through Mary, and so when we long for Mary, this is God's will. Jesus, too, we could say, "longed" for Mary, to create her and give Himself all to her. In addition, to long for Mary is also to long for God, because a longing for her is twofold: it is 1) a longing to be formed into Christ, and it is this we were created for, and 2) a loving longing that Jesus Himself imparts to us as He lives in us and loves her in us.

And Mary's Heart is God's Heart—to be in love with her Heart is to be in love with God. We see this at some level on earth, but highly mitigated and blotted by sin: when a man loves a woman, he loves a woman in whom there are traits that she picked up from her parents, and if those traits are lovable he is also brought to love her parents. Even at the level of the highly imperfect, where perhaps a father has abandoned the family and the mother raises her daughter on her own, that daughter will still have traits, positive and negative, from mother and father. To love her would still be at some level to know—and to love—her parents. This is, again, a terribly dim analogy, but much the same happens in regard to Mary, though on a level of total perfection: to love her, to know her, to see her, to be with her is to be with God. She is so like Him, so much His daughter, so much His Spouse, so much a theophany of the Third Person of the Holy Trinity that when we see and know and love her we see and know and love God. So much is He her Heart, so like God (without becoming God) that the Holy Trinity in her can assume to the Person of the Son a human nature drawn from her at her "yes." She always said "yes" to her Father...what is new in the Annunciation is not her "yes" to Him, but that this "yes" was a "yes" to a specific request: "Will you give me a human nature?" She gives flesh to the Eternal Word. Thus when we long for Mary, we truly long for Mary *as Mary*, and this is God's will! And when we long for Mary we are also longing for *God*, and this, too, is God's will.

Perpetual Virgin

Mary is the Mother of God. But she was first a virgin, not simply as a physical fact, but because she always belonged totally to God, indeed from the instant of her Immaculate Conception. She is Virgin in her soul and in her body, and because she is Immaculate, there is no disorder or disruption between body and soul. She does not simply *appear* absolutely pure and perfect but yet have a stain on her soul; nor is her soul absolutely pure and perfect but yet her body imperfect. Both are perfect and perfectly virginal. She is one whole person, Mary, who possesses as Mary absolute interior and physical purity and integrity and who totally gives herself to God. Mary's virginity as a gift of self to God then has two components (and is the model for all virgins):

1) physical integrity—this is essential, because the gift to God of self is total. It is not merely an interior gift, but a gift of one's entire person; thus this includes the body, and

this is further a sign of the next component...

2) interior integrity—this is the realm of the interior decision to belong completely to God, and with this decision one accepts virginity in its entirety, avoiding anything that might taint perfect virginity. It is a life wherein there is a supernatural motivation and no division within the person: one's body, senses, mind, and heart are God's, and where one's will is one with His.

Mary's virginity is *absolute* both physically and in her soul, and she experiences a completely exclusive and *absolute* spousal union with God. Mary's virginity is the outer physical manifestation of her Immaculate soul, and virginity when vowed to God, as in Mary's case, is a direct gift to God of oneself, entirely and without exception. St. Joseph's spousal union with Mary thus is, as mentioned earlier, merely a *participation* in God's spousal unity with her.[69]

And so *prior to and after the Annunciation she is Virgin.* There would be no miracle at all for a young married woman to conceive and bear a child. And Isaiah is clear: "Therefore the Lord himself shall give you a sign. Behold a virgin shall conceive, and bear a son, and his name shall be called Emmanuel."[70] Only God could give such a sign, because it is otherwise impossible for a virgin to "conceive, and bear" a child. She will both "conceive" the child (virgin prior to this) and bear (virgin in giving birth). In fact, as Bastero points out, "when the angel says, 'He will be born holy,' he is saying that the childbirth will be virginal."[71] He also points out another strong indication of a miraculous birth: Mary *immediately* tends to Jesus—there is no recovery time, no assistant, and nothing more than putting Him in swaddling clothes is required. Regarding this, Thomas writes that, "this is fitting as regards the effect of Christ's Incarnation: since He came for this purpose, that He might take away our corruption. Wherefore it is unfitting that in His Birth He should corrupt His Mother's virginity," and "it was fitting that He Who commanded us to honor our father and mother should not in His Birth lessen the honor due to His Mother."[72]

She also remains virgin after the birth of Jesus. In Scripture, there are mentions of *adelphos*, "bretheren" of Jesus, but the word was then used to mean both siblings and cousins, and since there is no mention of any other children of Mary, it is clear that "brethren" refers to "cousins."

Further, Mary is always, as the *Song of Songs* relates, "an enclosed garden." Thomas observes too that, "It is written (Ezekiel 44:2): 'This gate shall be shut, it shall not be opened, and no man shall pass through it; because the Lord the God of Israel hath entered in by it,'" and he again quotes Augustine:

> Expounding these words, Augustine says in a sermon (De Annunt. Dom. iii): "What means this closed gate in the House of the Lord, except that Mary is to be ever inviolate? What does it mean that 'no man shall pass through it,' save that Joseph shall not know her? And what is this—'The Lord alone enters in and goeth out by it'—except that the Holy Ghost shall impregnate her, and that the Lord of angels shall be born of her? And what means this—'it shall be shut for evermore'—but that Mary is a virgin before His Birth, a virgin in His Birth, and a virgin after His Birth?"[73]

She remains Ever-Virgin. Thomas says it would be out of the question that Mary, after a miraculous conception and birth of a child, during which God preserved her virginity miraculously, and wherein her womb is utterly sanctified, would then be desecrated by a fallen human person; her womb is a holy place—it would be totally inappropriate for anyone else to be there after God Himself was there, Who is the All Holy, and for she who is Immaculate and at enmity with the devil and all sin, to conceive a child who does not share her enmity, to clothe a soul in the state of original sin with her immaculate flesh. Thomas goes on to say that her perpetual virginity is proper and necessary too in that "as He is in His Godhead the Only-Begotten of the Father, being thus His Son in every respect perfect, so it was becoming that He should be the Only-Begotten son of His Mother, as being her perfect offspring. He provides three more reasons that are important to note:

1) Mary's womb is the "shrine" of the Holy Spirit. It did not cease to be a holy place consecrated to God alone.
2) She would appear as incredibly ungrateful to God to forfeit the virginity that God by miracle had maintained in her.
3) For St. Joseph to attempt to have natural children with her would be then a violation of a holy place and an act of incredible presumption.

Regarding Thomas's final point, this would be something unthinkable of this holy man, so holy that he was for Jesus an image of God the Father. It would have been a desecration of the true Ark of the Covenant (and if touching the first Ark meant instant death because it is so holy as to be the place of the very presence of God, what of Mary, the true Ark? To touch her in any remotely sensual manner would be unthinkable).

And she never ceases to belong to God *in toto*—she is ever Immaculate in her entire Person. Keeping in mind her integrity, her body always perfectly reflects her totally inviolate, "enclosed garden" soul: she is the Ever Virgin Mother of God.

—Notes—

1. Wilhelm and Scannel, Vol II of *A Manual of Catholic Theology Based on Scheeben's "Dogmatik,"* p. 126
2. CCC, 490, 493
3. Manteau-Bonamy, p. 17 and 57
4. *The Glories of Mary*, Disc. I, "The Immaculate Conception," p. 301
5. ibid, p. 299
6. ibid, p. 293
7. ibid, p. 291
8. *Mariology, Volume Two*, p. 138
9. Mrs. F. Raymond-Barker, *Bernadette,* p. 152
10. *Immaculate Conception and the Holy* Spirit, Manteau-Bonamy, p. 63
11. Richer, "Immaculate Coredemptrix Because Spouse of the Holy Spirit," p. 111
12. St .Thomas Aquinas, *Summa Theologica*, Part I, Qu. 37 & 38
13. "Jesus begins by entrusting his Mother to his disciple (Jn 19, 25-27); then, immediately afterward, he gives us his Spirit by dying for us and 'yielding up his Spirit.' (Jn 19, 28-30)…These two gifts made by Jesus: that of his own mother and that of the Holy Spirit, are intimately connected, inseparable from each other; the Spirit is present wherever the action of the Most Blessed Virgin takes place." Fr. Manteau-Bonamy, *Immaculate Conception and the Holy Spirit*, pp. 104-105

14. CCC, 490
15. Keeping in mind, of course, that the three Persons of the Trinity act together to assume a human nature to the Person of the Son, though the Person of the Spirit and Mary cooperate with each other in a particular way.
16. Manteau-Bonamy, *Immaculate Conception and the Holy Spirit*, pp. 17 and 57
17. That is, God created Mary such that she is able to share in these realities as far as a mere creature possibly can.
18. *The Meaning of Consecration Today*, p.151
19. *Summa Theologica*, Part I, Question 38, article 1
20. ibid, reply to objection 3
21. Manteau-Bonamy, *Immaculate Conception and the Holy Spirit*, p. 23
22. The Eucharist. As St. Augustine writes, "The Word is the Food of the Angels. Men have not the strength to feed It to themselves, nor need they do so. What is needed is a mother who may eat this supersubstantial Bread, transform it into her milk, and in this way feed her poor children. This mother is Mary. She nourishes herself with the Word and transforms It into the Sacred Humanity. She transforms It into Flesh and Blood, i.e., into this sweetest of milk which is called the Eucharist." (As found on p. 111 in the little book, *Jesus Our Eucharist Lord* by Fr. Stefano Manelli.)
23. Manteau-Bonamy, *Immaculate Conception and the Holy Spirit*, pp. 104-105
24. "Dominum et Vivificantem," n. 39
25. Manteau-Bonamy, *Immaculate Conception and the Holy Spirit*, pp. 17 and 57
26. Of note is the fact that at most apparitions Mary asks for a church to be built, where people can continue to receive the truth; she leads people to her Son.
27. We see this in her apparitions: at Lourdes, Fatima, and Kibheo, to name three approved apparitions where she speaks of the evil

of the world, the effects of sin and the need to do penance and make sacrifices.

28. In his *Mariology, Volume* II, Scheeben notes that St. Bernardine of Sienna teaches that, "…all gifts, virtues, and graces of the same Holy Ghost are administered by her [Mary's] hands to whomever she desires, when, in what manner, and to what degree she wishes" p. 271.
29. St. John Paul II, homily in Guayaquil, Ecuador, January 31, 1985. *"With Jesus": The Story of Mary Co-redemptrix*, by Dr. Mark Miravalle.
30. In his encyclical, *Dominum et Vivificantem*, par. 39, St. John Paul II explains the mission of the Spirit to convince the world of sin. In fact, here he speaks of invisible realities becoming "concertized": specifically, that in the crucified Savior there is made visible to the world how sin has wounded the Father, so to speak, in His heart. So deeply is God wounded by man's sin that He says, "I am sorry that I have made them." And it is in Jesus, "in whose humanity the 'suffering' of God is concretized."
31. This does not imply a limit on the Spirit's ability to "convince the world of sin," but simply says that in Mary the Spirit "convinces" in a visible manner.
32. Fr. Edward Caswall, translator
33. Laurentin, *The Meaning of Consecration Today*, p. 151
34. *Immaculate Conception and the Holy Spirit,* p. 95
35. ibid, p. 44
36. ibid, p. 4
37. Of course, Mary does not *comprehend* God; no finite creature could comprehend God in regard either to understanding God completely or in revealing God completely, since God is utterly beyond the comprehension of a finite creature.
38. As Kolbe points out, however, "Mary's nature and person are totally distinct from the nature and person of the Holy Spirit," p. 41. There is a union of "essence," but Mary is a human person who is

not self-subsisting being, and the Holy Spirit is the Third Person of the Trinity Who is self-subsisting being in union with the Father and Son.

39. Manteau-Bonamy, *Immaculate Conception and the Holy Spirit*, p. 44
40. Again, as St. Kolbe says, "These two gifts made by Jesus: that of his own mother and that of the Holy Spirit, are intimately connected, inseparable from each other."
41. On page 183 of his book, *The Mysteries of Christianity*, Fr. Scheeben writes of this motherly aspect of the Holy Spirit that, "As the mother is the bond of love between father and child, so in God the Holy Spirit is the bond of love between the Father and the Son." Since Mary is the "ectype" of the Holy Spirit, as mentioned on page 11 of this study, any divine maternal characteristics that belong to the Holy Spirit have certainly been impressed upon this Woman who has been created with such a deep *resemblance to* and *intimacy with* the Holy Spirit.
42. *Our Father, Our Mother: Mary and the Faces of God*, p. 140
43. p. 210
44. St. Paul says, "We see now through a glass in a dark manner; but then face to face. Now I know in part; but then I shall know even as I am known, (1 Cor 13:12)." In the Beatific Vision, we will see God "face to face." What does this mean, "face to face" and not "through a glass darkly"? We will see God. To see God face to face is to see *Him*, the *Persons* of the Trinity in Person.
45. Manteau-Bonamy, *Immaculate Conception and the Holy Spirit*, p. 94
46. We also find here a clue as to how the angel can say, "The Lord is with thee" even though she has not yet given her "*fiat*." This phrase doesn't refer specifically to Jesus living in her womb, but it can mean God *qua* God, and it can also refer to the Person of the Holy Spirit specifically, and in a special way in regard to the special relationship between Mary and the Holy Spirit; this certainly

fits with the sketch of Mary traced out in the Old Testament that this Woman would be one with God in such a way that union with her infallibly leads to union with God.

47. Luke 1:46
48. Manteau-Bonamy, *Immaculate Conception and the Holy Spirit,* p. 71
49. *In the Arms of Mary*, pp. 144-145
50. Manteau-Bonamy, *Immaculate Conception and the Holy Spirit*, p. 63
51. *Academic Dictionaries*
52. Manteau-Bonamy, *Immaculate Conception and the Holy Spirit*, p. 51
53. ibid, p. 70, "For the Holy Spirit is *her* spirit. Far from being alienated in her personality because of the dominance of the Holy Spirit, she is on the contrary more than any other creature in full possession of herself. It is characteristic of God that he acts in us in such a manner that our actions are truly ours."
54. John 14:9, "Jesus saith to him: Have I been so long a time with you; and have you not known me? Philip, he that seeth me seeth the Father also. How sayest thou, Shew us the Father?"
55. Manteau-Bonamy, *Immaculate Conception and the Holy Spirit*, p. 44
56. ibid p. 70, Fr. Manteau-Bonamy goes on to point out that St. Louis de Montfort, understanding this reality, thus calls Mary, "our link with God."
57. *Aesthetics*, p. 136
58. ibid, p. 136
59. ibid, p 136. Von Hildebrand continues on p. 138 to mention some essential points, and these clearly relate directly to the natural and supernatural beauty seen in the face of Mary:

    > ...the beauty of the visible is determined by certain visible factors and adheres directly to these, whereas the metaphysical beauty adheres to spiritual entities. This latter beauty is a fragrance, a radiance of personal, moral, and vital values. These manifest themselves in the visible, and in this way let the beauty become visible. Visible factors

allow these inner attitudes to appear in the face and are responsible for the expression. The expressed metaphysical beauty always remains the radiance of values that adhere to the inner personal realities; it always depends on these values, which are responsible for the metaphysical beauty in the same way as the corresponding disvalues are responsible for the metaphysical ugliness.

60. ibid, p. 136
61. Frisk, "The Holy Spirit and Mary," section entitled, "Mary as Image of the Holy Spirit."
62. *Crossing the Threshold of Hope*, p. 210
63. Manteau-Bonamy, *Immaculate Conception and the Holy Spirit*, p. 71, "Jesus is not merely divine; he is God, God the Son. Mary is not God, but she is fully divine because, as creature, she has no life except in her relationship with God: with the Father whose daughter she is; with the Son, whose mother she is; with the Holy Spirit, whose unique sanctuary she is."
64. *The Catechism of the Catholic Church* (493) puts the above quote this way: "The Fathers of the Eastern tradition call the Mother of God 'the All-Holy' (Panagia)."
65. 1 John 1: "That which was from the beginning, which we have heard, which we have seen with our eyes, which we have looked upon, and our hands have handled, of the word of life..."
66. Manteau-Bonamy, *Immaculate Conception and the Holy Spirit*, p. 31
67. St. Gemma Galgani (1878-1903), a young Italian girl who was a victim soul and bore the stigmata. In the latter part of her life she saw and spoke with her Guardian Angel daily, and she also frequently saw and spoke with Jesus, Mary, and St. Gabriel Possenti.
68. Cf. "Prayer to the Holy Spirit," by Cardinal Mercier, wherein he begins, "O, Holy Spirit, beloved of my soul..."
69. Letter from March 18, 1903, republished by Glenn Dallaire. This will become an important point in the section on consecration to

Mary. When a soul belongs to Mary in the exchange of hearts that consecration is, that soul experiences a participation in Jesus' own union with her, and our union with Mary could not exist unless God had so willed.

70. Isaiah 7:14
71. *Mary, Mother of the Redeemer*, p. 170
72. *Summa*, Part III, qu. 28, art. 2
73. ibid, Part III, qu. 28, art. 3

Chapter Two
The Immaculate Virgin is the Mother of God

Theotokos

The dogma of Mary as Mother of God demonstrates the title of this book remarkably: that Mary is God's Beloved. If you could make your own mother, you would make her the most beautiful, most wonderful, sweetest woman in existence. Her soul would be spotless, she would be filled with gentleness, kindness, compassion; she would never be angry or lose her temper; she would have eyes deep and full of beauty and mystery like the ocean, because those eyes will gaze into God's and God will gaze into hers; her lips would be perfectly formed to kiss her child; her hands gentle and full of grace to hold Him; her hair long and pretty and soft to hold—if you have ever held babies or very little children you know that they love to play with hair, or use it as a security blanket. All of this and more God does in regard to His Mother. But for God, He is also her Father: God is always transcendent, He is Mary's creator. She is also His spouse, because she belongs to Him so radically. She is the Woman He loves, just as she is the "world's first love," just as Venerable Fulton Sheen points out that each of us can say "she is the Woman I love!"[1] Note well—Sheen does not write that we each can say, in the deepest depths of one's heart, that Mary is "*one* of the women I love!" No, she is for each of us "*the* Woman," as God is "*the* Father." So for God, so for us. We could put it this way, in modern terminology: "If she's good enough for God, well, she's good enough for me!" The miracle is that God would make His Mother to be our Mother also.

The Greek word we use for "Mother of God," *Theotokos*, literally means "God-Bearer," and this word became extremely important in the year 431. At that time, a bishop named Nestorius had the idea that Mary was only the Mother of Jesus in His humanity, as he claimed Jesus was two distinct persons: a human person, Christ, and the Divine Person of the Eternal Word. Therefore, he claimed, Mary is only *Christotokos*, Mother of the human person only, not Mother of God the divine Person. Interestingly, had Nestorius applied to Mary his idea of two persons, he would have come up with something St. Maximilian Kolbe did in the 20th century, and Nestorious would have gone down in history as a great Mariologist; but this will be covered in the next chapter. Regarding Jesus, the Council of Ephesus (431 AD), with much thanks to St. Cyril, definitively proclaimed Mary as not merely Mother of Christ, but Mother of God, and for a crucial Christological reason: Jesus is *not* composed of two persons, as Nestorius held, but one Divine Person only, a Divine Person Who has assumed a human nature. He takes on a true human nature, He has a body and a soul the same as you and I, but here we have not a human person, but one Divine Person Who subsists in a Divine and a human nature. Thus we have the "Ephesus Syllogism":

Jesus is God,
Mary is His Mother,
Thus, Mary is the Mother of God

This dogma does not mean that Mary is the one who gave Jesus His *Divine* nature, and this reality can be compared to any human mother—no mother gives to their child a soul, only God does this, creating the soul *ex nihilo*. And yet, the woman who gave of her flesh and blood to form us really is our mother, though she does not give the soul. So with Mary: she really gives the Word of her flesh and blood (only hers, while for us we have elements of both a human mother and a human father), not His soul, and not His divinity. But like our mothers, she carried her child, nourished Him, clothed Him in her own substance; she is truly His Mother. And Mary always protects her Son, even in her dogmas and doctrines—they are not separate from Christology, but defend it and properly expound upon it.

Mary as Mother of God also concretely reveals Mary as God's Beloved in a special way:

> The fact that the Logos is really and truly the Son of Mary, confers upon the Mother the highest dignity to which a created person can attain, viz. a participation in the dignity of her Son. To fully appreciate this feature of the Divine maternity, it is necessary to consider it from a twofold point of view: as founded upon the natural operations of the Mother, and as the work of the spiritual and free operation of the Son.
>
> The natural operation of the Mother results in the pro-

duction of the absolutely most perfect fruit that can be produced; it "reaches the confines of the Godhead" by furnishing God with a new nature, whereas all other created activity reaches God only by knowledge and love; it is a co-operation with God's own internal activity, whereas the co-operation of other mothers in the production of the human soul by God, is only a co-operation with God's external creative activity. Hence the maternity of Mary is the highest ministry to which a creature can be elevated by God.

Again, the Mother of Christ is a relation by blood to Christ as man, and a "relation by affinity" to God Himself as pure Spirit. Man is related by affinity to persons who marry his blood relations, because such persons become morally or juridically one with the blood relations. Now, the humanity of Christ, related by blood to Mary, is united to the Logos more intimately than wife to husband; hence the affinity to God, contracted by Mary, is more intimate and perfect than any affinity among men.

The connection with God, based upon Mary's maternity, may also be conceived as an eminent and unique Divine filiation. Her title to a share in the good things of God, in His Life and Beatitude, is not merely owing to grace, as in the case of God's adopted sons; it arises from her substantial relations with the Divine Family. The "Seed of the Word of Truth," out of which the sons of adoption are born, is itself infused into Mary. The

> The Fathers, from this point of view, speak of Mary as...agna Dei (the little ewe-lamb of God), and as the only-beloved and only-begotten daughter of God.[2]

"...the only-beloved and only-begotten daughter of God": in other words, "like Father, like daughter." Fr. Scheeben says that Mary is "the most perfect image of the Father *ad extra*, after the incarnate wisdom. Thus she is to be regarded as a daughter whose daughterhood is the most perfect participation in and the most perfect image of the sonship of the eternal Son."[3]

Astonishingly, this daughter gives flesh to God, her creator. Thus ensues a physical relation, which comes not prior to, but after the fact that Mary is already one with God in her Heart and soul, and so her relation with God is not established at the Annunciation, but takes on a new, an additional form; as God the Father is truly the Father of the Son on the supernatural level, Mary really is the Mother of the Son on a biological level—Mary is a blood-relative of God! And because she is His Mother, just as the Father gives the Son His whole Self, Mary gives Jesus all she is—thus she is endowed with the Immaculate human nature, virtues and utter goodness that God would want Jesus as man to have.

With these elements in mind, we can form a little portrait of Mary as Mother of God...

A young Immaculate maiden of the human race—about fourteen years old—has been chosen to be the Mother of He Who is existence itself. She is thus related not only to God in regard to the humanity of Christ, but she is related rather to a *Divine Person*.[4] Fr. Garrigou-Lagrange, quoting St. Thomas, writes that, "The Humanity of Christ since it is united to God, the beatitude of the elect since it is the possession of God, the Blessed Virgin

Mary since she is the Mother of God—all these have a certain infinite dignity from their relation to God Himself, and under that respect there can be nothing more perfect than them since there can be nothing more perfect than God."[5] Fr. Lagrange goes on to cite Bossuet, who says, "the ineffable love which He had for you, O Mary, made Him conceive many other designs in your regard. He ordained that He should belong to you in the same quality in which He belonged to Himself: and in order to establish an eternal union with you He made you the Mother of His only Son and Himself the Father of yours."[6] And so no human nor angelic intelligence can fathom her; only God can plumb her depths to the very core. To *fully* comprehend the dignity of the Mother of God completely, one would have to fully comprehend the infinite dignity of God, and this we finite creatures cannot do, not on earth, not in Heaven.

—Notes—

1. *The World's First Love*, p. 24
2. Wilhelm and Scannel, Vol II of *A Manual of Catholic Theology Based on Scheeben's "Dogmatik,"* p. 126
3. *Mariology, Vol. I*, p. 174
4. Fr. Garigou-LaGrange writes on pp. 29-30 of *The Mother of Savior*,

> the dignity of the divine maternity is to be measured by considering the term to which it is immediately referred. Now this term is of the hypostatic order, and therefore surpasses the whole order of grace and glory.
>
> By her divine maternity Mary is related really to the

Word made flesh. The relation so set up has the uncreated Person of the Incarnate Word as its term, for Mary is the Mother of Jesus, who is God. It is not precisely the humanity of Jesus which is the term of the relation, but rather Jesus Himself in Person: it is He and not His humanity that is Son of Mary. Hence Mary, reaching, as Cajetan says, even to the frontiers of the Divinity, belongs terminally to the hypostatic order, to the order of the personal union of the Humanity of Jesus to the Uncreated Word. This truth follows also from the very definition of the divine maternity as formulated in the Council of Ephesus.

5. *The Mother of the Saviour, and Our Interior Life*, p. 31
6. ibid, p. 32

Chapter Three
Coredemptrix, Mediatrix, Advocate: a Natural Consequence of Motherhood

This doctrine is the link to authentic Marian devotion. It answers the question, "What does Mary have to do with me?" On a natural level, we could put it this way: "What does my mother have to do with me when I am due to be born and after I am born?" Anyone would say, "She suffers, then feeds me, clothes me, protects me, speaks on my behalf…everything!" And so we have the dogmas of her Divine Motherhood, her Perpetual Virginity, her Immaculate Conception, and her Assumption…and this doctrine completes those four. The first four dogmas speak of Mary in relation to God and about who she is at the core of her being; the 5th doctrine, which would be the 5th and final Marian dogma should it be proclaimed such (many appeals have gone to the Pope asking for this), applies the first four dogmas to her relationship with you and me. "What does Mary do with me while she spiritually gives birth to me at the Cross and after she is assumed into Heaven?" The answer is summed up in three short phrases:

1) She suffers for us—she is Coredemptrix.
2) She nurtures us—she is Mediatrix of all grace.

3) She intercedes, which means pleads, with God on our behalf—she is our Advocate.

It is important to point out immediately that of course Mary's participation in our Redemption is second to, and in participation with, the one absolutely essential mediation of Jesus, Who is God and man, and by Whom we are saved. Pope Benedict XVI puts the reality of Mary's participation very well in his "Act of Entrustment and Consecration of Priests to the Immaculate Heart of Mary," prayed at Fatima in 2010:

> Advocate and Mediatrix of grace,
> you who are fully immersed
> in the one universal mediation of Christ,
> invoke upon us, from God,
> a heart completely renewed
> that loves God with all its strength
> and serves mankind as you did.
>
> Repeat to the Lord
> your efficacious word:
> "They have no wine" (Jn 2:3),
> so that the Father and the Son will send upon us
> a new outpouring of
> the Holy Spirit.[1]

Coredemptrix

Mary's mission of Coredemptrix is seen from the Annunciation. At the most basic level, it is she who will enflesh the Word, enabling Him to suffer and die for us, to rise from the dead for us, to ascend into Heaven for us, and we see this in the beginning of Scripture, in Genesis 3:15, the prophecy of the Woman and her Seed. It is because of her *fiat* that Mary, Lady Wisdom in Proverbs chapter 9, can share her meal, the Eucharist, with us. Without her, we don't get to the meal. One either goes to Lady Wisdom, the Coredemptrix, the Lady who is with the Redeemer, or to Lady Folly, the lady who is with giants that throw us into the pit called Hell.

It is important, right at the beginning, to understand the parts of the word that compose the title, "Coredemptrix." "Co" means "with." Etymologically, it does not mean "equal to," though in English usage it can mean "equal." However, we also say, "a nurse cooperates with the surgeon in an operation." This does not imply the nurse is in any sense equal to the surgeon or sufficient of herself to perform the operation; it's obvious that this is not the case, and if it came down to picking the most necessary person for the operation, we would have to say that it simply goes nowhere without the surgeon. Like all analogies, this one limps a bit perhaps, but it gets the point across: the nurse is not a surgeon, but his helper; Mary is not God, but His handmaid. The word "redemptrix" is the female form of "redeemer." Put "Co" and "redemptrix" together and we have "Woman with the Redeemer," much the same as we have "nurse with surgeon."

Coredemptive Suffering

Her suffering, Fr. Garrigou-Lagrange notes, is measured "by her love of God Whom sin offended, by her love of Jesus crucified for our sins, and by her love of us whom sin had brought to spiritual ruin."[2] He goes on to point out that Mary's least actions, due to her great love, merited more than all the torments of all the martyrs. He ponders then what the worth of her sufferings in the plan of Salvation, especially at the Cross, must be! Surely they are past any reckoning, excepting God's ability to do so. This is her objective role—she really helped in securing the graces of salvation; we by our prayers and sufferings merely release those graces already won by Jesus and Mary, but Mary truly gives spiritual birth to us as Mother of the Son and our Mother: Jesus physically, us spiritually at Calvary, the Head (Jesus) and us (Members) making up the one whole Christ of Head and Body to Whom she gives birth. She is, to reiterate, "The Woman *with* the Redeemer."

The Doctrine of Co-Redemptrix in Lumen Gentium

"Without using the term 'co-redemptrix,' the Council clearly enunciated the doctrine: a cooperation of a unique kind, a maternal cooperation in the life and work of the Savior, which reaches its apex in the participation in the sacrifice of Calvary, and which is oriented towards the supernatural life of souls [...]" writes Vatican theologian Jean Galot.[3] In *Lumen Gentium*, chapter VIII, there are several phrases that speak to Mary's role as Co-Redeemer with her Son...

Adam and Eve

In setting forth the role of Mary in Salvation History, *Lumen Gentium* begins with our first parents in Genesis 3:15: "[...] she is already prophetically foreshadowed in the promise of victory over the serpent which was given to our first parents after their fall into sin."[4] Genesis 3:15 is a starting point. But to understand more fully the role of Mary as prophesied in Genesis 3:15, we need to look at what happened just prior to this promise of future redemption. What happened before this promise is a part of the whole picture.

The first hint at the role of Eve is found near the beginning of Genesis: "[…] 'And the Lord God said: It is not good for man to be alone: let us make him a help like unto himself.' And the Lord God having formed out of the ground all the beasts of the earth, and all the fowls of the air, brought them to Adam to see what he would call them […] but for Adam there was not found a helper like himself."[5] The key words here are "a help like unto himself." The word for "helper" is *ezer*, meaning someone who "helps, protects, aids, succours,"[6] and *kenegdo*, meaning "suitable."[7] What is made clear is that the woman is equal to the man *in dignity*, but has a *different role* than the man. Part of the woman's role is clearly to assist the man in facing trials, including, it would seem, trials of battle, since this was a possibility of which Adam was made aware immediately upon being given responsibility for the Garden of Eden: "And the Lord God took man, and put him into the paradise of pleasure, to dress it, and to keep it." In Hebrew, the word for "keep" is *Shamar*, the distinct meaning of which is to "preserve," "guard" and "protect,"[8] as in keep safe from some threat. And this role of "keeping" the Garden was specifically given to Adam. Adam and Eve each had their role to play, and that role was a part of their God-given nature. And so the role of a woman as *co-redeemer* is ingrained, so to speak, in Eve's very makeup, a suitable person to help Adam guard and preserve. Eve was to be Adam's great ally, to encourage him and lead him to fulfill God's commands, especially when times got tough.

And in Genesis chapter 3:1-15, times did get tough. Here, the devil usurps God's order by ignoring Adam and engaging Eve in what can only be described as an outright attack. Eve, rather than referring the devil to her husband, whose mission was to guard the Garden, battled the devil herself. Incredibly brave; but not incredibly wise. However, Adam remained silent while the devil attacked his bride and vilified God, his Father, and so in some sense Adam put Eve in a really bad spot. Had he spoken up, Eve probably would not have. But Eve is also at fault—she should have helped Adam to defend the Garden as God charged him to do, not by direct battle with the devil, but by being Adam's helper in this regard. Being a co-redeemer is clearly part of Eve's *very nature*. The New Eve and the New Adam will willingly undergo a *veritable replay* of the trial of Adam and Eve, and stand together in the greatest battle the world has ever seen. Pope John Paul II, in speaking of Mary as the New Eve in a Wednesday general audience, the 33rd installment in a series on Mary, sums up the situation:

> *Lumen gentium* recalls the contrast between Eve's behavior and that of Mary, described by St. Irenaeus: "Just as the former—that is, Eve—was seduced by the words of an angel so that she turned away from God by disobeying his word, so the latter—Mary—received the good news from an angel's announcement in such a way as to give birth to God by obeying his word; and as the former was seduced so that she disobeyed God, the latter let herself be convinced to obey God, and so the Virgin Mary became the advocate of the virgin Eve. And as the human race was subjected to death by a virgin, it was liberated by a Virgin; a virgin's disobe-

> dience was thus counterbalanced by a Virgin's obedience..." (*Adv. Haer.*, V, 19, 1).[9]

Mary's Fiat

"The Father of mercies willed that the Incarnation should be preceded by assent on the part of the predestined mother, so that just as a woman had a share in bringing about death, so also a woman should contribute to life. This is pre-eminently true of the Mother of Jesus, who gave to the world the Life that renews all things [...]" (*LG* VIII, 56).

As soon as Mary gave her "yes" to God she ushered in the New Adam, bringing Him to the battleground on earth and into combat with the devil. Her "yes" to the Incarnation, in other words, is also her "yes" to the Cross. It is what Eve was supposed to do. As Dr. Mark Miravalle writes:

> The yes of the Virgin of Nazareth is therefore in itself the yes to Calvary. There is no new invitation. The Archangel Gabriel does not come back and re-invite her to be "with Jesus" in the work of redemption. As Pope Benedict said recently in his February 11 letter to the Sick, Mary shares in the Passion of her Son as a continuation of her fiat at the Annunciation.[10]

With her "yes," Mary really does become responsible for God becoming man. Jesus is the Redeemer, but He makes His Incarnation dependent upon this young woman. It is an intimate union. Pope St. Leo XIII writes of this in his encyclical letter *Fidentem Piumque*, that

> She it is *from whom is born Jesus*; she is therefore truly His mother, and for this reason a worthy and acceptable "Mediatrix to the Mediator." As the various mysteries present themselves one after the other in the formula of the Rosary for the meditation and contemplation of men's minds, they also elucidate what we owe to Mary for our reconciliation and salvation. No one can fail to be sweetly affected when considering her who appeared in the house of Elizabeth as the minister of the divine gifts, and who presented her Son to the Shepherds, to the kings, and to Simeon. Moreover, one must remember that the blood of Christ shed for our sake, and those members in which He offers to His Father the wounds He received as "the price of our liberty," are no other than the flesh and blood of the Virgin; since "the flesh of Jesus is the flesh of Mary, and however much it was exalted in the glory of His Resurrection, nevertheless the nature of His flesh derived from Mary remained and still remain the same."[11]

In recent years, Dr. Joseph Seifert added to this, writing that not only is Jesus of Mary's flesh, she is also not simply a vehicle that Jesus uses. He obtains flesh from her because she freely consented to this:

> A dogma that declares Mary Coredemptrix would give a unique witness to the full freedom of the human person, as we have seen, and to God's respect for human freedom. This dogma would recognize in an ultimate way that a ***free decision*** of the human person of Mary,

> who was not even to become the Mother of God without her free ***fiat****—a* decision which was not exclusively caused by divine grace but was also the fruit of her own personal choice—was ***necessary*** for our salvation, or played at least an ***indispensable part*** in the concrete way of our Redemption chosen by God.[12]

And with that *fiat*, "She devoted herself totally, as handmaid of the Lord, to the person and work of her Son, under and with him, serving the mystery of redemption, by the grace of Almighty God. Rightly, therefore, the Fathers see Mary not merely as passively engaged by God, but as freely cooperating in the work of man's salvation through faith and obedience [...]"[13] (*LG* VIII, 56).

Mary's behavior at Cana is a prime example of this participation. Not only has the Savior come to earth through Mary, but now Mary encourages Him to begin His public ministry...and through her intercession, He does: "And the wine failing, the mother of Jesus saith to him: They have no wine. And Jesus saith to her: Woman, what is that to me and to thee? My hour is not yet come. His mother saith to the waiters: Whatsoever he shall say to you, do ye."[14] The hour for the New Adam to battle against the devil in open warfare has come, through the intercession of the New Eve.

Again, in all this there is the picture of what should have occurred in the first place. What Mary did is a total reversal of Eve's actions—Eve should have encouraged Adam to fight the devil. Mary reversed this at the Annunciation, and continues to at Cana and at the Cross.

"Thus the Blessed Virgin advanced in her pilgrimage of faith, and faithfully persevered in union with her Son unto the cross, where she stood, in keeping with the divine plan, enduring with her only begotten Son the intensity of his suffering, associated herself with his sacrifice in her mother's heart, and lovingly consenting to the immolation of this victim which was born of her."[15] St. Gemma Galgani also provides some insight into Mary's suffering, adding both to *Lumen Gentium* and to what has already been said in the previous section of this book:

> "I know very well that when a person hurts the son in the presence of a mom or dad, the pain hurts the son and also the parents. Therefore my Mom was crucified together with Jesus. And she never complained. Poor Mother!"
>
> "Oh God... Jesus is dead and Mom you are crying. Am I the only one that is so insensitive? I do not see anymore one sacrifice: I see two: one for Jesus and one for Mary! Oh Mother, if one could see you with Jesus, one would not be able to say who will be the first one to die: You or Jesus!"
>
> "Oh, wicked sinners stop crucifying Jesus, because at the same time you pierce His Mother!"[16]

And pierced she was. In the words of Dr. Mark Miravalle,

> What happened to Jesus in his body happened to Mary in spirit, in heart. Other contributors from the mystical tradition, and not simply Our Lady of All Nations, testify to Mary's spiritual and even invisible physical stigmata at Calvary in union with her son.

> John Paul II's theology of the body helps us to explain this. What does the theology of the body tell us? It tells us that the body expresses the person. Therefore Mary's spiritual stigmatization in her heart with Jesus would also be appropriately experienced in her body, but invisibly. Why? She would never constitute a distraction from her son. Her suffering would be mystically united to that of Jesus, of heart and body, but never causing humanity to take its eyes off its crucified God.[17]

This particular suffering of Mary seems even to be realized in some of her apparitions. In the apparition of Our Lady of All Nations, Mary has her arms extended, and grace is streaming from her hands…from her stigmatized hands, and at Akita the miraculous statue of Mary expressed a stigmata in her right hand. These apparitions of Our Lady show us that the grace of Jesus's Sacrifice comes to us through Mary as Coredemptrix and as a natural part of her role as Coredemptrix.

The Value of her Suffering

All that has been seen of Mary's suffering in this book would be senseless occurrences and cruel were they to bear no fruit, especially in light of the fact that aside from Jesus, she is the only innocent party, and it is precisely the two innocent ones who suffer beyond the bounds of all other human suffering. They are together from beginning to end, with Mary at crucial junctions acting in instrumental ways to bring about our salvation. St. John Paul II in his Apostolic Letter, *Salvifici Doloris*, n. 25 writes:

> In her, the many and intense sufferings were amassed in such an interconnected way that they were not only a proof of her unshakable faith, but also a contribution to the redemption of all.... It was on Calvary that Mary's suffering, beside the suffering of Jesus, reached an intensity which can hardly be imagined from a human point of view, but which were mysteriously and supernaturally fruitful for the Redemption of the world. Her ascent of Calvary and her standing at the foot of the cross together with the beloved disciple were a special sort of sharing in the redeeming death of her Son.

> And Mary's Motherhood continues:

> She conceived, brought forth, and nourished Christ, she presented Him to the Father in the temple, shared her Son's suffering as He died on the cross. Thus, in a wholly singular way she cooperated by her obedience, faith, hope, and burning charity in the work of the Savior in restoring supernatural life to souls. For this reason she is a mother to us in the order of grace.[18]

> And Mary "by her manifold intercession continues to bring us the gifts of eternal salvation."[19]

This is the behavior of a Mother who "cares for the brethren of her Son, who still journeys on earth surrounded by dangers and difficulties [...] Therefore the Blessed Virgin is invoked in the Church under the titles of Advocate, Helper, Benefactress, and Mediatrix."[20]

Mediatrix of All Grace

The nature of motherhood is to nourish, nurture, and mold a child who is given to her, a child to whom she is given. "No other person on earth is 'given' to us as our mother is; no one else so well as she personifies love in its most disinterested generous and devoted aspects."[21] Even the Saints can act as mediators between us and God as they pray for us. The "disinterested generous and devoted aspects" are of course that a mother gives of her very self, body and soul, in the nurturing of her child, and from the first instance of her child's conception. Indeed, motherhood and mediatrix go together, in the same breath, as it were: "Spiritual Mother" and "nourishing" go together, just as "physical mother" and "nourishing" do. "…Mary's mediation *is intimately linked with her motherhood.* It possesses a specifically maternal character, which distinguishes it from the mediation of the other creatures…" writes St. John Paul II in *Redemptoris Mater*.[22]

And what Mary mediates to us is grace. This begins at the Annunciation, and quite simply because by her "yes" she carries within her the one who is the source of all grace. The source of grace comes from Mary to us—and since we are talking about the very font of all grace, she is the one by whom God wants to mediate all grace. He doesn't change His mind; to obtain grace one goes to Mary, and this is more necessary than a newborn baby obtaining nourishment from his mom—a baby could nurse from another mom if the need arose, or from a bottle, but this cannot happen in regard to grace: the spiritual child-Mother relationship here is exclusive, and necessary for life.

We see her mediation to the unborn St. John the Baptist and

to St. Elizabeth in the Visitation, and she mediates grace in a physical way by carrying Jesus in the womb *and* via her voice! "And it came to pass, that when Elizabeth heard the salutation of Mary, the infant leaped in her womb. And Elizabeth was filled with the Holy Ghost…" In Bethlehem, she continues to mediate grace to the world as she lays the font of all grace in the manger, giving the Bread of Life to the world, and again there is a notable physical aspect to this mediation of all grace.

Conversely, there is an *antithetical mediation* in Genesis 3:15, one that is related in a certain way to Cana. Rather than mediate life by encouraging Adam to cling to God, his and her Father, and thereby helping Adam to exorcise the evil spirit and retain the life of their souls, Eve worked an anti-mediation as *Co-peccatrix* with the *Peccator*[23]—a knot that will remain tied until the Coredemptrix with the Redemptor unties that knot. In the article, "Pope John Paul II's Teaching on Marian Coredemption," Father Calkins cites St. John Paul II's words concerning this anti-mediation of Eve (although he does not use the term "anti-mediation") and how God reverses the situation:

> The Protogospel's words also reveal the unique destiny of the woman who, although yielding to the serpent's temptation before the man did, in virtue of the divine plan later becomes *God's first ally*. Eve was the serpent's accomplice in enticing man to sin. Overturning this situation, God declares that he will make the woman the serpent's enemy…[24]

The untying of this knot takes place in a particular way to the wedding at Cana. Eve should have sent Adam into battle; at

Cana, instead of keeping Jesus for herself—something, however, that Mary never did—she sent Him to defeat this same evil spirit by His public ministry and—on the face of it paradoxically—via His seeming defeat by suffering, death, and the scattering of those who should have stayed with Him.

But Mary is perfected as the Mediatrix of All Grace at Calvary. St. John Paul II writes in *Redemptoris Mater*, "If John's description of the event at Cana presents Mary's caring motherhood at the beginning of Christ's messianic activity, another passage from the same Gospel confirms this motherhood in the salvific economy of grace at its crowning moment, namely when Christ's sacrifice on the Cross, his Paschal Mystery, is accomplished."[25] The crucifixion finds Mary mediating all grace to the world as she freely offers the veritable well spring of grace, her Son, Who takes away the sins of the world—sacrificing her maternal right to protect Him. This is indeed the culmination of her *fiat* at the Annunciation where she knowingly consented to be the Sorrowful Mother of the Redeemer, to Whom she gave flesh in order to give Him as a Sacrifice, something we see characteristic of Mary's every action in Jesus' regard: she mediates all grace by saying "yes" to the Angel; she does the same when she visits Elizabeth; she does this again at Bethlehem, laying Jesus immediately in the manger for all; by fleeing to Egypt she preserves the source of all grace; at Cana she further mediates grace to the world as she starts Jesus upon His open ministry of healing the sick, casting out demons, and especially by forgiving sins; throughout the suffering and then death of Jesus she consents to all He experiences as she shares His love for us in an immolation that will definitively win our salvation; from Heaven God does not change His mind—she continues to be the one through whom all grace comes. Pope Benedict XV, in a letter from May 5th, 1917 during World War I, puts it this way: "And since all the graces which God deigns to bestow in pity upon men are dispensed through Mary, we urge that in this terrible hour, the trusting petition of her most afflicted children be directed to her…to Mary, the Mother of mercy, who is all-powerful in grace!"[26] Pope Pius XI in his encyclical on the Sacred Heart, *Caritate Christi Compulsi*, says the same thing as he places the Sacred Heart and the Immaculate Heart as "Mediatrix of All Graces" side by side: "Let them pray to Him, interposing likewise the powerful patronage of the Blessed Virgin Mary, Mediatrix of all graces, for themselves and for their families, for their country, for the Church…"[27] And St. Louis de Montfort writes, "God the Son has communicated to His Mother all that He has acquired by His Life and by His Death, His infinite merits and His admirable virtues; and He has made her the treasuress of all that His Father has given Him for His inheritance. It is by her that He applies His merits to His members, and that He communicates His virtues, and distributes His graces. She is His mysterious canal; she is His aqueduct, through which He makes His mercies flow gently and abundantly."[28]

Advocate

When people hear the word "advocate" they often think "lawyer." That's not far off, because an advocate is one who acts on behalf of another. Applied to Mary, she is acting like a lawyer in that she is with us before *the Judge*. But that's a blurry sort of idea if we leave the idea there. Mary is not any woman before God, as we've seen: she is His beloved daughter and spouse and Mother;

she's not simply a lawyer before a judge. More than that, God Himself made Mary *our* Mother as well: indeed she is our mother, our sister, the beloved of our hearts. *The beloved of her Beloved is the advocate of her beloved* (in a slightly less mind-twisting way, "Mary, the beloved of God, Who is her beloved, is the advocate of you, her beloved). There is no way, thank God, that when a soul lets Mary take his case before God that he will lose his case. He will only lose what he ought, that which is not good, burned off either here, in Purgatory, or in some combination of both, because the one Who is the Judge is *Abba*, Mary's Daddy, Who is also your Daddy and mine. This is like no worldly tribunal!

Every good mother and father knows this is how it works at the natural level as well. Usually, the father is the one who sentences after reviewing the evidence. Then the mother comes in and says, "how about we mitigate the punishment, for this and that reason, and he will be better in the future; let's take the punishment down a bit, or perhaps even entirely dispose of the punishment." But the supernatural level of motherly advocacy is far superior and more intense than anything on the natural level; Mary and Jesus offered the Blood of God to God for us, to wipe out our sins and the punishment due to those sins. When Mary pleads for us to Our Father, she does so red in the Blood of the Son Who is both hers and God's. And the Father allows Himself to be moved by her: prior to Mary's visits to the three children at Fatima, they were visited by an angel three times; in the first visit of the angel he taught them how God wanted them to pray, and the angel said to them, "The Most Holy Hearts of Jesus and Mary will be touched by your prayers."[29] If Jesus is touched by *our* prayers, what of Mary's prayers?

In the New Testament, we see Mary as Advocate at the Cana wedding. "They have no wine… Whatsoever he shall say to you, do ye."[30] Not only did the wedding guests get more wine, they got about 120 or more gallons of the best wine! When Jesus makes wine, no doubt He doesn't stint on the quality, and clearly when Mary is our advocate, she obtains results beyond our wildest dreams.

As well in the Old Testament there are types of Mary as advocate. Queen Esther acts as advocate on behalf of her people, the Jews, before her husband, King Assuerus: "And he commanded her (no doubt but he was Mardochai) to go to the king, and petition for her people, and for her country... And do thou call upon the Lord, and speak to the king for us, and deliver us from death. And on the third day she laid away the garments she wore, and put on her glorious apparel." She so affects the king by her beautiful and gracious presence that he immediately writes a letter on behalf of the Jews, not only saving their lives, but greatly extolling them.

When Mary advocates on behalf of the people at Cana, she not only intercedes as Mother, but as Queen Mother, as the Mother of the King of Kings. She, like Esther and Bathsheba, knows how best to present petitions to the King, because she knows Him better than anyone. In fact, she makes her petition beautiful by the sheer beauty of her presence. A request from a poor dirty beggar, rude of manner, smelling of filth, and who does not know the king at all is not going to move the king much in his direction. But what of Esther and Bathsheba?

Esther

First we read this:

> Queen Esther also, fearing the danger that was at hand, had recourse to the Lord. And when she had laid away her royal apparel, she put on garments suitable for weeping and mourning: instead of divers precious ointments, she covered her head with ashes and dung, and she humbled her body with fasts: and all the places in which before she was accustomed to rejoice, she filled with her torn hair.[31]

This sounds bad at first, but in fact it's very good. First, find favor with the Lord! Esther first tends to purifying her soul. Mary's soul was already pure from her Immaculate Conception, and so we don't read of anything like this at Cana. But when Esther *appears before the King*, we read this:

> And on the third day she laid away the garments she wore, and put on her glorious apparel. And glittering in royal robes, after she had called upon God the ruler and Saviour of all, she took two maids with her, And upon one of them she leaned, as if for delicateness and overmuch tenderness she were not able to bear up her own body. And the other maid followed her lady, bearing up her train flowing on the ground. But she with a rosy colour in her face, and with gracious and bright eyes…[32]

Bathsheba

From Queen Esther's beauty of soul and body, which is a focus in her intercession, we come to Bathsheba, and the focus is on her sheer advocacy power as Queen and Mother:

> And Adonias the son of Haggith came to Bethsabee the mother of Solomon. And she said to him: Is thy coming peaceable? he answered: Peaceable. And he added: I have a word to speak with thee. She said to him: Speak. And he said: Thou knowest that the kingdom was mine, and all Israel had preferred me to be their king: but the kingdom is transferred, and is become my brother's: for it was appointed him by the Lord.
>
> Now therefore I ask one petition of thee: turn not away my face. And she said to him: Say on. And he said: I pray thee speak to king Solomon (for he cannot deny thee any thing) to give me Abisag the Sunamitess to wife. And Bethsabee said: Well, I will speak for thee to the king. Then Bethsabee came to king Solomon, to speak to him for Adonias: and the king arose to meet her, and bowed to her, and sat down upon his throne: and a throne was set for the king's mother, and she sat on his right hand. And she said to him: I desire one small petition of thee, do not put me to confusion. And the king said to her: My mother, ask: for I must not turn away thy face.[33]

In the situation above, King Solomon, for various reasons, does not actually fulfill the request of the Queen Mother (he has the fellow killed), but that is beside the point. Clearly there is a precedence of the Queen Mother bringing petitions to the King and being heard. Further, as with all types, Mary supersedes and brings to perfection all good that we see in those types. Mary far exceeds the beauty, gentleness, graciousness and intercessory power of her types, and knows her own Son far better, and loves Him and is loved by Him practically to an infinity more than prior holders of the office of Queen Mother.

Now let's come back to the New Testament, to the very end of the Bible. It's a short, potent verse: "And the spirit and the bride say: Come. And he that heareth, let him say: Come. And he that thirsteth, let him come: and he that will, let him take the water of life, freely."[34] This should sound reminiscent of two things: Mary's "one sole life" unity with the Holy Spirit ("the *spirit and the bride* say: Come"), and Lady Wisdom's meal ("And he that thirsteth, let him come: and he that will, let him take the water of life, freely")! The spirit and the bride seem to say "Come" with one voice, and in this we see advocacy as well: when the Queen says, "Come" one ought to do so, and it means we *can* do so—she is helping us to Heaven by issuing the invitation with the Holy Spirit. And it is really a dialogue as well—in the next phrase, those who hear (you and I), reply, "Come." Two lovers call to each other: Mary (in absolute unison with the Holy Spirit) calls to the soul and the soul calls to her (and thus to the Holy Spirit), and then the soul is invited to "take the water of life, freely." Mary and the Holy Spirit, as one Advocate,[35] issue the invitation.

Pope Pius XI phrases Mary as Advocate succinctly, writing, "Trusting in her intercession with Christ, who whereas He is the 'one mediator of God and men' (1 Timothy ii, 5), chose to make His Mother the advocate of sinners, and the minister and mediatress of grace, as an earnest of heavenly gifts and as a token of Our paternal affection we most lovingly impart the Apostolic Blessing to you…"[36]

Chapter 8 of *Lumen Gentium* goes into a bit more detail, and encompasses Mary as Coredemptrix, Mediatrix and Advocate:

> 61. …She conceived, brought forth and nourished Christ. She presented Him to the Father in the temple, and was united with Him by compassion as He died on the Cross. In this singular way she cooperated by her obedience, faith, hope and burning charity in the work of the Saviour in giving back supernatural life to souls. Wherefore she is our mother in the order of grace.
>
> 62. This maternity of Mary in the order of grace began with the consent which she gave in faith at the Annunciation and which she sustained without wavering beneath the cross, and lasts until the eternal fulfillment of all the elect. Taken up to heaven she did not lay aside this salvific duty, but by her constant intercession continues to bring us the gifts of eternal salvation.

And as always, there are Saints to consider. St. Alphonsus quotes several Saints in regard to Mary's powerful advocacy. Here are a few:

St. Bernardine of Sienna: "At the command of Mary, all obey, even God," which means, says St. Alphonsus, "God grants the prayers of Mary as if they were commands."[37]

St. Anselm: "Our Lord, O most holy Virigin, has exalted thee to such a degree that by his favor all things that are possible to him should be possible to thee."[38]

Richard of St. Laurence: "Yes, Mary is omnipotent…for the queen by every law enjoys the same privileges as the king. And as…the power of the son and that of the mother is the same, a mother is made omnipotent by an omnipotent son."[39]

St. Alphonsus goes on to quote St. Antoninus, who says that God has placed her not only as patroness of the entire Church, but has placed the Church "under the dominion of Mary."[40] After all, Mary is not only Queen in the sense that the New Adam is the mystical spouse of the New Eve, she is His *Mother*, and Jesus perfectly fulfills the Ten Commandments, glorifying and obeying His Mother; the glorified Jesus does not suddenly stop being Jesus, Son of God *and* Son of Mary.

In fact, Mary's Queenship extends to the entire created order, including the Church Militant (on earth), the Church suffering (Purgatory), and the Church Triumphant (Heaven). Indeed, Mary has a tremendous effect on those in Heaven. For one thing, the glory that those in Heaven possess is due to the merits of Jesus and also of Mary.[41] Further, Mary continues to give light to the souls in Heaven, and their joy is increased because of her;[42] she is like the moon that makes the light of the sun something we can see without our eyes being destroyed. Even those in Hell, as would be expected, are under her dominion; after all, she has crushed the ancient serpent, and overcome sin by her Immaculate Conception and death by her glorious Assumption into Heaven.

—Notes—

1. "Act of Entrustment and Consecration of Priests to the Immaculate Heart of Mary"
2. *The Mother of the Savior and Our Interior Life*, p. 188
3. *Fifth Marian Dogma*,"Mary Coredemptrix Mediatrix Advocate: A Response to 7 Common Objections"
4. VIII, n. 55
5. 2:18-20
6. *Strong's Hebrew* 5828
7. ibid, 5048
8. ibid, 8104
9. *Guayaquil (Ecuador)—Thursday, January 31, 1985* Wednesday general audience, the 33rd installment in a series on Mary.
10. "Mary Co-redemptrix and the Fifth Marian Dogma: Perennial Christian Truth; Contemporary Call of the Lady of All Nations." Address at Amsterdam Conference by Dr. Mark Miravalle May 31, 2008.
11. n. 3
12. Josef Seifert. "Mary as Coredemptrix and Mediatrix of all Graces—Philosophical and Personalist Foundations of a Marian Doctrine." Version: 6th January 2003.
13. *Lumen Gentium*, VIII, n. 56
14. John 2:1-3
15. *Lumen Gentium*, VIII, n. 58
16. Excerpts from her writings and ecstasies, from the book *La Povera Gemma* written by Padre Enrico Zoffoli C.P.
17. Dr. Mark Miravalle, "Mary Co-redemptrix and the Fifth Marian Dogma: Perennial Christian Truth; Contemporary Call of the Lady of All Nations." Address at Amsterdam Conference, May 31, 2008.
18. *Lumen Gentium*, VIII, n. 61
19. ibid, n. 62
20. ibid

21. Manteau-Bonamy, *Immaculate Conception and the Holy Spirit*, p. 23
22. n. 38
23. Miravalle, *Mary Coredemptrix, Mediatrix, Advocate*, p. 8
24. *Theological Foundations II*, p. 130
25. n. 23
26. Fr. Apostoli, *Fatima for Today*, p. 8
27. n. 31
28. *True Devotion*, n. 24
29. Chanoine C. Barthas, *Our Lady of Light*, p. 8
30. John 2:3, 5
31. Esther 14:1, 2
32. ibid, 15:4-8
33. 3 Kings (1 Kings) 2:13-20
34. Revelation 22:17
35. By calling the Holy Spirit and Mary "one Advocate" is not meant of course that they are one Person—they are two, one human (Mary) and one divine (the Holy Spirit). Fr. Garrigou-Lagrange cites Servant of God Marie de Sainte-Therese, a Flemish mystic, who wrote, "It is of the nature of love to unite itself to the object loved . . . Thus tender, burning and unifying love draws the soul which loves Mary to live in her, to be united to her, and to other effects and transformations . . . Then God shows Himself in Mary and by her as in a mirror" p. 270.

    Further, in note 16, chapter 5 of Part II in his book, *Life of Union with Mary*, Fr. Neubert writes, "Mary of St. Theresa speaks of contemplation of God and Mary as a single object."

    We might also note a contemporary, personal account from Fr. Dwight Longenecker, a convert to Catholicism from Evangelicalism. He writes that prior to his conversion he had had no direct experience with Mary, until one day: "A Catholic friend who was a Benedictine oblate suggested that I might like to visit a Catholic Benedictine monastery. While there I told one of the monks that during a time of contemplative prayer I had sensed God's presence in a very real, but feminine way. The femininity disturbed me because I knew God isn't feminine. The monk smiled and said, 'Don't worry. That's not God. It's the Virgin Mary. She is the Mediatrix. She wants to help you with your prayers and bring you closer to God.'"

36. Encyclical, *Miserentissimus Redemptor*
37. *The Glories of Mary*, chapter VI, part I, p.181
38. ibid
39. ibid
40. ibid
41. Fr. Garrigou-Lagrange, *The Mother of the Savior*, p. 237
42. ibid

Chapter Four
The Assumption: We Are Not Left without a True Mother

This dogma proclaims an obvious point straight away: we have a Mother who *has a body!* She has a glorified body, which is a true body, and she is more alive than we are now in our mortal bodies. This is incredibly important for us as human beings and our relationship with Mary, and that God pays attention to this detail demonstrates His immense love and regard for us. The fact is, it would be much less consoling if Mary were our Mother yet could not be physically close to us; motherhood *demands* physical closeness. Though we usually do not see Mary with our mortal eyes or touch her, nothing stops her from being truly close to us spiritually *as well as physically*. It is the mother's heart, her soul, loving us and also loving us in a bodily fashion, with exquisite tenderness that makes a complete mother. And so we have a Heavenly Mother we can relate to in every regard: we can talk with her and tell her of our feelings, emotions, likes and dislikes, dreams, difficulties, and with *her ears* she can hear us; with *her eyes* she can see us wherever we are and whether we are happy or sad, physically well or in great distress; with *her hands* she can caress us; with *her lips* she can kiss us.[1] Jesus does not leave us with a beloved who does not have a body, who is not complete and who could not be completely present to us as our Mother! Indeed, the relationship we have with *both* Jesus and Mary is spiritual, but there is also an immediate physical sense—not carnal, since of course that kind of love is not found here (and is surpassed). In the Eucharist, we come into physical contact with Christ Glorified, He Who is flesh of Mary's flesh. In the Eucharist, we are one with Jesus and thus one with Mary in the most intimate bonds, as one flesh, in a mystical/spiritual (again, not carnal) manner, but in a true manner. [2]

It makes eminent sense, of course, that like Jesus, Mary would receive her glorified body prior to the rest of us; after all, His flesh is her flesh, both are immaculate, utterly pure, without ever having carried the stain of original sin and thus not subject to the penalty of death, a penalty that particularly concerns bodily decomposition. Jesus did will to be subject to death as regards the separation of the body and soul in order to die for us, but it was not proper for Him or Mary in their immaculate flesh to be subject to disintegration. Further, Mary is "full of grace," and she is perfect—to be without a body in Heaven is not yet to be 100% perfect…and we know that Mary lacks no perfection. Pope Pius XII in his proclamation of the Assumption as a dogma writes this:

> In like manner St. Francis de Sales, after asserting that it is wrong to doubt that Jesus Christ has himself observed, in the most perfect way, the divine commandment by which children are ordered to honor their parents, asks this question: "What son would not bring his mother back to life and would not bring her into paradise after

> her death if he could?" And St. Alphonsus writes that "Jesus did not wish to have the body of Mary corrupted after death, since it would have redounded to his own dishonor to have her virginal flesh, from which he himself had assumed flesh, reduced to dust."[3]

The Pope then goes on to quote various Saints, Doctors, Fathers and holy theologians of the Church, including the Mariologist Francis Suarez:

> At the same time the great Suarez was professing in the field of mariology the norm that "keeping in mind the standards of propriety, and when there is no contradiction or repugnance on the part of Scripture, the mysteries of grace which God has wrought in the Virgin must be measured, not by the ordinary laws, but by the divine omnipotence."[4]

Thus the Assumption of Mary is a natural effect of her Immaculate Conception, her fullness of grace, her dignity as Mother of God, and as the beloved daughter and spouse of God. And of course, as the best Son, Jesus, a Divine Person, would honor His Mother and mystical Spouse, the New Eve, in the most perfect way possible. Further, her death was not because her body was aging and corrupting, and thus leading to physical death. As with us, God determined when to call Mary home, but what caused the separation of body and soul was her incredible, longing love for God.

Mary, as the beloved Golden Thread of Scripture, is of course seen in Scripture (as she is in her other dogmas) regarding her Assumption, and Pope Pius XII points out the following:

Genesis 3:15: Mary and her seed both share in the victory over the devil. They have enmity with the devil and are thus in total opposition to the devil, sin and death. In her Immaculate Conception Mary overcomes sin; in her Assumption she overcomes death.[5]

Psalm 131:8 [132:8 RSVCE]: "Arise, O Lord, into your resting place: you and the ark, which you have sanctified."[6]

Song of Songs 8:5: "Who is this that comes up from the desert, flowing with delights, leaning upon her beloved?" Of this the Pope quotes St. Bonaventure, who said, "From this we can see that she is there bodily...her blessedness would not have been complete unless she were there as a person. The soul is not a person, but the soul, joined to the body, is a person. It is manifest that she is there in soul and in body. Otherwise she would not possess her complete beatitude."[7]

Song of Songs 3:6: "Who is she that goeth up by the desert, as a pillar of smoke of aromatical spices, of myrrh, and frankincense, and of all the powders of the perfumer?"[8]

Luke 1:28: "And the angel being come in, said unto her: Hail, full of grace, the Lord is with thee: blessed art thou among women."[9]

Revelation 11:19 to 12:18:[10] In 11:19 we read, "And the temple of God was opened in heaven: and the ark of his testament was seen in his temple, and there were lightnings, and voices, and an earthquake, and great hail." The Ark is seen in Heaven—not a picture of the Ark, not a spirit of the Ark, but the actual Ark, who we know is Mary (the Ark of the Covenant, made of incorruptible wood, being for a time a place where the presence of God was and also a type of the true Ark to come). Physical presence is denoted here, and this continues in the next phrase, 12:1: "And a great sign appeared in heaven: A woman clothed with the sun, and the moon under her feet, and on her head a crown of twelve stars…" It is clear this verse continues the physical aspect of the Ark; after all, the Woman—who John clearly is tying to Mary, as he speaks of her in his Gospel as the "Woman"—is clothed, standing, and wearing a crown. Only someone with a physical body could do these things! And of course, her feet and head are mentioned. This is a "great sign"! If the Ark were there in Heaven merely in the sense that the soul of the one who is the Mother of God is there, we would say, "Well sure, but Revelation speaks of other souls in Heaven as well, and Jesus opened Heaven, so yeah, she would be there." Of course this sign is "great" in various ways, but one major aspect of this is that Mary is not in Heaven only in regard to her soul, but *body and soul*, in her glorified body, possessing the *fullness* of life. She's clothed (has a body), has feet and a head. This Woman assumed bodily into heavenly glory is a "great sign" of triumph over both sin and death: the Woman has crushed the ancient serpent's head.

Another verse speaks to this bodily assumption as well: "And there were given to the woman two wings of a great eagle, that she might fly into the desert unto her place, where she is nourished…"[11] In several places in the Bible the eagle is mentioned as a bird of amazing power and agility with the ability to renew its vigor, even its youth, as in Psalm 102:5 [103 *RSVCE*], which is reminiscent of Mary's ever-youthful beauty: "thy youth shall be renewed like the eagle's." The wings of the Eagle may be angels bearing Mary in her glorified body up to Heaven (as would be proper for a queen), and we see this theme in Exodus 19:4 as well, and which is also reminiscent of Mary's Assumption: "You have seen what I have done to the Egyptians, how I have carried you upon the wings of eagles, and have taken you to myself." Deuteronomy 32:11-14 refers to how God, like an eagle, cared for Jacob:

> He found him in a desert land, in a place of horror, and of vast wilderness: he led him about, and taught him: and he kept him as the apple of his eye.
>
> As the eagle enticing her young to fly, and hovering over them, he spread his wings, and hath taken him and carried him on his shoulders. The Lord alone was his leader: and there was no strange god with him. He set him upon high land: that he might eat the fruits of the fields, that he might suck honey out of the rock, and oil out of the hardest stone, Butter of the herd, and milk of the sheep with the fat of lambs, and of the rams of the breed of Basan: and goats with the marrow of wheat, and might drink the purest blood of the grape.

The Glorified Body

One day, God have mercy on us, we will be in Heaven body and soul, as Jesus and Mary are. What the glorified body is like is a mystery of which we understand very little.[12] We do know it is a physical body—we don't become angels or ghosts. Jesus is very clear about this:

> Now whilst they were speaking these things, Jesus stood in the midst of them, and saith to them: Peace be to you; it is I, fear not. But they being troubled and frightened, supposed that they saw a spirit. And he said to them: Why are you troubled, and why do thoughts

> arise in your hearts? See my hands and feet, that it is I myself; handle, and see: for a spirit hath not flesh and bones, as you see me to have. And when he had said this, he shewed them his hands and feet.
>
> But while they yet believed not, and wondered for joy, he said: Have you any thing to eat? And they offered him a piece of a broiled fish, and a honeycomb. And when he had eaten before them, taking the remains, he gave to them.[13]

A glorified body is a *physical body*: a body with flesh and bones, a person who can eat and talk, move and touch. But yet, it is at the same time totally spiritualized and can pass through material things (walls, doors, etc.); i.e., it possesses the quality of *agility*. Apparently, one can alter one's appearance as well: we know from history that in the lives of the Saints Jesus appears sometimes as a man and other times as a little child; Mary sometimes has eyes that are one color or another, and her hair is often brown but at other times blonde/golden (uncommon, but Mary appeared with flowing gold hair to Adele Brise in Wisconsin at what is currently the only fully approved apparition of Mary in the United States of America).[14]

There is also a quality that is new and different. We can't credit Jesus with any deceit, so when St. Mary Magdalene thinks He is the gardener and the two disciples on the road to Emmaus simply fail to recognize someone they should *immediately* recognize, this tells us there is something physical yet unlike what we have previously known.

Of course, we know that another difference in a glorified body is that after this life and after the resurrection those glorified will never become sick or die, hunger or thirst, nor suffer in any way. The glorified body is as eternal as the soul, ever young, beautiful, healthy, whole, and will become entirely and perfectly a reflection of the soul—the two will be integrated perfectly. While on earth, however, we still suffer from dis-integration, the body fighting against the soul, the soul against the body. But we do have a glimpse on earth—however miniscule—of this integration of the whole person in Heaven. For example, look at a photo of Blessed Mother Theresa of Calcutta, who with all her wrinkles somehow shines with a beauty that transcends the physical; this is the beauty of a soul united with Christ reflected in her. The face of holy people, especially in the face and around the eyes, often have a sparkling, lively, beauty that is, contrariwise, lacking in the face/eyes of a someone who lives in sin. The person who is pure seems light (body follows soul—if the soul is "light" of sin, the body will reflect this; for some Saints they literally float, like St. Joseph of Cupertino, the "flying Saint"), while the person steeped in sin seems to be heavy, weighed down, earthy clay rather than heavenly spiritualized.

The Summa

We can know still more of the glorified body though, and thus more about Mary's glorified body and soul in Heaven. St. Thomas in the *Summa* notes seven qualities of the glorified body: identity, integrity, quality, impassibility, subtlety, agility, clarity.[15] Let's begin, however, with the last and work back to front:

Clarity

This results from the overflow of the soul's glory into the body. This spiritual clarity of the soul is received and seen in the body. Given the difference of clarity in each soul, everyone will appear differently, and what this means is that in the body of each person the glory of that person's soul will be visible. We might think of diamonds, which differ in color and clarity and are ranged from having blemishes of various sorts to the very rare diamond that is totally flawless. Some diamonds reflect light better than other diamonds. The body will be a true body, and exist in perfect obedience to the person, but the density of the body will not hinder clarity any more than the body of a diamond, or a crystal in Thomas' example, hinders clarity. And so the person will be seen in the body in a way not possible to our mortal bodies, and yet the glorified body "will retain the color due to it by reason of the nature of its component parts, but in addition to this it will have clarity resulting from the soul's glory. Thus we see bodies which have color by their nature aglow with the resplendence of the sun, or from some other cause extrinsic or intrinsic."[16]

Thomas also here gives a clue as to how Jesus or Mary can appear in one way or another, in that all these varieties reflect an aspect of their glory (so there is a certain specific glory to Jesus in His childhood, and a certain specific glory to Jesus in His manhood, in that He willingly becomes a baby completely relying on a human Mother, and later as a man gathers the Apostles and sends them out, and then at age thirty-three is nailed to the Cross): Thomas writes that, "the color of the glorified body will be completely in the power of the soul, so that it can thereby act or not act on the sight. Hence it will be in its power to hide or not to hide a body that is behind it."[17] Although he is speaking about the glorified body being visible or not, it seems accurate to say that indeed the particular aspect of the soul's glory revealed to the person seeing the glorified body is changeable as one wills, though the person does not change: Jesus as a baby is the same Divine Person as Jesus when a grown man; His life includes all these moments, as my life includes the moments of my childhood and my adult years, each being of the same person yet distinct in terms of decisions, grace, and merit, etc.

Agility

The glorified body will not be subject to the difficulty of slowness (or, we could add, clumsiness, or any other imperfection). That is, the body will be in total subjugation to the glorified soul, and the body will in fact be adapted to this subjugation, such that there will be nothing in the body that will resist whatever the spirit wills; to be here or there, to be visible or invisible, to sense or not to sense, and so on. Movement will be no sooner willed than done. Even in this life we see that athletes, by dint of training, become more agile, meaning their bodies become quicker to respond to their will. Movement won't be literally instantaneous, nor will a body be in two places at the exact same time; but, the time required for any movement is so stunningly short that it is altogether imperceptible, and only appears to be instantaneous.[18] The reason is that the body remains a body, even though glorified; "…the glorified body will never lose its corporeity, and therefore it will never be possible for it to be moved instantaneously,"[19] Thomas writes. And so Mary may go anywhere she likes, quick as thought, and yet she remains, consolingly, an embodied creature to whom we can be close.

Subtlety

Subtlety refers to the spiritualization of the body. While a true body, the glorified body will be able to pass through doors, walls, stone, and so on. There will be no impediment for the glorified body which is totally subject to the soul. Yet Thomas says it will be "palpable," "tangible." That is, both sensible to the sight and something that can be touched, or vice-versa one could not permit being touched:

> …yet since the body is altogether subject to the spirit, it is in its power thereby to affect or not to affect the touch. In like manner it is competent by its nature to resist any other passing body, so that the latter cannot be in the same place together with it: although, according to its pleasure, it may happen by the Divine power that it occupy the same place with another body, and thus offer no resistance to a passing body. Wherefore according to its nature the glorified body is palpable, but it is competent for it to be impalpable to a non-glorified body by a supernatural power. Hence Gregory says (Hom. xxv in Evang.) that "our Lord offered His flesh to be handled, which He had brought in through the closed doors, so as to afford a complete proof that after His resurrection His body was unchanged in nature though changed in glory."[20]

Impassibility

One day, there will be no more pain, suffering, depression, sadness or disaster. We will not be hungry or thirsty, hot or freezing; we will be able to enjoy food, as Jesus ate a fish, but we will not have to eat or drink out of necessity and none of the attendant frailties of our current physical situation will exist anymore.[21] Neither will our glorified bodies experience old age or disintegration—the true fountain of youth is the life of Christ in our souls! We will be ever young, ever vigorous, ever passionate in all the best ways. The joy we experience in God's eternal "now" will be spiritual, yes, but it will also encompass our bodies and senses, and although there will not be carnal pleasure, the pleasure that there is in Heaven both spiritually and physically (encompassing the whole human person) will completely surpass anything of this world; we never lose anything by being chaste, pure, and virginal—any pleasure given up in this world is found in a transcendent manner in Heaven.

Quality

The glorified body is impassible—it can never be sick, sorrowful, age or die, as mentioned above. *Quality* specifically concerns the element of youth, and in fact most perfect youth. "Man will rise again without any defect of human nature, because as God founded human nature without a defect, even so will He restore it without defect."[22] Yet, with this youth, there will be concurrent with it the reverence due to old age, which Thomas points out is not due to deterioration of the body in the aging process, but due to the wisdom gained (ideally) over a lifetime. In Heaven, we will retain the wisdom and the reverence due to age, but it will be combined not with a failing body, but a perfect and perfectly youthful body.

Of crucial importance as well is the reality of male-female complementarity. Men will have glorified male bodies, women will have glorified female bodies. There will be no difficulty nor shame, Thomas says, in seeing each other, for as he points out, this intimate co-existence of glorified men and women, precisely because we will be *glorified* men and women, does not include lust or any sort of disorder. The beauty of complementarity is part of God's creation, and in Heaven we will understand the mystery of what it is to be a man/what it is to be a woman, and how and why we complement each other. Each will understand their manhood and womanhood in a way not possible prior to the resurrection.

Integrity

Related to the above, all the parts of our bodies will exist in our glorified bodies. The soul is the form of the body, and the body has various faculties because of something the soul possesses. When Mary appears with her beautiful flowing hair, this is not a mirage—it really is her hair, and it really is physical hair. When St. Catherine Laboure knelt next to Mary and placed her hands on Mary's lap, it was upon Mary's physical lap that she placed her hands. When St. Padre Pio was visited by Mary, it was into Mary's physical eyes that he gazed. The manner in which the bodily functions will work in a spiritualized-glorified body, however, is a mystery; we only know it will be a true human body with flesh and bone, hair and nails, skin and nerves, eyes and lips, nose and ears. All of these are required for the perfection of the human person. The heart, the brain, the blood, the hands and feet and so on are present, Thomas points out, to accomplish the operations of the soul, the form of the body; these are primary functions. But functions like hair and nails, which "are directed to the safe-keeping of the other parts as leaves to cover fruit,"[23] are secondary functions, yet the human person is perfected only with primary and secondary elements both, as God created us to have.

Identity

At the resurrection, the body we receive glorified is the same body in all essentials as the one we have now, minus all imperfection. Thomas compared the difference to grain/seed: the plant that grows from the seed is the seed grown up—they are identically the same, but what a difference![24] Now we are mortal and prone to weakness and a disintegration that takes myriad forms and causes myriad problems (hair loss, vision loss, hearing loss; deformed or missing limbs; asthma; scoliosis; schizophrenia and dementia; etc.), but then we will be immortal and our bodies will exist in perfection as our souls do, and in perfect unity. If you are a man, you will rise as an ever-young, whole man; if you are a woman, you will rise as an ever-young, whole woman. The inner life of a woman will still be particular to a woman, with all her charm, beauty, sense of humor, manner of speech, desire to nurture, and so on; a man will still be attracted to women (though not in any lustful way). Men will still maintain their mode of thought and ability to solve problems, their desire to protect and cherish, their own sense of humor and manner of speech, and so on. Women will still be attracted to men (though not in any lustful way). Somehow, complementarity will be perfected, which is implied in identity, since each will rise as a man or woman and with all that this entails, and further as "that particular man, that particular woman."

Physical Mediation of Grace

Mary was and is "full of grace." We don't say, "Mary's soul is full of grace," because the person is not just a soul, but a body-soul unity. It is *Mary* whole and entire who is "full of grace." Given this, somehow Mary almost certainly not only mediates grace in the sense of interceding for us as Advocate, but physically gives us grace as well (we already saw that she does this in various ways in Scripture). Grace then actually passes physically through her, coming to us truly from her hands. This seems most appropriate: again, she is not only our Mother in her soul, but as a whole human person who is body and soul. Mary, body and soul, is our mother, the whole Mary, and when she cares for us, "nurturing us with grace" we could say, she does so as every true mother does, but she does this in a most perfect way. No truly good, loving, earthly mother—if she has any choice in the matter—has someone else feed her baby; she does it herself! And babies need that intimate closeness. Therefore, it would seem that Mary does not relinquish what any natural mother does when it comes to her baby; Mary nourishes us by grace, without which we cannot live any more than a baby without natural food will live, and without whose closeness we cannot thrive any more than a baby deprived of his mother's love can thrive. When Jesus proclaimed her our Mother from the Cross, He did not put exceptions on it, saying,

"Behold your Mother, except when it concerns…" and He did not mean her to be any less perfect than a natural mother; rather He made her incomprehensibly more perfect. Does God deny to Mary (Immaculate and full of grace) on the supernatural level what He does not deny to the natural mother (fallen and not full of grace) on the natural level? In this way, Mary glorified bodily perfectly fulfills her role as Mother to us embodied creatures on earth: from a Mother with a truly physical body to we her children who have true physical bodies. The closeness between our Mother and each of her children is thus properly intimate and befitting. This is no earthly queen who gives her children to the nanny—as St. Therese said, "she is more Mother than Queen."[25]

This is the course that grace takes, as taught by St. Bernardine of Siena: grace comes from God, to Christ, to Mary, to us. We return to God precisely along this route: to Mary, to Christ, to God.[26] We can be even more specific: "Grace begins in the Divine Nature, passes through the Sacred Humanity of Christ (a physical instrument), passes through Mary (also a physical instrument), and finally passes through the sacrament (also a physical instrument). So we have here another argument for the view that Mary serves as a physical instrument of grace."[27]

As Mother, of course Mary needs to know her children intimately. She forms us into Christ, and thus needs to know all the details of our lives. She watches over each in particular, she visits each in particular, she imparts grace to each in particular, she listens to each and comforts each, not as if pouring water from a hose onto the whole garden, but as a mother cares for each child individually because each is a wholly unique person. In fact, each of the blessed in Heaven, in the vision of God, will see all that pertains to them: "For every created intellect knows in the Word, not all simply, but so many more things the more perfectly it sees the Word. Yet no beatified intellect fails to know in the Word whatever pertains to itself."[28] What pertains to Mary? Each of us. Indeed, *everything*—she is Queen of All Hearts, of Heaven and of Earth. And the extent of her knowledge (as for us all, Thomas says), depends on not only how much we know (the number of things), but also the quality of our knowing, "the clearness of the knowledge." After Christ, no soul sees more clearly than Mary.[29] It seems as though In His Fatherly Providence God has in some way placed Providence in the hands of Mary, and thus all the experiences of our lives carry her sweet scent.

Conclusion

All of these elements mean that our relationship with Mary is human, warm, comforting, because she is glorified, not less human, but *more* human; not less Mother, more a Mother. Not less close, but intimately close. She can go, physically, to anyone, anywhere, at any time. When she comes to bring those who have loved her to Heaven, she comes to comfort them as they pass from this life to the next. And every aspect of her immense beauty on earth is highlighted beyond all bounds now that she is in Heaven. Some see her with their physical eyes here on earth, and touch her and talk to her. In Heaven, at the end, we will all be able to do so, in a constant rapture of love. For now, her physical eyes are watching over you; her hands send you grace; her Heart ever beats with love for you; her lips speak to you (so quietly…in your heart, in inspirations, in good thoughts) and of you to God, and smile upon you; she walks by you and sometimes sits next to you; the love of the Holy Spirit, with Whom she lives "one sole life," flows over on to you from her as she keeps you in the crossing of her arms. Oh the joy, that begins even now, of being the child of Mary!

—Notes—

1. Cf. Thomas, *Summa*, Supplement, Qu. 82, art. 4—all the sense of the glorified body will be actual; see also *Part III*, Qu. 84, art. 1, obj. 3 and reply to obj. 3
2. Once St. Bernadette was asked, "What would please you more, to receive Holy Communion, or to see the Madonna in the grotto?" She answered, "What a strange question! The two cannot be separated. Jesus and Mary always go together." And as Fr. Manelli writes, in chapter 6 of *Jesus Our Eucharistic Love*, "The Madonna and the Holy Eucharist are by the nature of things united inseparably 'even to the end of the world.'"
3. *Munificentissimus Deus*, n. 35
4. ibid, n. 37
5. ibid, n. 39
6. ibid n. 26
7. *Munificentissimus Deus,* n. 32
8. ibid, 26
9. ibid, 25
10. ibid, 27
11. Revelation 12:14
12. For further reading, see Dr. Petr Kreeft's *Everything you wanted to know about Heaven*, chapters 6-8 in particular as concerns the glorified body.
13. Luke 24:36-43
14. Edward Looney, "Call the Evangelize: The Story of Adele Brise

and the Mariophany that Changed her Life"

15. See *Part III, Supplement*, questions 82-85 respectively
16. *Summa*, Qu. 85, art. 1, reply to obj. 3
17. ibid, reply to obj. 2
18. ibid, Part III, *Supplement*, Qu. 84, art. 3
19. ibid, reply to obj. 3
20. ibid, Part III, *Supplement*, Qu. 83, art. 6
21. ibid, Qu. 80, art. 3 and Qu. 81, art. 4
22. ibid, Qu. 81, art. 1
23. ibid, Qu. 80, art. 2
24. ibid, Qu. 79, art. 1
25. *St. Therese of Lisieux, Her Last Conversations*, p. 161 "How I love the Blessed Virgin! If I had been a priest, how I should have spoken of her. She is sometimes described as unapproachable, whereas she should be represented as easy of imitation. She is more Mother than Queen. I have heard it said that her splendor eclipses that of all the saints as the rising sun makes all the stars disappear. It sounds so strange. That a Mother should take away the glory of her children! I think quite the reverse. I believe that she will greatly increase the splendor of the elect… Our Mother Mary… How simple her life must have been."
26. Fr. Wiliam Most, *Mary in Our Life*, chapter V, "All Grace Through Her Hands"
27. ibid
28. Thomas, *Summa*, Part III, Qu. 10, art. 2
29. ibid, reply to obj. 3

—Section Four—

Consecration to Mary

CHAPTER ONE
The Roots of Consecration to Mary

Consecration to Mary does not exist in a vacuum, and to speak of such a reality without establishing the foundation for it would be similar to a little boy saying to a young lady whom he has just met, supposing after Sunday Mass, "I think you are the most beautiful girl I have ever seen. Will you be my mother?" At most, she could say to the little fellow something like, "Aw, that is so sweet, but you have a mother already. We can be friends though, okay?" Love for a beautiful young lady does not and cannot make that young lady one's mother. There is simply no basis for it, regardless of desire or devotion; even adoption, while constituting a true sort of motherhood, would not make the child in our example the flesh and blood of the young lady's flesh and blood.

How then to explain consecration to Mary? In fact, that explanation has already begun: all that has been written thus far has served to pave the way for understanding Marian consecration, and from this healthy soil we can discern three main roots of the precious plant that is union with Mary.

First root: eternity

The roots of consecration to Mary are deep. In fact, they couldn't be deeper, because they are found in the eternal mind of God. In speaking about Jesus, Thomas says this:

> ...by one and the same act God predestinated both Christ and us. But if we consider predestination on the part of its term, thus Christ's predestination is the cause of ours: for God, by predestinating from eternity, so decreed our salvation, that it should be achieved through Jesus Christ.[1]

What he is saying is that from eternity, in *the same act*, God's will is for us to be one with Christ. God willed you and me to be one with Christ in the same decree that He willed that the Second Person would assume a human nature. There is no separating the Head—Jesus, the Second Person of the Holy Trinity—from His Body, of which we are members. And there is no Incarnate God without Mary. If God willed to become Incarnate in Mary, and He willed us to be one with Him, then He willed that we, with Him, belong totally to Mary. This is the deepest root of consecration to Mary. God's will is for us to be one with Christ, thus it is God's will for us to be one with Mary, because He is.

Second root: the womb

Pope St. Pius X speaks of the next root, and it flows from the first root. From his encyclical, *Ad Diem Illum* (art. 10) of February 2, 1904:

> Wherefore in the same holy bosom of his most chaste Mother, Christ took to Himself flesh, and united to Himself the spiritual body formed by those who were to believe in Him. Hence Mary, carrying the Savior within her, may be said to have also carried all those whose life was contained in the life of the Savior. Therefore all we who are united to Christ, and as the Apostle says are members of His body, of His flesh, and of His bones (Ephes. v., 30), have issued from the womb of Mary like a body united to its head. Hence, though in a spiritual and mystical fashion, we are all children of Mary, and she is Mother of us all. Mother, spiritually indeed, but truly Mother of the members of Christ, who are we (S. Aug. L. de S. Virginitate, c. 6).

He goes on to say, "If then the most Blessed Virgin is the Mother at once of God and men, who can doubt that she will work with all diligence to procure that Christ, Head of the Body of the Church (Coloss. i., 18), may transfuse His gifts into us, His members, and above all that of knowing Him and living through Him (I John iv., 9)?"[2]

The *whole Christ* is the Head (Jesus) and the Body with all its members (His Church, and each belonging to it). It is a peculiar thing then that some members of Jesus' Body forget the Mother! The Head does not forget her and she is ever the apple of His eye, but various members of the Body, as if experiencing paralysis, hardly incline toward her, if at all. Why is this? The situation is similar to paralysis in a physical body. When someone has a serious neck injury, it can happen that the body and the head don't communicate as they should, because there has been damage to the connecting nerves and communication between head and body is disrupted. In regard to the Mystical Body of Christ there is a similar injury—a disconnect between Jesus and His members due to injury caused by sin and inadvertent blocks we place in the way of grace. There is also the activity of the devil, who is constantly attempting to destroy love of Mary in souls. When a city is under siege, supplies are cut off, and when it comes to souls, the devil attempts to cut off the aqueduct of grace, Mary, from the soul, thus placing the soul in a precarious and potentially deadly situation. These three elements—sin, blockades, and the subtle attacks of the devil—render the main point of union with Jesus and Mary, reception of the Eucharist, either nonexistent (soul does not go to Holy Communion or receives knowingly in a state of mortal sin) or extremely diminished (the heart is so full of self and world that union is impeded). It must be borne in mind that to receive the Eucharist is to receive the Body, Blood, Soul and Divinity of Jesus, and when we receive this Heavenly Food we become one with Christ: this means that Mary and the communicant also become "one flesh"—In Jesus we are bone, flesh and blood of her bone, flesh and blood. This unity between the soul, Jesus, and by Communion with Him, Mary as well, is so staggering that it ought to be pondered day in and day out. We forget who we are otherwise! And if one does not have the Heart of Jesus, which is received in Holy Communion—His Heart, that is His whole Self, His mind, affections, eyes, ears, thoughts—then it is no wonder that some members of the Body of Christ are so slow or else totally immobile when it comes to Mary. And yet there is the flip side as well: if we do not hear of Mary, read about her, think about her, pray to her, how will we be brought to Christ? It is a mathematical certainty that where love of Mary wains, faith goes by the wayside, because it is she who brings souls to her Son. Mary (our secondary end) leads to the Eucharist (Jesus, our primary end), and the Eucharist in turn leads back to Mary, strengthening love of her, because when we put on Christ He gives us His Heart and Its dispositions. In fact, the entire Holy Trinity loves Mary—while Jesus is the Divine Person Who assumes a human nature, the actual act of assumption is via the power of all three Persons, as all three assumed a human nature to the Person of the Son via Mary and by her consent.[3] In Jesus we find the active love of all the Trinity for Mary. And if this is true for us—"And I live, now not I; but Christ liveth in me,"[4]—then each of us by that fact ought to say of Mary in exultation, "Mary is the Woman I love!"

Yet, often the imitation of Christ is considered in every aspect except for Mary, and yet Mary is the utterly crucial aspect of Christ. What, after all, does the Son of God do in time? He totally gives Himself over to Mary: He is formed by her, breathes her air, takes her flesh and blood, lives in her atmosphere from His conception in her womb until His death. He dedicates *thirty years* simply to living with Mary, and then three years in His public Ministry (which she consents to and signals Him to begin, and then closely follows), and three hours on the Cross (where again we find Mary consenting and standing by Jesus). Thirty years living a domestic life with Mary. That's how He spent most of His time on earth. At the Cross He suffers with her, and it is with her that He redeems us. We, too, if we wish to become Christified, must totally give ourselves to her—and this is not only something to be done out of love, but out of justice, since God has given her to us and us to her in Christ from eternity. The verse, "Saul, Saul, why persecutest thou me?"[5] tells us there is one whole Christ, the Head attached to the members. Does one love one's earthly mother with the head, but neglect with one's arms to give her a hug, or make her a Mother's Day card with one's hands, or give her a kiss with one's lips? How like Christ are we if we are not in love with her? Recall the *Song of Songs*! St. Louis de Montfort writes that those who are bound for Heaven (as opposed to those who are not), "are subject and obedient to our Blessed Lady, as to their good Mother; after the example of Jesus Christ, who, of the three-and-thirty years He lived on earth, employed thirty to glorify God His Father, by a perfect and entire subjection to His holy Mother."[6]

Third root: Birth

From all that has been said, this root comes as no surprise. We move from eternity, to Mary's womb, to birth. At Calvary we find the full flowering of the roots of consecration to Mary: this is the revelation of a reality that already existed, just as in natural birth we are not talking about the conception of a baby, but the birth of one already in existence and who is now unveiled: "Woman, behold thy son…"[7] Here Jesus hands the child—each of us in the person of John—to the Mother. We are not the architects of this consecration. From eternity we have belonged to Mary, in time we were safely carried in her womb, and we have come forth from her as her own. It would have been sheer presumption to "take" Mary for our own if she had not been made ours by God, and we could never have done it in any case. And so here at the Cross there is a new revelation: the children of Mary, His brethren, you and I. We are placed in Mary's arms: "behold thy Mother."[8]

Notice that this is not an option! Jesus did not say, "If you'd like, she can be your Mother." The Incarnate God gives a command—"Behold your Mother!" In a true sense we can say that at the end of time there is but the New Adam and the New Eve: Jesus and Mary, inasmuch as we are one with Christ, and so one with His Mother as she is the Mother of the whole Christ. We can also put it this way: in the end, each of the saved is three together, an *alter sacra familia*—the soul is one with Christ, and thus one with Mary, and if one with Mary then one with Christ. As in natural marriage there are "three to get married," the couple and Jesus with them, so on the heavenly level there are for each soul "three to get married." Despite our unworthiness, we, like Joseph, must also humbly heed the words of the Angel: "...take the child and his mother, and go into the land of Israel."

Consecration

Lady Wisdom. As we saw in Proverbs 9, she leads immediately to her meal, the reception of the Eucharist, her bread and mixed wine; she doesn't bring one to her home and then sit and read a book with her guest, or serve some hors d'oeuvres first. Rather, the effect of being set aside for God because one is joined to Mary is instantaneous. Hence, between Jesus—a Divine Person—and us we have a Mediatrix with the Mediator: Mary is a *human person* who is utterly in union with God, and this is such a union that God can and does become incarnate in her. No other human person exists in as great a union with God as Mary does, and thus there is no better way to belong to God than by Mary.

In fact, it is the only way, because it is the way God chose from eternity as He destined us and Jesus in one and the same divine decree. Specifically, when a person is Baptized, he begins to live the life of Christ; he is brought into union with God by sanctifying grace residing in his soul, and thus he is entrusted in a special way to Mary, who is Mother of this part of Christ's Body just as she is Mother of the Head of that Body. No mother says to her baby, "I formed your head, but as for your body…"

We could say then that by God's will for Jesus to be formed whole and entire, head and body, by this Woman, it is by this Woman we are consecrated to God. We simply cannot become part of His Body—consecrated to Him—without her. The Holy Spirit forms Jesus within her, and she with the Holy Spirit shapes and carries Him and us in her womb, and thus rightly does Jesus give each soul to her; not to do this at the Cross would have been to withhold from Mary the children who are rightfully hers. And so she is the human person who links us to the Three Divine Persons. She is truly Mediatrix: God converges at this still point (Mary) from Heaven, we converge at this same still point from earth, and in her and through her we are brought into union with Christ, and thus into the very Divine Life of the Holy Trinity.

Mary's spiritual motherhood to us, then, is also a crucial element of consideration in regard to consecration to her. Given that her spiritual motherhood is a true motherhood, which began at the Annunciation[9] and culminates with her giving most painful spiritual birth to us at the Cross, she has a right to us; we belong to her, and we have an obligation to willingly be formed by her (as was Jesus Himself—"The disciple is not above the master, nor the servant above his lord. It is enough for the disciple that he be as his master, and the servant as his lord."[10]). Consecration then is a logical conclusion: does a child belong to its mother? Yes; certainly to God first, but entrusted by God to that Mother. When that Mother is radically united to God[11] and is His own Mother, and is given by God to men as theirs too, in this light consecration to Mary—which we could call a ratification of the spiritual mother-child relationship—is seen as a reality that is necessary, not by nature but by God's will.

Yet this foundational understanding of Mary's motherhood is in general quite lacking (thus so is an understanding of consecration to Mary). According to Fr. Emil Neubert, "A great number of Christians, even those devoted to the Blessed Virgin, have but an imperfect and narrow idea of it. Since Mary's spiritual motherhood is the basis of our filial love toward her, this love itself can only be narrow and imperfect if her motherhood is not clearly understood."[12] There are, says Neubert, two "incomplete ideas"[13] that people have of Mary's motherhood:

1) "Metaphorical Motherhood."[14] For some, Mary is called our Mother because "she helps us and loves us *as if* she were our Mother." It is a motherhood that is, to such people, "merely figurative, and not a real one." Building on this theme, he links it to mediation—that is, nourishment, nurturing, and forming a child:

> …she showers upon us so many spiritual favors… she even surrounds us with so many natural favors in health and sickness, in all circumstances of our life, that never has a real mother done as much for the most cherished of her children. And yet, is a woman who merely feeds a child, though it be with her own milk, really its mother?[15]

2) "Adoptive Motherhood."[16] For some, Mary adopted us at Calvary as her children, when Jesus said to her, "Woman, behold thy son," and to St. John, "Behold thy Mother."[17] She then treats these children given to her as though they are her own natural children. Yet as Neubert says,

> But to see the basis of her spiritual maternity in this expression alone is to have a very superficial idea of that motherhood. For it would be something purely accidental, depending on a word which our Savior could have failed to pronounce; at any rate something extrinsic to Mary and to us. An adoption is only a legal fiction—it gives to the adopted one the rights of a child, but [...] cannot make him receive his very nature from the father or mother who adopts him.[18]

"The true meaning: Mary Transmits to Us Supernatural Life."[19] Mary's motherhood is not a legal matter, it is *true* spiritual motherhood. "This spiritual motherhood means that Mary has given us supernatural life just as truly as our mothers have given us natural life."[20] And in the next sentence, in one breath as it were, Fr. Neubert concludes, "What our mothers do for our natural life, Mary does in the supernatural order, nourishing, protecting, increasing, and developing our life so as to bring it to maturity."[21]

In fact, she is more Mother to us than our biological mothers: Mary carried us with Jesus in her womb, though in a different way from Christ (for Jesus physically, for us mystically), and the reality of Mary as Mother to us precedes that of our natural mothers—indeed it is only after Mary carries us in her womb that our natural mothers carry us in theirs; Mary suffered incomparably more in giving birth to us than all the pain of all biological mothers in childbirth from the beginning to the end of time; the life Mary gives us is the very life of God and that life she gives is eternal, ever-merry and youthful, while our biological mothers give us life that is temporary and filled with weakness and difficulty; Mary never leaves us and never abandons us, and even when we reach adulthood she remains with us, while our biological mothers cannot (and sometimes will not) do so; Mary brings us to supernatural life in Baptism and she can renew that life even should we die due to mortal sin, though it be seven times seventy times in a week, while our biological mothers can only give us life once; Mary loves us more than any Mother, and her love is perfect and of infinite value since to give us life she consented to offering up her Son's Blood of infinite worth.

The bond between Mary and the soul is also superior to anything in the natural mother-child relationship, though there are similarities. We give to Mary, says St. Louis de Montfort, "(1) Our body with its senses and members; (2) Our soul with its faculties; (3) Our present material possessions and all we shall acquire in the future; (4) Our interior and spiritual possessions, that is, our merits, virtues and good actions of the past, the present and the future."[22] This goes far beyond both natural mother-child relations and what is promised in a natural marriage, since one cannot give to a biological mother or even an earthly spouse all one's "spiritual possessions," and certainly not one's very soul and eternal welfare (implied in de Montfort's "we give ourselves entirely to her"); such precious treasures, which bear upon our eternal salvation, could be given to no fallen human being, and certainly not in an absolute way, as one is able to give all to Mary.

Further considerations demonstrate still more the difference between both natural mother-child and spousal relationships. In a merely biological mother-child relationship, there is eventually a "going forth from," a going out on one's own. By contrast, the union of Mary with the soul is a *total* mutual self-giving of selves in a true exchange of persons that is permanent (indeed meant to be eternal), and wherein the "one shared life with Mary" both increases with one's spiritual growth and increases one's union with her Son. This is quite different in its essence from the natural mother-child bond (though we can say that "grace builds on nature": there is a true mother-child relationship between the soul and Mary, but of a supernaturalized character, the epitome of the natural mother-child relationship). Further, in biological motherhood the union of heart and mind may not endure. In a natural marriage, there is union of heart and mind (however imperfect) wherein the spouses live *one* life in this world, though it is limited (again, one cannot wholly entrust one's soul, spiritual goods, formation of soul, etc., to one's spouse, however holy, in any natural marriage). Regarding relations between human persons, the summit of the mother-child relationship, and *in a sense* of the spousal relationship, is thus found only between Mary and the individual soul in a transcendent, supernaturalized, mystical relationship.

—Notes—

1. *Summa*, Third Part, Qu. 24, Art. 4
2. *Ad Diem Illum*, n. 11
3. *Summa*, Third Part, Qu. 3, Art. 4: "I answer that, As was said above (Article 1), assumption implies two things, viz. the act of

assuming and the term of assumption. Now the act of assumption proceeds from the Divine power, which is common to the three Persons, but the term of the assumption is a Person, as stated above (Article 2). Hence what has to do with action in the assumption is common to the three Persons; but what pertains to the nature of term belongs to one Person in such a manner as not to belong to another; for the three Persons caused the human nature to be united to the one Person of the Son."

4. Galatians 2:20
5. Acts 9:4
6. *True Devotion to Mary*, n. 197
7. John 19:26
8. ibid, 19:27
9. From the pen of Pope St. Pius X we have this paragraph from his encyclical, *Ad Diem Illum* (art. 10) of February 2, 1904: "Wherefore in the same holy bosom of his most chaste Mother Christ took to Himself flesh, and united to Himself the spiritual body formed by those who were to believe in Him. Hence Mary, carrying the Savior within her, may be said to have also carried all those whose life was contained in the life of the Savior. Therefore all we who are united to Christ, and as the Apostle says are members of His body, of His flesh, and of His bones (Ephes. v., 30), have issued from the womb of Mary like a body united to its head. Hence, though in a spiritual and mystical fashion, we are all children of Mary, and she is Mother of us all. Mother, spiritually indeed, but truly Mother of the members of Christ, who are we (S. Aug. L. de S. Virginitate, c. 6)."
10. *Douay-Rheims,* Matt 10:24-25
11. Not only as mother indeed, but as daughter of the Father, mother (and mystically spouse) of the Son, and spouse of the Holy Spirit.
12. Fr. Emil Neubert, *Mary in Doctrine*, p. 46
13. ibid, p. 47
14. ibid, p. 47

15. ibid, p. 47
16. ibid, p. 47
17. *Douay-Rheims*, John 19:26-27
18. Fr. Emil Neubert, *Mary in Doctrine*, p. 47
19. ibid, p. 47
20. ibid, p. 48
21. ibid, p. 48
22. *True Devotion*, n. 121

Chapter Two
I and Thou: Consecration is a Covenant

Dr. Scott Hahn has a concise definition of "covenant": "…a covenant calls for the exchange of persons ('I am yours and you are mine'), creating a shared bond of interpersonal communion."[1] Marriage is perhaps the most obvious form of this type of covenant that we see. One of the forms of Catholic marital vows goes like this: "I, (name), take you, (name), to be my wife. I promise to be true to you in good times and in bad, in sickness and in health. I will love you and honor you all the days of my life."[2] Consecration to Mary has this sort of tenor to it, such that we can call consecration to Mary a "covenant." This covenant is the ratification of a true mother-child relationship. Yet, this relationship also has a spousal aspect to it since both parties fully consent to give themselves each to the other in a permanent union of life in time and eternity (keep in mind that this is a mystical-spiritual relationship, and so "mother" and "spouse" are not understood in an earthly/biological sense, thus the two relationships are not mutually exclusive). This total and irrevocable exchange of selves results in a union of life with Mary and her Son that has eternal duration and consequences.

Blessed Mother Theresa of Calcutta recognized the inherent covenantal aspect of consecration to Mary and called it a "covenant of consecration."[3] St. Louis De Montfort writes of this union, "…we give ourselves entirely to her… She also gives her whole self, and gives it in an unspeakable manner."[4] This is why St. John Paul II can write in his poem, *Totus Tuus*, "Live in me, act in me… Think your thoughts in my mind… Possess my soul… Take over my entire Personality and life, replace it with yourself…keep me in this union always."[5]

A recurrent theme of this union is its totality. "Total, entire, whole…" In the life of a Catholic the phrase "total consecration to Mary" has probably been used so much that when we do come across it the gravity of the statement isn't striking. "Total" means just what the definition leads us to believe though, and if we stop to think about it we'll realize it is radical: it means everything, without diminution, without diluting, comprehensive and encompassing all. Jesus Himself made a total gift of self to Mary. He gave her His grace, His love, His Body, His soul, His obedience, His thoughts, His affections and so forth. In sum, His whole Heart, the "heart" meaning His whole Self. What do we give? Whatever we have! This includes: prayers, merits, thoughts, bodies, souls, senses, finances, vocation, duties of our state of life, sense of humor, sadness, joys, travels, vacations, jobs, relationships with others, Holy Communions received, graces given, breath, sleep, beats of the heart, whatever we read, what we say to others and to ourselves, all property, all plans, one's death, those entrusted to our care (living and dead), pregnancy, smoking a pipe, the swings of a golf club, disasters encountered (which may be the same as swinging a golf club), sewing ripped clothing and picking up a gum wrapper on the floor. In fact, as Queen and as our Mother, everything is in her purview because as Mother she is forming us into Christ—and everything in our lives impacts this reality. The smallest event has eschatological gravitas: not only our eternity but that of others is shaped by the way we live each event of daily life. Every moment of time must be accounted for, and all of it comes to us as a gift by which we are fashioned into a saint; even picking up a gum wrapper is an event weighted with some amount of gravity—it's an action that might be done out of love for God and while exercising the virtues of patience and humility, or it may be done in anger and frustration and swearing. Mary wants whole lives, not parts of lives. What we don't give, she asks for. She doesn't do things by halves.

A common question, however, is this: "What of my obligations?" Suppose your sick uncle needs prayers, but you have given everything to Mary…and that includes all of your prayers! That means she can and will apply your prayers as she sees is best. But knowing Mary a bit, we have to ask ourselves: "Would she really let me fail in my obligations? Would she do harm to my Uncle by not helping him when I pray for him?" Mary knows our obligations better than we do, and she is keener than we are to see they are taken care of in such a way that God will be most pleased! Maybe you pray a Rosary for your Uncle, but she sees that some poor fellow in the mountains of Nepal is dying and will die unrepentant unless someone prays for him, so she applies a decade of the Rosary for him and his soul is saved. We detect a very small amount of what passes in the world, and that which is right in front of us often escapes our concern. Of about 7 billion people on the planet, we know almost none. Suppose you know 100 in the closest bonds of family life and friendship: 100 out of 7 billion is infinitesimal. Of the few people in one's immediate family—suppose you have a family of seven—you perceive only an incredibly small percentage of their interior life, but Mary knows each of their most intimate secrets, movements of will, daydreams, and emotions. Giving Mary our prayers and sufferings causes them to be sweetened by her and made presentable to the King, and she applies those prayers and sufferings in ways that are unimaginably fruitful. This makes you, with her, unimaginably fruitful, something you won't see much perhaps in this world, but you will when this mind-bogglingly short life is over. We never lose by giving all to Mary. It is like giving one dollar to a stockbroker who is absolutely sure to turn that into several million dollars, tax free—it would be insanity not to give him the dollar. Think what good could be done. And that's just money, worthless compared to what Mary can achieve.

In this regard, a total gift of self to Mary is also incredibly freeing: if Mary is literally taking care of everything, to the minutest detail—which we saw in Proverbs 31—there is nothing to be anxious about. In this way, consecration to Mary illuminates this passage of Matthew, 6:25-31:

> Therefore I say to you, be not solicitous for your life, what you shall eat, nor for your body, what you shall put on. Is not the life more than the meat: and the body more than the raiment?
>
> Behold the birds of the air, for they neither sow, nor do they reap, nor gather into barns: and your heavenly Father feedeth them. Are not you of much more value than they? And which of you by taking thought,

> can add to his stature by one cubit? And for raiment why are you solicitous? Consider the lilies of the field, how they grow: they labour not, neither do they spin. But I say to you, that not even Solomon in all his glory was arrayed as one of these. And if the grass of the field, which is today, and tomorrow is cast into the oven, God doth so clothe: how much more you, O ye of little faith?
>
> Be not solicitous therefore, saying, What shall we eat: or what shall we drink, or wherewith shall we be clothed? For after all these things do the heathens seek. For your Father knoweth that you have need of all these things. Seek ye therefore first the kingdom of God, and his justice, and all these things shall be added unto you. Be not therefore solicitous for tomorrow; for the morrow will be solicitous for itself. Sufficient for the day is the evil thereof.

A primary way that God cares for us is precisely via Mary, who is both our Mother and the Queen of Heaven and all the created world, seeing all most keenly and handling everything most adeptly. She says to her Son, “they have no wine,” and Mary brings the grace of her Son into our lives, and the water becomes the best wine. We give her ourselves, stained with sin and wounds such that we would be shocked to see it were God to show us, and she gives us herself—she becomes one’s Queen, Mom, Princess, Beloved, Nurse, Sister, Constant Companion, Sweetness, Hope, Beauty, Refreshment, Love, Advocate, Guardian, Banker and the Treasure of Treasures from the hand of the Holy Trinity. She is the Woman we see in portraiture in the Old and New Testaments and in the Teaching of the Church (dogma and doctrine). The real fear is not the "total" element of consecration, but the *disvalued response* of giving her only "some," even should that some be 99.9%.

I-Thou

There is a crucial facet to Marian consecration that is unlike the natural mother-child relationship and quite like marriage. This aspect is seen clearly when Lady Wisdom shares her meal. The meal is her Son, and in that she nourishes each of us with Jesus, the font of all grace, this is the action of a Mother; but, in that she is giving to each of us the Heart of her Heart (Jesus) in an intimacy that is placed antithetically to the adultery of Lady Folly, this is the action of one's beloved, a sort of spousal action. Sirach 15:2-3 speaks to this: "She [Lady Wisdom] will come to meet him like a mother, and like the wife of his youth she will welcome him. She will feed him with the bread of understanding..." (*RSVCE*); in this passage too we see Lady Wisdom sharing her meal with the intimacy of a mother and of a spouse. This could be called the *I-Thou* aspect. It could also be termed a "conjugal *I-Thou*" aspect, though not in the traditionally understood sense. The word "conjugal" first and primarily pertains to an exclusive union of hearts; "conjugal" does not necessarily mean the physical expression of marriage as many believe, and the word "conjugal" is simply Latin for "yoked together." The conjugal *act* is a physical expression of marriage (not a strictly necessary one, contrary to what the world believes), and neither natural marriage nor its physical expression concerns us here. Rather, it is this exclusive "yoking together" of hearts that concerns us, and it exists on an altogether different plane than natural relationships, and thus consecration to Mary does not preclude the Sacrament of Marriage, for example. How then is consecration to Mary exclusive on the higher, supernatural plane? Because as a total and irrevocable gift to Mary, this means one has said "no" both to living life on one's own terms and to living a life of sin. It is saying "yes" to Mary as the essential factor in one's life in every respect. And except for one's relationship to Christ, there is no more intimate "yoked together" than the soul's relationship to Mary.

But what, specifically, is an *I-Thou* relationship, and why does it pertain to Marian consecration? Dietrich Von Hildebrand defines the *I-Thou* relationship this way:

> Not only the heart but the entire personality is given up to the other…in conjugal love there is an aspiration not merely for a return of affection in general, but for the unique love whereby the beloved belongs to the lover in an entirely exclusive manner, as he in turn wants to belong to the beloved. This love tends to a unique union and even partly constitutes it: a community where two persons constitute a closed union which can exist only between them. Conjugal love establishes a relationship in which the regard of each one of the two parties is turned exclusively upon the other.[6]

Thus the *I-Thou* relationship is quite distinct in quality from any other relationship. This is not the simple "we" of friendship, where friends are side by side moving through life together; rather, in the *I-Thou* relationship a man and woman move through life as *one*.

Further, while in every relationship there is an incommunicability—a uniqueness that cannot be replicated—in the *I-Thou* relationship that incommunicable uniqueness is of an altogether higher level of intimacy, wherein the gaze of each is upon the other and "one" gaze is established between the two and arises out of this mutual regard as each lover is immersed in the beloved. In natural marriage, the two then live, as one, a life for and with Christ as a single entity composed of two distinct persons who are separate and yet intimately united as one whole. This does not inhibit each individual's relationship with Christ of course, since in the *I-Thou* relationship there is not a literal morphing of two individuals such that they mix, each separate person ceasing to exist—in fact, that would destroy the *I-Thou* relationship since there would no longer be either an "I" or a "Thou" to relate to and so no immersion of one in the other! But a oneness of life does begin to exist between the man and woman once they are joined in conjugal love. In consecration to Mary, the soul and Mary also share an *I-Thou* oneness of life, but this in regard to the spiritual life and with some key differences that differentiate it from any natural marriage: the "one gaze" consists not in Mary coming to share our gaze, but in we coming to share hers. Further, we become like her, not she like us—she imparts her dispositions, thoughts, ideas, likes and dislikes and so on. Thus more and more, within the matrix of this intimate union with Mary, the soul begins to become like her and sees what she sees, becomes immersed in her eyes and in her gaze, and this gaze always leads to Christ: He becomes the focus of the one gaze of Mary and the soul, He becomes "our Jesus." As this conformity to Mary grows, the conformity to Christ grows, because she is like Him, and the soul she forms she forms into an *alter Christus*. This amounts to a quite similar yet distinctly different conjugal *I-Thou* than anything in natural marriage, and a quite similar yet distinctly different mother-child relationship than anything in biological motherhood. This is both an *I-Thou* and a Mother-child union! "For as a young man marries a virgin, so shall your sons marry you..." [7]

There is one more similarity-yet-difference in this Marian *I-Thou* relationship. An *I-Thou* relationship implies a *definite decision* to embrace the *exclusive* giving of oneself to *one particular* "other," and accepting the exclusive giving of self that is offered by the other. So it is in consecration to Mary. But there is one major difference too: the *I-Thou* relationship in regard to consecration to Mary involves *three* persons, not two: it is always Jesus, the soul and Mary. It is not simply that one united Christo-specific gaze is established between the soul and Mary, it is also that union of the soul with Mary=union of the soul with Jesus, and union of the soul with Jesus=union of the soul with Mary. Consecration to Mary cannot be other than eschatological triumvirate with Jesus as the central gathering point.

Now, this *I-Thou* relationship between Mary and the soul is a substantial relationship; it is absolutely unique and unrepeatable and cannot be communicated to another. This may be a clue to the mysterious line of Revelation, "To him who conquers I will give some of the hidden manna, and I will give him a white stone, with a new name written on the stone which no one knows except him who receives it."[8] Whatever that stone is, why is it that only the one who receives it knows the new name? Perhaps, in part at least, because it speaks of this exclusive and incommunicable relationship. No two Jesus-Mary-soul relationships are the same, though the essential elements will be common to all: the Christifed soul has the Heart of God, and for God's Heart Mary is the Beloved. For this reason, we can say that it is not only that we go "to Jesus through Mary,"[9] as St. Louis de Montfort rightly states, but also that we go "to Jesus with Mary" as well, and vice versa, "to Mary with Jesus." It's crucial to highlight this since so many people seem confused by the word "through." St. Louis did not mean that Mary is an object of use, a door only, a thing forgotten once Jesus is obtained. We do not lose Mary by being united with Jesus through her, but we remain united to Jesus with her, and remain united to Mary with Jesus. Once we put on Christ, we find ourselves with Him in her arms.

Slavery in the I-Thou relationship

St. Louis brings up another phrase as well that needs to be seen in the light of love, but is often understood more as "willing object of use," and that phrase is "the slave of Mary."[10] On the face of it, this sounds quite opposite to an *I-Thou* relationship. This is not, however, a "slave" in the sense we often think of it, though some aspects of slavery—such as being entirely at another's disposal—do exist, but as love, not as use. Again, the soul consecrated to Mary lives with her in *mutual* and total self-giving love. Jesus too, says St. Louis, was "a slave in the bosom of the divine Mary,"[11] and God is not an object and cannot be used! We can think of "slavery" in this regard in terms of "in-loveness." That is, when someone is in love, he or she basically says, "I'm your slave, I want to do what will make you happy, tell me what I can do for you," and so on. Very little children, who are in a particular way "in love" with Mom and Dad, want to do whatever Mom and Dad say. There is also a certain, but no less true, "in-loveness" with God and with Our Lady, where we say, "My heart is on fire with love for you—how can I make you happy? Command me, I am yours and I will do it!" It is the devil, master of illusion, who takes words pertaining to holy things and distorts them. It is sheer speculation, but it is possible the word "slavery" began life with Adam as he said to Eve, "I am yours to command, you are my love." The devil, the ultimately self-centered creature, perhaps took the word "slavery" and applied it to impersonal, selfish domination, thus using a word that represents a holy thing in a mocking, desecrating way, defining "slavery" rather as "using people like objects."

The gift of one's self to Mary and Mary to that person in a "holy slavery" of love is, as mentioned above, both *complete* and *mutual*, as an *I-Thou* relationship must be. Blessed Mother Theresa in this regard points out some interesting realities concerning consecration to Mary. For one, we have duties toward her…but she also has duties toward us! The relationship is reciprocal. Among other duties of Mary that Blessed Mother Theresa lists she notes, "To give of her spirit and heart," "To possess me," and "…Union with her heart…"[12] And ours? "Total gift of all I have and am… Right to enter into her heart, to share her interior life."[13] This is what St Louis de Montfort says when he writes of one consecrated to Mary that, "He belongs all to Mary, and Mary belongs all to him…'All that I have is thine, and all thou hast is mine.'" Imagine that! It is not only that such a person belongs to Mary—she also then belongs totally to that person! This is not hyperbole, but reality, and so truly the case that she even shares her interior life. Think of that: most people will not share their interior life with you—who they are deep down, their desires and aspirations, their joys and sorrows, their mind and heart and thoughts; but Mary shares the depth of her Heart with us. This beyond merely sharing goods, even spiritual goods—this is the bond of unique and exclusive love. A queen might give presents to a stranger, but only with one who is her chosen loved one does she open her interior life.

The Decision

Although an exclusive relationship with Mary is truly present by the very fact of being one with Christ in Baptism, consecration to Mary does not happen automatically; one must ratify this decision, and the decision for consecration to Mary is a sort of nuclear bomb of the spiritual life. And just as a nuclear bomb cannot be launched unless multiple keys are turned, so it is with this exclusive *I-Thou* love relationship with Mary. Jesus and Mary have turned the first key. We have to turn the second key of *total* gift of self to Mary. Once a baby exists in the mother's womb, a relationship exists. But suppose that despite being carried in her womb the baby is born and then could, were it possible, not really be interested in her, not really nurse much, not really snuggle much, and mostly spend time not paying attention to her. This would be a lacking mother-child relationship! Yet not only lacking—it would not be normal, proper, or particularly healthy. Or what of a groom, who although truly having consented to marriage, goes off to other countries, leaves his bride and barely ever communicates with her? The marital relationship exists, but has hardly been ratified by the husband by lifestyle, just as the baby in the example has hardly ratified it. But, once that baby or that husband decides to accept the unitive reality fully as it pertains to Mom or bride, what a change! Health, goodness, happiness, love, companionship, contentment—*life*—really takes off, and in ways so wonderful they could hardly be expected were they not experienced. But to get to the experience one must make the leap—the giving of self to Mom or bride, and accepting the life of Mom or bride as theirs as well in one unified life.

But we have to ask: is consecration strictly necessary? Perhaps surprisingly, no. A life of union with Mary may exist apart from consecration, and thus consecration is not absolutely indispensable. A characteristic of all Saints is their love for Mary, but not all Saints made an explicit act of consecration to Mary. Indeed she is our Mother apart from an explicit act of consecration, and loving her is a natural result of the life of Christ in us. Fr. Neubert has Christ saying to us each, "You live by me. My dispositions must become your dispositions… You love my Mother; no, it is no longer you who love her, it is I who love her in you. Do you understand now why you are so happy in loving Mary? It is I in you who am happy in loving her."[14] By dint of constant prayer, fasting, Holy Communion and study of Scripture, some Saints became so like Christ that their hearts, conformed to His in an incredible likeness, loved Mary as Jesus does. But for most of us, that path is strewn with difficulty such that we could say they followed an extraordinary path in that regard. For most, the surest path is that of Consecration, an astonishingly powerful means of concretizing one's relationship with Mary, *of accepting it with full thought and deliberation*, and of allowing her to act in one's life. Consecration to her is, St. Louis de Montfort says, "easy, short, perfect and secure."[15] It must be said too that in our days, the wickedness and snares of the devil have become so outrageous, so subtle yet at times so blatant, that perhaps the wisest thing to do at this point in history *for anyone* is to consecrate oneself to Mary. The need far surpasses that of any other time in history.

Taking the Leap

St. Louis de Montfort recognized that embracing consecration to Mary is a truly serious step to take. It's not game, not the whim of a passing moment, not something based on fickle emotions that are on fire one moment and desolate or bored the next. A true spiritual reality takes place that did not exist before, one between you and Mary, and it is by nature permanent in this life and in the next—and so more permanent than the bonds of natural marriage, which end with the death of the spouse. Although Mary awaits our "yes" to be nested with her "yes" to us, as two halves of one pendant, it is important that one knows as much about this as possible, and it is important to be as ready as possible, in order to give as perfect a "yes" as possible. After all, you are about to give yourself to Mary as her own (to that beautiful Princess of Heaven!) and, oh blissful joy!—she is about to give herself to you. This is why St. Louis de Montfort sets aside four weeks of preparation prior to the wondrous leap of consecration. No one marries without a) getting to know the person involved, b) praying and thinking about it, and c) setting a date and preparing. Strictly speaking, if one knew enough and was ready enough the consecration could be made on the spot—there is no magic time frame, no magic formula. St. Louis de Montfort and St. Maximilian Kolbe each have various consecration prayers, building on essential elements of this covenant made with Mary, and one could even form one's own prayer, preferably incorporating the elements that these great Marian Saints saw as worthy of inclusion in a consecration to Mary. Nevertheless, ordinarily a serious preparation, as St. Louis recommends, should be made, and the date of a special Marian Feast upon which to finally make this covenant with Mary set, to which you can look forward with eager anticipation. Not only do we look forward to that date with a sort of sweetly impatient love, Mary as well longs for that moment!

There is something that is enchantingly fairytale-like about all this, and it makes sense that there would be. Fairytales and myths incorporate reality in various ways using symbols. The prince wins the princess; Gorgons, like Medusa, are horrifyingly ugly and are full of hate and death for all who come too close; ancient and mysterious weapons appear for the hero to use against the forces of evil; knights defend the defenseless; the prince gets a princess. *These are faint images of reality*! There *is* a Princess to win, fairer than any you will find on earth; there *are* monsters to avoid and to defeat, more horrific and more deadly than any Gorgon; ancient and mysterious weapons to battle against evil *do* exist; there are people, defenseless against evil creatures, who will end up in Hell unless we pray and sacrifice for them. Fairytales are much truer than we realize, and much easier to live out than those in books, which are faint visages of the fairytale you are living right now. Granted, the evil beings we fight are usually (not always) invisible—but the effect of their activity is obvious for any with eyes to see. Those who "marry" the Princess, however, fight with the Woman who crushes the enemy's head. "I am all yours," says this Princess and Mother to each of us, "will you be all mine? *Ego diligentes me diligo*." And this Princess will make us pure, the very image of her Son, and she will make our souls ready for eternal bliss. We were paupers, grimy and ill-mannered, but now we can make the words of Shakespeare's Romeo our own:

> The measure done, I'll watch her place of stand,
> And, touching hers, make blessed my rude hand.
> Did my heart love till now? forswear it, sight!
> For I ne'er saw true beauty till this night.[16]

While Waiting—an important addendum

While preparing oneself for this consecration, however, it may happen that one's past sins begin to haunt, wretched creatures that we are, and a sense of unworthiness may strike. Various difficulties may thrust themselves into one's life. These are a good sign and to be expected—the devil is about to experience vastly diminished power in your regard, and so he causes various troubles. But St. Alphonsus provides a consoling true story for trials such as these, and it's important to impress it on our minds. The Saint tells of a man who loved Mary and had given himself to her, and she seemed to have disappeared. He was horribly troubled by the devil. Suddenly, just prior to his death, Mary revealed her presence to his physical eyes to help him as he lay there fearing for his eternal welfare. She said to him, "My own beloved Adolph, thou art mine, thou hast given thyself to me, and now why dost thou fear death so much?"[17] Immediately all fear and dismay left him, and he died in joy as he was finally united forever with his Lady and her Son. What she says to Adolph she says to every soul who belongs to her or desires to (a desire that comes from God).

Just replace the name "Adolph" with your own. Engrave this line in your heart, because Mary, Our Mom and the Princess of Heaven, does say it to those who love her, and we can reply in kind: "My own beloved, thou art mine, thou hast given thyself to me…"

—Notes—

1. Dr. Scott Hahn, *A Father Who Keeps His Promises*, p. 26
2. USCCB, "The Marriage Vows," *For Your Marriage*
3. Fr. Michael Gaitley, *33 Days to Morning* Glory, p. 114
4. St. Louis De Montfort, *True Devotion*, p. 89, art 144
5. "Immaculate Conception, Mary my Mother, Live in me, Act in me, Speak in me and through me, Think your thoughts in my mind, Love through my heart, Give me your dispositions and feelings, Teach, lead me and guide me to Jesus, Correct, enlighten and expand my thoughts and behavior, Possess my soul, Take over my entire personality and life, replace it with Yourself, Incline me to constant adoration, Pray in me and through me, Let me live in you and keep me in this union always. Amen."
6. *Marriage: the Mystery of Faithful Love*, p. 8
7. *RSVCE* Isaiah 62:4, 5. The *Douay-Rheims* has, "For the young man shall dwell with the virgin, and thy children shall dwell in thee." The word translated in the *Douay-Rheims* as "dwell" means "marry"—"dwell" is taken in that sense.
8. *RSVCE* Revelation 2:17. The *Douay-Rheims* has "counter" instead of "stone." They are both saying the same essential thing, with differing nuances. This "stone" is a small pebble, in this case white, and was used for voting, white meaning a "yes" vote; and the "white" spoken of here is a brilliant white, something altogether white. See *Strong's Hebrew* 5586 for "stone" (*pséphos*) and 3022 for "white" (*leukos*).

9. *True Devotion*, Week 2, "Obtain Knowledge of the Blessed Virgin"
10. ibid, n. 244
11. ibid, n. 243
12. Fr. Michael Gaitley, MIC, *33 Days to Morning Glory*, p. 114
13. ibid
14. *Life of Union with Mary*, p. 44. Later in this chapter he writes, "By uniting ourselves to Jesus when praying to Mary, we help Him love His Mother; we are for Him a 'supplementary humanity' in the exercise of His filial love for her who is so much more dear to Him than all other creatures. What great joy we may thus give Him!" and "Just as our awareness of loving Mary in the name of Jesus obtains an increase of joy for Jesus, for Mary, and for us, so also our awareness that Mary united herself to us in order to love Jesus increases her joy, the joy of Jesus, and our own."
15. *True Devotion*, n. 152
16. Shakespeare, *Romeo and Juliet*, "Act I, Scene V, a hall in Capulet's house."
17. *The Glories of Mary*, Section III, "Our Life, Our Sweetness"

Chapter Three
Consecration as Espousal of Hearts[1]

In his book, *The World's First Love*, Venerable Fulton Sheen writes that subconsciously all women want to be *like Mary*, and that all men when they love a woman really *love Mary and want to marry her*: "She is the one whom every man loves when he loves a woman—whether he knows it or not. She is what every woman wants to be when she looks at herself. She is the woman whom every man marries in ideal when he takes a spouse…she is the way every woman wants to command respect because of her goodness of body and soul."[2] Sheen's laconic and deeply profound insight is this chapter in super-condensed form; it is an idea that is an ultra-compact pin-point of theology that speaks to the souls' relationship to Mary in consecration, and points to a particular model of consecration.

St. Louis de Montfort, as mentioned earlier, spoke of a holy "slavery" to Mary. This is one emphasis of consecration, and one that can work in tandem with other emphases. St. Maximilian Kolbe's idea of consecration to Mary is that one becomes her "property." He felt that "property" denotes the absolute and irrevocable gift of self to Mary in a way better than that of slavery, yet also includes the idea of holy slavery. "Property" does indeed go further than "slavery," since a slave may retain something of himself—his own ideas, inclinations, etc. The slave may even suggest to his master this or that perspective; but one does not say to one's table, "Do you mind if I put you here or there?" or, "What are your feelings about this?" or, "We must keep in mind your rights." The table does not complain, nor has it a right to. It is quiet and obedient, it does not question, it does not grumble. Both the words "slave" and "property" work as models of consecration. Neither, however, are entirely comprehensive of the reality of consecration, and Kolbe speaks of this. He said that if a better, more suitable phrase could be found to describe consecration, if a clearer lens could be found through which to view it, that phrase ought to be used. In relating this, Kolbe speaks of the difference between the words "slavery" and property." He writes,

> It might be said that de Montfort's expression "slave" implies that one still possesses some personal rights; but this cannot be said of "property." And if there can be found other expressions which go even farther in the direction of self-sacrifice and oblation, such expressions will be all the more in conformity with the spirit of the Militia Immaculatae.[3]

The phrase "spousal" certainly seems to fit as going "even farther," and it is an idea I have pondered for some time. I add this personal detail because I was surprised to see recently an article by Jayson M. Brunelle, published in 2013, that highlights this same idea, an article I will cite further on in this chapter. I do not know this Catholic gentleman and had previously never heard of him, and so it seems no coincidence but rather the workings of Providence that people unbeknownst to each other are coming to the same conclusion: consecration as espousal; we could call it the "espousal emphasis" of consecration just as we say de Montfort's is the "slavery emphasis" and Kolbe's the "property emphasis."

Before continuing, it's important to note that by "espousal" is not meant what we understand by the Sacrament of Marriage, though there are similarities. This is a mystical espousal, and so not one that deals with the body as an earthly marriage does. Yet it does include two distinct persons who give their hearts to each other totally, which is what happens in any model of consecration. Of course, it's important to reiterate, *only God is the Spouse of Mary properly speaking*, and St. Joseph himself but shared in God's spousal unity with Mary. Concerning this, Luigi Gambero cites St. Peter Chrysologus: "Mary's divine marriage with her Son is compared to the human marriage she was going to contract with Joseph. The text excludes any incompatibility between the two types of marriage, because they take place on two different levels."[4] Similar to St. Joseph, we participate in God's relationship with Mary in a spiritual way, and at the spiritual level reality works at a deeper and more vast scale: Jesus is truly the "spouse" of every soul, too, and clearly this is not meant in any natural sense. Further, it is precisely because of this union with Jesus that a soul is able to experience unity with Mary in any regard—union with Jesus includes union with Mary *ipso facto*.

Now, why is "espousal" a better term? As "slave" still implies some rights, "property" implies a loss of will and mere use, while "espousal" implies that one has utterly aligned one's will with Mary's will and continues to do so *knowingly* and *deliberately* in a continuously lived and affectionate bond of love that is returned by her. Her concerns become my concerns; a table has no concerns. If she desires some suffering or some project, I too desire it—I do not merely accept quietly like the table, I *will what she wills*—this contains within itself acceptance and obedience without grumbling, like "property," but goes further than "property." It is doing whatever the beloved wants, but includes willing what the beloved wants as Mary and the soul live "one life" in an *I-Thou* relationship; this is much the same as a man, of one heart with his wife, who willingly and with love does whatever she asks, or very like a little child who will likewise lovingly do anything for his mom. And so "espousal" binds together and includes in itself the other two emphases, "slave" and "property," since a spouse is, properly understood, both of those things, but in a way determined by love, not by use. Further, "espousal" better fits with the reality of union with Mary as displayed in the Wisdom literature of the Old Testament. In Proverbs 9, we saw that there is a spousal intimacy between the soul and Lady Wisdom as the soul shares the meal that comes from her, the Eucharist, and this meal is shown in contrast to a situation of adultery with Lady Folly. Clearly those two situations are opposed, and not opposed as one of mere true friendship to false friendship, but rather a true though mystical bond of *espousal* compared to a false illicit bond that is *adultery*. To wit, the opposite of adultery (illicit intimacy) with Lady Folly is marriage (licit intimacy) to Lady Wisdom in an "I-Thou-mystical-conjugal" union of hearts.

Consider again St. Joseph. He, better than anyone, participated in God's spousal love of Mary. She is properly spouse only of God; Joseph is given the grace to participate. In this way, Joseph is the human person exemplar (Jesus is the Divine Person exemplar) of how a human person should love Mary. She was Joseph's beloved beyond the love of any other human person for Mary. But we are all called to imitate him, to "take the Child and His Mother,"[5] as he did.

Male and Female difference in regard to espousal to Jesus and Mary

There are two ways that "espousal" to Mary—no doubt a new horizon of reality for some!—may be understood. Both of these ways are based on the fact of complementarity of the sexes: men and women "complement" each other, they fulfill each other, and this reality does not reside at the merely natural level, and certainly not at the merely sexual level, but goes to the heart, to the soul. A man's experience of Mary's beauty will differ from a woman's experience of Mary's beauty, because a man remains a man and Mary remains a woman. A woman's experience of Mary is something like, "I want to be like that, and I want to be in union with that beauty, and that beauty will make me beautiful like her, and I will find my destiny in her and with her, together we two, and in this way she completes me, she renders me a true woman, and we will walk side by side; by contemplating her I become an icon of her." By contrast, a man says, "I love this beauty I see and want to belong to her, defend her, and to melt into this beauty who will hold me in her arms, to be one with her and find my destiny with her who will make me a strong and good man; she completes me, and I find joy and sweetness in contemplating her." In fact, for the man, he can take the words of the bridegroom in the *Song of Songs* as his own: "Thou hast wounded my heart, my sister, my spouse (4:9)…" A woman sees Mary and wants to be like Mary; Mary's inner and outer beauty, all of a unity, humbles a woman and she stands in awe of Mary, and measuring herself against Mary, wants to be like her. A man sees Mary and her beauty wounds him to the heart, and only the love of this beauty entering into and reposing in the man's heart and his in hers will heal him. At the risk of being soppy, there is a beautiful song by John Denver that, inadvertently, speaks to this (part of these lyrics even compare the woman he loves to various elements of nature, a la St. Alphonsus: characteristics of Mary are intrinsic to the fabric of the natural world); Denver writes, "let me love you, let me give my life to you, let me drown in your laughter, let me die in your arms, let me lay down beside you, let me always be with you."[6] While a romantic song, it does capture the love of a man for Mary, but this song as well captures the love of a little child for his or her mom. Where does every soul want to be? Where did Jesus want to be? With her, His mother and spouse, in life and in death and after death, in childhood and in adulthood, at home, in the world, on the Cross, in Heaven…with she who is the New Eve.

This differing appreciation of beauty of course does not imply, again, anything of the sexual realm. To a highly sexualized culture of death, an attractive woman can only equal *sexual* attraction for a man in most cases. But the fact is, female beauty need not necessarily be equivalent to sexual attraction. A boy's mother may be stunningly beautiful, and it will strike him in an altogether different fashion than it will a girl, though not at all in any sexual way, just as a girl will experience the handsomeness of her father in a way different than his son.

Thus for a girl and Mary, the experience of union is one of spiritual union in the sense of *likeness*. The girl learns from Mother how to be a woman and they share a certain vision and outlook in life as they are both female. She learns too from her Mother about her beauty and charm, what it is and what it is for, how to use it and how not to use it. A contemporary description from a mother concerning this union between mother and daughter will make this clearer:

> When the nurse brought my baby in, I looked into her face and saw myself—her eyes, her skin, her expressions, her spirit. She looked up at me and smiled her first hello… Wynonna and I were instantly one, a partnership, a team—just the two of us against a frightening and unknown world. On that spring day…we began our wonderful duet, a blend of heart, mind and soul that continues to this day.[7]

This is a spiritual union, and while there is a oneness of flesh, it is, though physical at one level, a sort of mystical oneness, a oneness of heart.

For a boy, the experience of union with his mom is likewise a union of both flesh and heart, but in the sense not of likeness but of *complementarity*. Her beauty strikes him not as like his own, but as a gift to him, a gift to love, enfleshed beauty, one who nourishes him and encourages him to do great things, and his natural desire is to cherish and protect her. He is not like her, but understands himself via an oppositional relationship, wherein he more deeply understands himself and his role in the world. So it is in his relationship with Mary. Unlike Mary as model of life as she is for girls, as a relationship of *identification*, for a boy there is a relationship of *complementarity*, one in which, in a purely mystical way (as opposed to carnal), this spiritual relationship may blossom into Mary as both Mother and, so to speak, sweetheart—on the spiritual level, there is no contradiction between Mary as Mother and Spouse of one person, just as for a man and a woman both Jesus is "spouse": contradictory at the natural level, of a different type and meaning on the mystical level. Women will "espouse" Mary's Heart after the fashion of women, men after the fashion of men, both in a totally pure, spiritual sense.

Vive le Difference: Complementarity

Espousal may be taken in a more restricted sense, however. Whereas for both men and women Jesus is "spouse of the soul," and whereas both men and women can "espouse" Mary's Heart, there is a more specific reality to deal with as well: Jesus is a man, Mary is a woman. This does not change in Heaven. At the level of the soul a woman is properly feminine and a man properly masculine. We do not, at the level of the soul or in Heaven, become androgynous or turn into angels. Indeed, the soul is the form of the body, and if the body is male or female, it is because the soul has these specific qualities that make one physically a man or woman.

Given this, women can be "brides of Christ," and this is taken not in a carnal way, but in a mystical, *yet true*, manner. Women thus imitate Mary in a particular way. They imitate Mary's womanhood as any daughter looks to her mother as her example of womanhood, and women imitate Mary in her relationship with Christ and participate in Mary's spousal relationship to Christ as

New Eve to New Adam. Even aside from becoming a female religious who is a "bride of Christ," women relate to Jesus as women, not as men.

A man *cannot* be a "bride of Christ." The necessary complementarity does not exist between a man and Jesus even on the spiritual level. Neither does a man look to Mary as a model of manhood. He may imitate her virtues, attitudes, and outlook, and in this way act like her, learn from her, and become a man who clearly has been affected in his very being by her.[8] But this never authentically morphs into a man looking to Mary as a model of what a man is. He does not imitate her in the way a woman does. Rather, as women imitate Mary looking to her as the perfect model of womanhood in everything that properly belongs to womanhood, and as they also imitate in their womanly way her virtues and attitudes and outlook, so a man looks to Jesus in this way—He Who has assumed to Himself a perfect manhood. As a woman in some sense becomes an image of Mary, men are meant to become an image of Jesus, as He is the exemplar of both a human being and also of a man.

And so for men and women both, consecration to Mary leads to union with Jesus, and union with Him leads also to deeper union with Mary. But how this belonging to Mary is lived out certainly differs according to one's gender, just as belonging to Jesus also differs in how it is lived out according to one's gender. For example, I have seen how women, lay women and nuns, pray to Jesus, look at His pictures, and touch statues of Him—as a man, that's just not how I relate to Him. I have seen on the other hand how men pray to Mary, look at her pictures, and touch her statues, and that I can relate to, because I am a man and I relate to Mary as a man relates to a woman.

Given the intrinsic role of complementarity that exists between men and women, consecration to Mary will differ essentially in the sense that men and women relate to Mary precisely as *men* and *women*. Consecration to Mary is not an androgynous spiritual reality any more than the soul is not an androgynous spiritual reality. The general facet holds true of course: in Christ we are all "sons in the Son," we all live His divine life, we are all formed into another Christ. But in this, women do not become men. Likewise, Mary is the Beloved of every person, but this does not vitiate the reality of complementarity.

And so there are the commonalities of consecration, facets that are for both men and women, even while men and women live out this consecration differently. A short review of these will set the following treatment of espousal to Mary specifically in regard to men in a clear light. In general, all little children, boys and girls, see Mom as their beloved sweetheart, both Mom and baby experiencing a special form of "in-loveness." Further, Mom and baby live "one" life, they cannot be separated, and it is like a sort of marriage. In regard to Mary, since we are all in Christ and thus related to Mary because we are His members, the verse, "For as a young man marries a virgin, so shall your sons marry you"[9] is true for all. One cannot be one with Jesus and not with Mary, they are two Hearts united. Christ is her mystical spouse, and thus in Christ as His Body we participate in this in some mystical way. We are all, men and women, "sons in the Son." Consecration to Mary then can be considered both as a child-Mother union that leads to union with Christ, as well as a species of mystical espousal inasmuch as there is a mystical life of utter intimacy and union wherein the soul grows together with Mary as she forms that soul into Christ and she shares her Heart with that soul. This type of consecration as espousal is open to both men and women. But beyond these general realities, we must continue to contend with complementarity.

Men consider Mary as "Beloved" as *men*. A boy relates to Mary as a boy, not as a girl, and as he grows into a man he relates to Mary as a man. And while the man remains her child, and a little child at that, there is concurrent with this a beautiful fulfillment of the man as a man, something he finds only in relation to a woman. We can go so far as to say that just as it is only with Jesus one can understand true manhood, only in Mary can one understand true womanhood: How ought one view a woman? How ought one relate to her? How should women be treated? Not only are these questions answered for a man in a special way within a relationship with Mary, she provides the grace to live such that he treats women as they ought to be treated. "No Mary" means not only that we do not find Christ, it means a distorted view of reality, and so "no Mary" leads to a warped view of women, one that the devil, the master of illusion, is all too ready to foist on us. It is by intimate spiritual union with Mary that a man becomes pure and chaste, a man like St. Joseph, just as it is due to Mary that St. Joseph became the holiest human person after Mary.

In light of this, men often enough come to see themselves as knights of Our Lady. Children still, yes, the "babe to Mom relation" never ceases and never shall cease for eternity. But in addition to this there is a sort of courtly "knight-to-lady" love that comes to the heart, a role proper to man who is created by God as a lover, protector and provider for woman. The knight of Mary thus seeks to obey her in all things and to lay all he is and has at her disposal, and he loves her both as child to Mom and as knight to Lady, ready even to die for her and to ever defend her honor and cause others to love her as well. Yet there is a still deeper relationship that a man may have with her.

Manly Espousal

While it has been mentioned by some Saints in relation to priesthood, there is no need for this deeper relationship with Mary to be restricted to that sphere. The mystical relationship of a man with Mary is one that can exist along with natural relationships and is analogous to them, just as Mary is truly God's spouse and yet this does not prevent St. Joseph from being espoused to her in a natural marriage.

For religious, natural marriage is totally passed over. A nun, a bride of Christ, skips the natural marriage aspect and claims only the mystical—this state is superior to natural marriage. Priests (usually) skip natural marriage as well, and accept a superior reality—that of being married to the Church; yet there is another reality here—priest as spouse of Mary.[10] Despite the fact that religious life is a superior state of life, this does not rule out a mystical-spousal relationship based on complementarity between a woman living in a natural marriage and Jesus, and a married man in a natural marriage and Mary. Indeed, such a close relationship with Jesus and Mary will augment and beautify a natural marriage! Saint Catherine of Genoa is an example of a Saint who experienced a natural spousal unity with her husband and concomitantly a spousal unity with God. Pope Benedict XVI points this out in his Wednesday Audience of January 12, 2011, writing that, "From her conversion until her death there were no extraordinary events but two elements characterize her entire life: on the one hand her mystical experience, that is, the profound union with God, which she felt as spousal union, and on the other, assistance to the sick..." These two spousal unions, one natural and one mystical, are different in quality and not mutually exclusive.

But it must be made clear: objectively, the man or woman who chooses the life of a religious or priest chooses a state that is superior to natural marriage, and this relationship with Jesus and Mary that excludes any earthly spouse certainly renders the one choosing that state more open to a deeper relationship with Jesus and Mary. Thus, while objectively speaking the relationship of a man or woman living in a natural marriage will not objectively have the pointed focus and perfection in a relationship with Jesus and Mary that one embracing the religious state does have objectively (and may have subjectively in a way much deeper than one in a natural marriage, though one in a religious state may not, on a subjective level, accept such depth of relationship), there is no contradiction for a married man moved by grace to accept consecration as a spiritual espousal to Mary, since one relationship is natural, and the other mystical, one the imperfect image, the other more perfect and thus bringing greater perfection to the natural, as in the case of St. Catherine of Genoa. This relationship with Mary thus moves from child of Mary, to knight of Mary, to the espoused of Mary, with this higher level of intimacy not excluding but wonderfully including the others.

We find this espousal of Mary prophesied in Ecclesiasticus (Sirach) 15:1-3 as well as in Isaiah 62:5, mentioned above, where we read of Lady Wisdom, "He that feareth God, will do good: and he that possesseth justice, shall lay hold on her, And she will meet him as an honourable mother, and will receive him as a wife married of a virgin. With the bread of life and understanding, she shall feed him…" In a man's consecration as espousal to Mary there is a sort of fulfillment of these prophecies, but this is especially fulfilled in the life of St. Joseph, the exemplar of a man espousing Mary's Heart:

> Reverend Stanley Smolensk, contemporary Josephologist, explains this point: "[Joseph's] interior life was based on his singular union with Jesus through Mary. He was consecrated to Jesus through Mary by his espousal to her … Thus, Joseph's consecration is the epitome of all consecrations to Jesus through Mary." Thus, we can understand Joseph's sanctity as the fruit of his union with the two hearts, based on his espousal union with the heart of Mary. And we, too, can model our total consecration to Jesus through Mary on St. Joseph's "spousal" union with Mary. We, like Joseph, are called to "espouse" the Immaculate Heart of Mary; to give Mary our hearts undividedly and take her heart as our own.[11]

This is a particularly powerful model of relation to Mary, for women as women, and for men as men. And how men need Mary as their spiritual spouse in these days, when men are under tremendous attack, brought into the slavery of impurity, forgetful of the immense dignity and beauty of women, and forgetful of their own dignity and role as men. Sadly, however, the world today has been so sexualized that many men cannot think of a woman or of marriage in anything but a sexual context. This is a horrendous, hellish diminution of male-female relations; certainly no natural marriage that is based upon sexual expression will thrive. In this regard, Dr. James Keating writes,

> Some might argue it is "better" to relate to Mary as mother because she "forms" one into Christ. It is also, however, a powerful role of the woman to "form" the man she marries into her "spouse." There is in the woman a formative power ordered toward the complete man, son and spouse. Since Mary is the New Eve, the Woman (Jn 2:4; 19:26), she desires to order men correctly toward their spousal-masculine identity. [12]

Only Mary has the ability to do this. Thus as a man spiritually espouses Mary's Heart to his, he will become a better man, a better husband, a better priest, a better brother, a better son, because in this utterly close and intimate union with Mary she will form men into pure images of her Son, into another Jesus, *the* Man. She literally formed Jesus in her womb and she literally brought Joseph into union with Jesus. In regard to both Jesus and St. Joseph, we find espousal to Mary, the natural and the mystical. We also see this reality in St. John at the Cross, and thus aside from Jesus as *the* exemplar we have St. Joseph, *a married layman*, and St. John, who, while standing for us all at the Cross, is *a priest*: there is then an example for both laymen and priests in regard to a man as espoused to Mary.

It is also important to note that there are examples of male Saints who have experienced a direct and literal mystical marriage to Mary that has been sometimes (though not always) accompanied by extraordinary phenomena; yet the form itself is quite similar in various respects to that of Marian consecration as espousal:

> Saint Edmund of Canterbury, of the Premonstratensian Saint Hermann–Joseph of Steinfeld, and of the Dominican Alain de la Roche. In the seventeenth century, Saint John Eudes wrote of Our Lady as the spouse of priests, and bound himself to her by means of a marriage contract. Does not the liturgy attribute to Our Lady the words of Wisdom in the Book of Proverbs: "I love them that love me" (Prov 8:17)…[13]

Further, in a painting that accompanies the article cited above, the author points out that,

> …just above Saint Robert and a little to his right, none other than Saint Joseph is looking on! He is pointing to his staff, the top of which has flowered into a pure white lily. What does this mean? Saint Joseph is saying that intimacy with the Virgin Mary is the secret of holy purity. He is pointing to his flowering staff to say that one bound to Mary, as if by a marriage bond, will be pure…[and]… will find that she communicates the grace of a fruitful purity to those who bind themselves to her in a permanent and exclusive way.

This espousal between a man and Mary is perhaps a key—an essential key—to the purity of men in our day, where impurity, and the false promise of intimacy implied in that impurity (the lying seduction of Lady Folly), is flooding the world like a sewer and threatening to drown him in it. In fact, it is no accident that the hands of the bride in the *Song of Songs* are dripping with myrrh: "I arose up to open to my beloved: my hands dropped with myrrh, and my fingers were full of the choicest myrrh."[14] Recall that myrrh is mentioned as a gift from the wise men at the Nativity as well. The word "myrrh" means "bitter," and refers to the Sorrowful Mother and her crucified Son. But myrrh was also used for cleansing, that is purifying and sweetening, and it is fragrant. We read in Esther, "Now when every virgin's turn came to go in to the king, after all had been done for setting them off to advantage, it was the twelfth month: so that for six months they were anointed with oil of myrrh..."[15] The *RSVCE* has "beautifying" instead of "advantage." What is happening here is a purification of the young women for their meeting with the king. In the *Song of Songs* then it is no small detail that the bride's hands are simply dripping with myrrh—that's a lot of myrrh oil if one is *dripping* with it. That is, if you want to be pure, go to Mary—she is simply overflowing with purity, and when a person chooses to live intimately with her, that myrrh flows from Mary's hands to the one close to her, and purifies. How can a man be pure today? Go to the Lady who is overflowing with purity and spiritually espouse her Heart to yours in the bonds of love. In the book of *Wisdom* Solomon says this very thing, realizing that in order to obtain purity he must marry Lady Wisdom: "...there is great delight in her friendship, and inexhaustible riches in the works of her hands, and in the exercise of conference with her, wisdom, and glory in the communication of her words: I went about seeking, that I might take her to myself[16]... And as I knew that I could not otherwise be continent, except God gave it, and this also was a point of wisdom, to know whose gift it was: I went to the Lord, and besought him…"[17] And what Solomon beseeches from the Lord in order to obtain the gift of continence—he doesn't simply ask the Lord for the gift of continence—is for Lady Wisdom, and *by her* he will obtain continence! "For if one be perfect among the children of men, yet if thy wisdom be not with him, he shall be nothing regarded[18]… Send her out of thy holy heaven, and from the throne of thy majesty, that she may be with me, and may labour with me, that I may know what is acceptable with thee: For she knoweth and understandeth all things, and shall lead me soberly in my works, and shall preserve me by her power."[19]

Minus this exclusive union with Mary, there is disintegration of the person: "But he that shall sin against me, shall hurt his own soul. All that hate me love death."[20] This disintegration of the person becomes visible, often, in the physical bearing of a person, especially in the eyes. Spiritually, it is like pouring acid on one's face, though worse, since it affects one's soul, and a dis-integrated soul is the true death of a person. Impurity has the effect of the strongest acid on the soul and leads to a corruption that causes that soul to reek; espousal to Mary's Heart leads to integration, health, joy and indescribable sweetness.

In the same article cited earlier, Dr. Keating explores some of the effects that come with this particular Marian union. While he relates this to the priesthood (again, in the sense of male/female complementarity), it certainly speaks to any man's mystical union with Mary, lay or religious, in terms of male/female complementarity and how important such a union is:

> Beyond Christ and St. Joseph, a third figure emerges who is related to Mary's spousal character: St. John the evangelist at the cross of Christ. Joseph Ratzinger noted that the apostle John allowed the fullness of Mary's feminine identity to be received into his heart at the cross (Jn 19:27: "He took her into everything that was his own"). This taking "implies a … personal relation between the disciple … and Mary; a letting of Mary into the inmost core of [his] own mental and spiritual life; a handing [of himself] over into her feminine and maternal existence; a reciprocal self-commitment that becomes the ever-new way to Christ's birth and brings about Christ's taking form in man."[21]

Of course, the reality behind any consecration-covenant to Mary is precisely this idea of a chosen permanent life with her, wherein the soul is pledged utterly to her and her to the soul. A mystical marriage such as mentioned in the life of St. Hermann Joseph is indeed rare: Mary appeared to him, put a ring on his finger, called him her new spouse and gave him the second name of "Joseph." Nevertheless, consecration to Mary as espousal is open to all, both in the sense of complementarity and in the sense first described as it applies to both men and women. Certainly not all receive the inspiration/grace to take consecration to this level. Some are more inclined to the "holy slavery" model, some to the "property" model. Some, perhaps men especially, will receive the grace to consecrate themselves to Mary in the sense of espousal—living their lives in total union with Mary's Heart so as to be as close to her as possible. This can only benefit the world.

A final note: all forms of consecration to Mary are Christocentric

Fr. Gambero points out that Jesus as Spouse of Mary has deep roots: "Ephrem is the first Christian author to call Mary spouse of Christ…" and he cites St. Ephrem, who writes of Jesus and Mary, "For she is Your mother—she alone—and Your sister with all. She was to You mother; she was to you sister. Moreover, she is Your betrothed with the chaste women."[22] With this in mind we have to ponder Jesus' words to Saul/St. Paul when Saul was persecuting Christians: "Why do you persecute Me?"[23] There is a mystical association: we are one with Him (He is our primary end), forming His mystical Body; there is not a separate (one might say "beheaded") Head and Body. That is, since Jesus is the New Adam and we form one Body with Him, "it is not now I who live but Christ Who lives in me." As mentioned in the last chapter, Jesus gives each individual soul His Heart, and thus Mary is loved by the soul with Jesus' own Heart. This gives immense happiness to Jesus, since through you and me He is able to love Mary anew, and Mary is able to love Jesus anew. But this is a dual reality: the soul with Mary loving Jesus, and the soul with Jesus loving Mary. In both cases the primary union is with and oriented to Christ, and then out of that primary union, the soul finds union with both Jesus and Mary. "When we say 'Mary' we put into this cry not only all that our soul feels for her, but also and more especially all that the soul of Jesus feels for His Mother. When we say 'Jesus' it is Mary who, through us, prays and loves her Son…"[24]

We go to Jesus *through* Mary and *with* Mary, and then we go to Mary *with* Him as we are one with He Who is our Life. This tri-union of souls will be found in every saint in Heaven, but it will especially shine in those consecrated to Mary as her "slave," her "property," her "spouse."

—Notes—

1. By "espousal" is *not* meant the highest levels of union with God known as the "Unitive Way," which is experienced by those extremely far advanced in holiness and which includes mystical espousal and marriage to God Himself. As will be discussed in this chapter, "espousal" in the sense of consecration to Mary is a certain way of experiencing one's consecration to Mary as a most radical *gift* of one's heart to Mary and *acceptance* of Mary's Heart to him or her. Indeed this is a spiritual reality, a mystical reality, and as such, is something that can be experienced by men or women; as we do not speak here of the "Unitive Way," neither do we speak of any sort of "natural marriage." However, there is the issue of complementarity, and thus consecration as espousal to Mary will differ between men and women, which will also be discussed in this chapter.
2. p. 24
3. Manteau-Bonamy, *Immaculate Conception and the Holy Spirit*, p. 111
4. *Mary and the Fathers of the Church*, p. 297
5. Matthew 2:13 and 20. This is important. There are two identical phrases, except for the destination: Verse 13 reads, "Arise, and take the child and his mother, and fly into Egypt," and verse 20, "Arise, and take the child and his mother, and go into the land of Israel." Wherever we go, in whatever circumstances, whether we seem to be sent into exile or into the Promised Land, we must "take the child and his mother" with us, as St. Joseph did.
6. "Annie's Song"

7. Naomi Judd, "A Team of Two," from *The Love Between a Mother and Daughter is Forever*, p. 42
8. This is crucial for any child of Mary, which means all Christians, especially those consecrated to her: "He who does not works of his mother, abjures his lineage," says St. Alphonsus Liguori in his book *Glories of Mary* (section IV, "Mary is the Mother of Penitent Sinners," in the section entitled "Mary, our Queen, our Mother") quoting St. Peter Chrysostom.
9. Isaiah 62:5
10. Hilda Graef, *Mary, a History of Doctrine and Devotion*, p. 308
11. Jayson Brunelle, "To Jesus Through Mary, in the Spirit of St. Joseph: The Wheat, the Rose, and the Lily"
12. Dr. James Keating, "Imagination, Prayer and the Spousal Gift"
13. Fr. Kirby, "I Love Them That Love Me"
14. 5:5
15. 2:12
16. Wisdom 8:18
17. ibid, 8:21
18. ibid, 9:6
19. ibid, 9:10, 11
20. Proverbs 8:36
21. Dr. James Keating, "Imagination, Prayer, and the Spousal Gift"
22. Fr. Luigi Gambero, *Mary and the Fathers of the Church*, pp. 117 and 118
23. Acts 9:4
24. Fr. Emil Neubert, *Life of Union with Mary*, p. 47

—Section Five—

Apparitions of Mary

Chapter One
A Short Note on Apparitions

An apparition is simply an "appearance." We could even say it is a "sensible visit." In the course of these appearances, Mary often defines herself in some way (as we saw in a particular way at Lourdes), makes various requests, shares secrets (some of which are personal secrets for the one whom she is visiting), and foretells something that either will happen unless people repent of their sinful lives, or something that is certainly going to happen at some point. One of the requests she often makes is for a chapel at the site of the apparition, and here we see that Mary does not cease to be Lady Wisdom! Lady Wisdom continually invites us to her house of seven pillars, the Church of Seven Sacraments, which is where she shares her Eucharistic meal, bringing us into union with her and her Son.

Yet there is a personalistic aspect to these apparitions. Just as Mary is to each of us "a personal romance," so each apparition is personal as well. Mary never deals with us as a mere "crowd" of people, but as individuals. Similar to how St. John represents each of us, we can say that the one who receives the visible visits of Mary represents each of us. Mary's visit is truly to that person who sees her, personally, but her visit is in a certain way for each person as well. Thus we can take the words Mary says to St. Bernadette, "I cannot make you happy in this life, only in the next," as said "to me personally." At the Cross we saw how utterly personal the Sacrifice of Jesus is for each of us, and how Mary offered it, knowing us each, for each of us, one at a time in a miraculous way (via infused knowledge). She has not changed her ways in Heaven or in her appearances on earth. Each apparition is for me and for you, and her love for each of us overflows onto us with each visit.

And the actual words of Mary in her apparitions help us to know her better, and beyond the specifics of some messages in her appearances, her words are timeless. This is how her appearances should be understood—not merely as distant historic happenings, but as words from her to us *now*, each a personal love note from her. Usually, she works quietly, though incessantly, with us and upon us, shaping us into an image of her Son, allowing this or that in our lives (often some suffering) in order to root out bad habits, remnants of sin, and attachments; making us humble by showing us what we really are (e.g. that home project that should have taken you one hour but took you five, with all manner of inexplicable troubles…and you saw that you are not as patient, kind, or pure as you started to believe yourself to be!); strengthening virtues in us.

We do not see her, and perhaps often we do not sense her, though we are in her arms. Sometimes though, she does let someone see her, hear her, even touch her, and in her dulcet voice so sweet and gentle our lovely Lady tells us things via these people we call "seers" or "visionaries," those who have the blessing of receiving a tangible visit from Mary. She whispers to us as well…

Chapter Two
Tepeyac (Mexico), Rue de Bac and Lourdes

Tepeyac, 1531

Mary's words to St. Juan Diego are perhaps the most consoling words she has spoken to us in any of her apparitions. Her words reveal a love that is so personal, so intimate and so close that they leave us stunned, overjoyed, at peace, content, and attachments to this world simply melt away. When a little baby is upset for being overtired and hungry, when the baby needs love, comforting touches, closeness, the arms of Mom immediately console, and sweet union causes all problems to melt away as baby, so to speak, melts into Mom, baby's head resting on Mom's heart.

From the first words she utters, Mary treats Juan Diego as her most precious little one, as if there were no one else in the world for her. "'Juanito…Juan Dieguito,' she called affectionately…"[1] His name is of course "Juan," but she is speaking to him with incredible intimacy; it is like a conversation between two best friends, Mother to child, or sister to brother, because it *is* such a conversation. At the same time she shows him a reverential courtesy that doesn't quite come through in the translation into English.[2] She continues, "Juanito, my son, where are you going?" She is interested in everything we are doing. If you come upon someone you know, especially someone you love, and you see them walking somewhere, of course you say, "Hey, where are you off to?" He tells her he is going to Mass; she smiles, and says,

> Know for certain, dearest of my sons, that I am the perfect and perpetual Virgin Mary, Mother of the true God… I ardently desire a teocalli [a church] be built here for me where I will show and offer all my love, my compassion, my help and my protection to the people. I am your merciful mother, the Mother of all who live united in this land, and of all mankind, of all those who love me, of those who cry to me, of those who have confidence in me. Here I will hear their weeping and their sorrows, and will remedy and alleviate their sufferings, necessities and misfortunes.[3]

Immediately, Mary reveals several things: he is her dearest child, she is the Mother of God *and* our Mother, and she tells us how we should act toward her. First, love her! Everything follows from this; it is from our love for someone that we do kind things for them, think of them and so on, especially when there is a close relationship, and this is what comes next—it is only with those extremely close to us that we "cry" to them and have "confidence" in them, and only a person who is so close to us will "hear" us in our weeping and sorrows and necessities. This is the first apparition. The second and third apparitions concern her helping Juan Diego to do what she has asked him to in the face of various difficulties.

She doesn't leave him unaided, and she comforts him as he sets out to do what she asks—she never leaves us to ourselves when we are intent on remaining close to her. At the fifth apparition, however, when it seems that finally something has gone so badly wrong that he will not be able to meet her as she requested, she speaks those words that have consoled countless souls for near 500 years:

> Listen and let it penetrate your heart, my dear little son. Do not be troubled or weighed down with grief. Do not fear any illness or vexation, anxiety or pain. Am I not here who am your Mother? Are you not under my shadow and protection? Am I not your fountain of life? Are you not in the folds of my mantle? In the crossing of my arms? Is there anything else you need?[4]

There are several intriguing elements in this small passage…

First, "Is there anything else you need?" Only Mary can say this! If anyone else were to say, "You need nothing else but me and what I have to offer you," they would be either lying or deluded. But Mary can say this, because she truly is our "fountain of life"; again we see Lady Wisdom. When we find her, we find God; if we go to her, we share her meal, the only meal that is a "Who," not a "what." She is the fountain where we find the water of eternal life, and only from this fountain does that water proceed. She gives life to our souls.

Second, we are *in* the fountain, *at the Heart* of the fountain! This is what is meant by "in the folds of my mantle…in the crossing of my arms." This is an expression of the closeness between mother and baby. At the time of Juan Diego, in the fold of the mantle (or for a man, like Juan Diego, his *tilma*), a woman could carry precious cargo safely, and she would especially save this spot for carrying her baby. It was essentially "a portable crib,"[5] and kept the baby safe from the world. Here too the closeness between Mom and baby remains secretive, hidden from prying eyes just as each of our spiritual lives, generally speaking, is something hidden from others. The next phrase, however, is still more astonishing and sheds more light on this privileged place: in the original language of the Aztecs, the words for "crossing" meant two sticks that were rubbed together in order to start a fire, but it also described, in a vivid way, how the mother held her child, crossing her arms behind him and thus pressing the child up against her heart.[6] This little place is a world, the coziest, safest and most pleasant of worlds, where the fire of the mother's love completely encompasses her child. It is here that Mary carries us.

Third, this puts us under her "shadow and protection." Whatever may happen in our lives—whatever you can think of—it can never truly be out of control, an unmitigated disaster, any more than a man who lives in a fountain of fresh water is in danger of dying of thirst; such a man has no anxiety of being thirsty. There is nothing to fear! Psalm 23 seems to speak to this:

> The Lord is my shepherd, I shall not want; he makes me lie down in green pastures. He leads me beside still waters; he restores my soul. He leads me in paths of righteousness for his name's sake. Even though I walk through the valley of the shadow of death, I fear no evil; for thou art with me; thy rod and thy staff, they comfort me. Thou preparest a table before me in the presence of my enemies; thou anointest my head with oil, my cup

> overflows. Surely goodness and mercy shall follow me all the days of my life; and I shall dwell in the house of the Lord for ever.

What is the green pasture? The still waters? What is the table that He prepares? How does the cup overflow? Where do we find His goodness and mercy? What is the house of the Lord? All of this seems to be implied in Mary's words, "Am I not your fountain of life?" She is the green pasture and the fountain of life-giving water that fills the cup to overflowing; the Lord is with her, St. Gabriel told her, and so we find in her the goodness and mercy of the Lord, she who is His very house. In the very midst of our enemies we receive the Eucharist. All we have to do is love her in return, cry to her, have confidence in her, and let her carry us against her Heart. What comfort we have from hearing and feeling the beat of her Heart! What sweetness will flow into us! What hope! What confidence! What secrets will she share with us? That depends on the ear that is against her Heart, and how well that flower—we are all her flowers—opens up to the sun shining from her.

This message is also a sort of basis for the apparitions of Mary that will come in the 19th and 20th centuries. It is fundamental to first love her, and in that love cry to her, and in that crying have complete confidence in her. Mary's post-Juan Diego apparitions are best understood with her words to Juan Diego deeply impressed within our hearts.

Rue De Bac, Apparitions of the Miraculous Medal, 1830

After making it clear in Mexico the type of relationship we

should have with her, we find Mary appearing to St. Catherine Laboure in Paris, France. On July 18, around 11:15 at night, her guardian angel, appearing to be about four or five years old, led her to the chapel. All the lights were lit as if for the Christmas Midnight Mass! There she waited, until finally her angel told her that Mary was coming. There was the sound of a silk dress rustling, and Mary appeared and sat in a chair by the altar. St. Catherine did what anyone would do who loves, cries to and has confidence in her mom—she ran to her side, knelt down right by her and put her hands on her knees.[7] They talked for two hours, and she said it was the sweetest moment of her life. Much of that conversation we will never know, but Mary did tell her about the evil times coming, and, in complete intersection with her words to St. Juan Diego, to deal with whatever sufferings God sends meekly, patiently, and even joyfully: "Do not be troubled or weighed down with grief. Do not fear any illness or vexation, anxiety or pain. Am I not here who am your Mother?"

November 27th of 1830 found St. Catherine receiving another visit from Mary, this time appearing as the image we see on the Miraculous Medal. Grace, appearing as light, is pouring from rings on Mary's hands onto a globe, of which she says, "This globe represents the entire world, including France, and every person."[8] Upon this globe Mary showers graces; the very source of grace has given Himself over to her, and she nourishes us with this grace as something belonging to her. But, we have to ask for many of these graces and not erect elements in our lives that would block that grace from being effective in our lives (again, we have to "cry" to her and remain in her crossed arms, resting on her Heart):

> She had three rings in [on] each finger; the thickest ring

> near the hand; a medium size ring in the middle, and the smallest in the extremity. From the precious stones, rays of light flowed downwards; filling all the bottom area. While Sister Catherine was contemplating the Virgin, she (Mary) looked at her and said to her heart: "This globe you see—at the feet of Mary—represents the whole world, specially France and each soul in particular. The rays symbolize the graces that I give to those who ask for them. The pearls that don't have rays are the graces of the souls who don't ask.[9]

In some way, the apparitions of Mary to St. Catherine are a spiritual picture of what closeness with Mary looks like.

> Our Lady…grants the gift of having a familiar relationship with Mary of mother-daughter: she sees her and comes near to Mary with familiarity and simplicity, she touches the Virgin and Mary sits down so that Sr. Catherine can come closer and place her arms and hands on the knees of the Queen of Heaven.[10]

Intimacy with Mary. This is a crucial foundation for what will come at Lourdes and Fatima; but it's a foundation that is frequently forgotten, and when we back away from Mary, we do so to our great peril and that of others—as a baby is in danger and useless of achieving anything on its own, so are we without Mary. The Eternal Word Himself chose to be dependent on her—she fed Him, changed His clothes, snuggled Him to her Heart, got Him to sleep, listened to Him, loved Him and received His love. We need Mary, though we can choose to leave her; but choosing things God

Himself does not choose is always a bad idea. The evil effects that come from lack of union with Mary will be crystal clear at Fatima.

Lourdes, 1858

After the appearances of Mary to St. Bernadette were concluded, the devil became very active at Lourdes. Mary appeared there identifying herself as "The Immaculate Conception," and the ancient serpent writhed as a snake whose head is stepped on by a crushing force. Many people—children mostly—were tormented by disturbing visions, even at the grotto where Mary spoke to St. Bernadette. It was an effort to discredit the apparitions.[11] But why go to such lengths? Certainly one reason was to discredit Mary's self-revelation. As outlined in the previous section, the dogma of the Immaculate Conception is of essential importance in knowing who Mary is in her deepest being and to better understanding how she unites us to God. Those demonic happenings were then also an attempt to stop people from putting the messages into action: praying the Rosary and performing penances, two crucial elements to these apparitions.

In the third apparition, after laughing when Bernadette asks her to write down her name, Mary speaks her first words to Bernadette: "There is no need to write down what I have to say. Will you do me the favour of coming here for a fortnight?" After an affirmative reply, Mary then sets everything in the right place—"I do not promise to make you happy in this world, but in the next." A warped view of reality makes this sound rather dim! Yet it goes with what Mary told St. Juan Diego: "Do not fear any illness or vexation, anxiety or pain." She doesn't say there will be no trouble, and she doesn't say we will be temporally well off. But we don't have to worry about it, because she will work it all to our eternal good, and we'll suffer these things in her arms. When a little child is suffering, Mom's arms are exactly the place to be.

The next messages build upon this trust and upon our situation in this world, which is one of suffering not only for ourselves but for others as well: "Penance, penance, penance, pray for sinners" Mary says, and she says this while Bernadette is in the midst of perplexing actions: digging in the dirt, drinking muddy water, eating bitter weeds, and smearing mud on her face. People in the crowd called her crazy. But this is penance, for herself and especially for sinners; Mary is fashioning her as well into an *alter Christus*. The official Lourdes sanctuary website expounds on this:

> These actions are biblical actions. Because "the Lady" asked her, Bernadette acts out the Incarnation, the Passion and the death of Christ. **Moving on her knees at the back of the Grotto: this action recalls the Incarnation, God lowers himself to become human.** Bernadette kisses the ground showing us that this act of humility is an action of the love God has for his people. **Eating bitter grass at the back of the Grotto:** when the Jews in the Old Testament wanted to show that God had taken on himself all the bitterness and all the sins of the world… **Smearing her face with mud:** when the prophet Isaiah wanted to speak to us about the Messiah he called him "the suffering servant." Because he carried on himself all our sins his face no longer appeared human…mud disfigures Bernadette and the crowd cries out "she has gone mad."

We are carried by Mary as Jesus was; we suffer like Jesus did as well. This bears out the reality that to be Mary's children means to be one with her Son, a member of His mystical Body, and that our relationship with her is based on His. The servant is not above the Master, but rather becomes like Him. Every step of the way, however, is Mary with us while we, like living statues, suffer the chisel blows and sandpaper of the sculptor.

Many Apparitions, One Mother, One Message

Tepeyac, Rue de Bac, Lourdes: all part of one message from the same Mother, and in perfect order:

1) Tepeyac: Mary reveals intimate mother-child closeness and safety. Even in difficulties she makes everything sweet. She shows us in a vivid way that we are each her beloved and carried by her as a most precious treasure. (*Here we are simply carried.*)
2) Rue de Bac: the mother-child love revealed at Tepeyac also means Mom lavishing love and nourishing upon her baby. She pours grace upon us, nourishing our souls, though for some we have to ask. (*Now we see more activity expected on our part, including more prayer.*)
3) Lourdes: Mary has established the solid, stable and essential foundation of loving security in her arms. Thus assured of her love and closeness, she can then begin to impart to us more details of what it means to belong to her. We know already there is nothing to be anxious about, whatever happens, and what is going to happen to us in her arms is our souls being formed into a likeness

> of Jesus. Hence: "I do not promise to make you happy in this world [exceedingly temporary/short], but in the next [exceedingly permanent/eternal]." (*From resting in her arms, to asking for graces, we now come to a still greater responsibility: performing penances; the sculpture is beginning to take on greater dimension as its contours more and more replicate those of Jesus. Further, the prayer becomes more intense and specific: the Rosary.*)

At Fatima Mary will carry on as our mother-sculptress, and in a manner more intense than in any previous apparition, while the appearances of Mary at Kibeho will reinforce all aspects: intimacy with Mary, prayer and penance.

—Notes—

1. Francis Johnston, *The Wonder of Guadalupe*, p. 26
2. ibid, p. 49
3. ibid, pp. 26-27
4. ibid, p. 33
5. Monsignor Angel Garibay, *Handbook on Guadalupe*, "The Spiritual Motherhood of Mary," p. 14. He provides an incredible exposition of Mary's message based on the original language and culture.
6. ibid
7. Hilda Graef, *Mary, a History of Doctrine and Devotion*, p. 345
8. "The Apparitions of the Miraculous Medal," Official chapel website, *Chapelle Notre-Dame de la Médaille Miraculeuse*
9. *Pierced Hearts*, "The Miraculous Medal"
10. ibid
11. Cf. Trochu, *Saint Bernadette Soubirous*, chapter 16, "Devilry and Counterfeit"

Chapter Three
Fatima

Fatima, Portugal, 1917. The world has gone from bad to worse since 1531, and many souls are now in such outrageous danger that Mary comes to reveal the unprecedented precarious situation the world is in. The miracle of the sun points to this: "But never before has she performed a public miracle at an appointed hour and spot. In fact, not since her divine Son predicted His resurrection on the third day, as a predetermined sign of His divinity and messianic mission, has anything of this kind been wrought."[1] The situation calls for more generous prayer as well: at Lourdes Mary came as the Immaculate Conception and St. Bernadette prayed the Rosary; at Fatima Mary comes as "The Lady of the Rosary," tells us to pray the Rosary every day, and adds a prayer to be said after each decade. Along with the Rosary the Brown Scapular is given to the world anew. Three sayings of Mary to the children also demonstrate that from Mexico to Rue de Bac, and from Lourdes to Fatima, there has been a ratcheting up of the need to live our lives in union with Mary, and in doing this to become an image of the suffering Christ, ever while in Mary's arms:

> You are suffering very much, but do not be discouraged. I will never forsake you. My Immaculate Heart will be your refuge and the way that will lead you to God.[2]
>
> Sacrifice yourself for sinners, and say often, but especially when you are making some sacrifices: O Jesus, it is for love of You, for the conversion of sinners, and to repair the offenses against the Immaculate Heart of Mary.[3]
>
> Pray, pray very much, and make sacrifices for sinners, for many souls go to Hell because there is nobody to make sacrifices and to pray for them.[4]

Sacrifices help make reparation for sins and draw graces down on sinners. Note that Mary does not say, "many souls *will*," but many souls *do* go to Hell…unless we make sacrifices for them and pray for them. And Mary wasn't content simply to talk about Hell, she showed the three children Hell, and there they saw not only demons but damned human souls. It was so horrifying that had not Mary already promised all of them that they were going to Heaven they would have died of terror. This is a tremendous—and tremendously frightening—aspect of being a Catholic. I don't refer to Hell—that should be terrifying for everyone. No, I mean terrifying in that we are supposed to be other Christs! God invites us to participate in His work of Salvation, and we can say "yes" or "no." It is an immense thing, that other souls depend on us, and it would be a crushing one were it not for Mary's comforting presence and wise tempering of the weight of our responsibility, such that our crosses are just the right size. Our reaction must be the same as the children's though: stay close to Mary in every way, constantly going back to 1531:

> Listen and let it penetrate your heart, my dear little son. Do not be troubled or weighed down with grief. Do not fear any illness or vexation, anxiety or pain. Am I not here, I, who am your Mother? Are you not under my shadow and protection? Am I not your fountain of life? Are you not in the folds of my mantle? In the crossing of my arms? Is there anything else you need?

It is by her Heart that we suffer. Nevertheless, the reality of Hell is a disturbing thing to ponder—and souls go to Hell because so many people do *nothing*. Now, we could also put it like this, by analogy: "A parent's children die when they don't feed them." Our reply would be, "Well of course! A parent naturally is supposed to feed their kids—how could they just *not* do that? It's their responsibility, and not an impossible one!" So for us—and it needs to be emphasized, because we hear it so little. But we have sufferings of one sort or another every day, and so the words above become addressed to us: "Well of course! A Catholic naturally is supposed to help Jesus and Mary save souls—how could they just *not* do that? It's their responsibility, and not an impossible one!"

Here the connection between Mary's apparitions and consecration to Mary becomes still more evident: everything we have—including our sufferings, sacrifices and prayers—by consecration to Mary *have all been given to her*. All our lives are hers to do with as she likes, and she takes, by our total consent, all our sufferings and prayers as belonging to her. It is good to pray the prayer she gave to the three children, but doing so at every ache and pain is impossible. It is easier to do when there is a deliberate sacrifice—for example, "I won't put sugar in my coffee this morning—Mary, use this to save souls." But in addition to this, since all is hers to do with as she pleases, not one single headache, not the smallest splinter, not the slightest backache comes along that she does not use to some soul's eternal advantage, because we belong wholly to her. When we try always to accept these things by saying, in word and action, "I will what you will—if you will this suffering, I will it too, save souls with it," then it becomes still more efficacious (often we take back our sufferings or our time, by complaints and grumblings, as if we still owned it, despite the fact that we have given her all… "all" means "all").

The deeper reality is this: the person who is united to Mary brings forth spiritual children with her—some souls will be in Heaven because *you and Mary*, in Christ and with Him as a member of His Body, got them there! Some things God determines will only happen if asked for. As Mary told St. Catherine, there are many graces that never leave those rings on her fingers because *no one asks*. That is, Jesus and Mary obtained all the grace of salvation; by our prayer and sufferings we play our part—offered to Mary they obtain more grace flowing from those rings. Everyone is called to be a mother or father in a spiritual sense, and this includes not only religious but laity as well. A husband may, in the sufferings and prayers that he gives to Mary, save with Mary many souls; likewise his wife may do this. As St. Elizabeth of the Holy Trinity writes, we "must be resolved to share *fully* the Master's passion. It is one of the redeemed who in turn must redeem other souls."[5]

How do we come to God? With Mary. How with Mary? By union with her Immaculate Heart, which is our refuge. There she forms us into Christ, and as Mary formed Christ and with Him as Coredemptrix brought salvation to souls, so we are invited by

Mary to have union with her Heart, be formed into an *alter Christus* and in this union save souls.

St. Gemma Galgani

St. Gemma Galgani is a good example of this union with Mary and saving souls. Few are called by God to St. Gemma's level of participation, but she is a vivid portrait of living what Mary said at Fatima. We could say St. Gemma's charism is one of a "coredemptive" life, and it is no accident that St. Gemma and her charism appeared at the dawn of the 20th century, a sort of herald who preceded Mary's appearances at Fatima, in some sense preparing the way. But how can "coredemption" be applied to anyone but Our Lady? The truth is that only Mary can be *the* Coredemptrix, only she and Jesus,

> [...] work jointly and directly for the ransoming of mankind from the slavery and death of sin, paying with their suffering and death on Calvary the price of the ransom (the passion for Christ, the compassion for Mary), meriting in such wise the acquisition of redemptive grace for the entire human family, past, present and future.
>
> This salvific work, achieved by the Redeemer and Coredemptrix, is called precisely objective Redemption, or more properly, Redemption in actu primo, that is, in the primary act of acquisition of redemptive grace, historically linked to the life, passion and death of Christ and His Mother.[6]

Thus any participation in the roles of coredemption must be understood as meaning participation in a *subjective* manner, a *tertiary* manner.[7] As St. Elizabeth of the Trinity said, we must be redeemers (co-redeemers) with the Redeemer. And so Gemma, while participating in a subjective way in *suffering* for, *obtaining graces* for (through her prayer and suffering), and *interceding* (advocate) for souls, is not a coredemptrix equal to Mary, she is a coredemptrix alongside and with Mary; she participates in Our Lady's office of Coredemptrix. This is similar to a toddler breaking eggs for her mother to help bake bread—the toddler breaking the eggs and dropping them into the mixing bowl is neither necessary nor an essential participation in the creation of bread, but this participation is willed by the mother and is effective in this small way toward the goal—again, only by the express will of the mother, and so there is nothing strictly necessary here, and yet the bread will never exist if the child does not break the eggs. In a similar way, Jesus allows us—and still more, desires us—to participate in His one mediation: Mary in an objective fashion as Coredemptrix, and everyone else in a subjective fashion as a "mini-coredemptrix."

This is what Mary is telling us at Fatima: many souls will be saved if Catholics in the state of grace offer prayers and sacrifices for sinners. Thus an element of the apostolate of every Catholic soul is to save souls from eternal ruin; and this is to do, in some way, what St. Gemma did. St. Gemma's spirituality is thus of utmost importance for the world in these times.

How to Suffer

Mary taught Gemma how to suffer in union with Jesus via her own example. The following three quotes form a mini-dissertation on Mary as Coredemptrix, and contain crucial information on how people should live this spirituality of coredemption. The first quote is from a letter that Gemma penned to Fr. Germanus on April 7th, 1900:

> What a sight You saw Mom when Jesus died!... When You placed Him in the tomb! And you could not be with Him anymore? How is it possible that You suffered so much because of me? How did You do it? Poor Jesus!... Tell me, how did You stand seeing Jesus being crucified to the Cross? My Mom…let me know the cross… Who will understand You, oh Mother? I see that You continue to look at those wounds. How could I not have compassion on You?... Oh how great was Your pain!... You cannot recognize Jesus. What did You do?... Oh God...Jesus is dead and Mom You are crying. Am I the only one that is so insensitive?... I do not see anymore one sacrifice: I see two: one for Jesus and one for Mary! Oh Mother, if one could see You with Jesus, one would not be able to say who will be the first one to die: You or Jesus![8]

In this second example, during one of her ecstasies, Gemma saw and spoke with Our Lady, saying,

> Why are You crying? What causes Your cry? If You

> cry because they offend Jesus, oh, my Mom, be consoled!... I will do all I can so that He will not be any more offended. I will do all I can so that they will leave Him be...do not worry my Mother, I will sacrifice everything: words, thoughts, sacrifices, so that He will be less offended... Oh, wicked sinners stop crucifying Jesus, because at the same time you pierce His Mother.[9]

If one didn't know any better, it can be thought that Gemma was living out Mary's requests at Fatima in this straightforward exposition of suffering. But what of Mary being consoled? This, too, is an aspect of Fatima. Sr. Lucia said that Mary was intensely sorrowful over the loss of souls. Given this, the consolation St. Gemma mentioned is due to the reparation made for sin and for the salvation of souls that occurs because of Gemma's subjective participation in the work of Redemption. If a passerby spots a house on fire and runs in and saves parents and children, the parents will be thankful—consoled—beyond the telling. Imagine the consolation of Mary when the passerby prevents her children from burning forever. This is part of our dignity as Catholics. Jesus and Mary won the war, and we participate in their glory by winning battles. As Shakespeare writes:

> All the world's a stage,
> And all the men and women merely players:
> They have their exits and their entrances;
> And one man in his time plays many parts.[10]

> I hold the world but as the world, Gratiano;

A stage where every man must play a part,
And mine a sad one.[11]

But the sadness is only for this short life, not the next forever life, and the sadness of suffering as we run into the fire, so to speak, is worth the joy and smile of Mary, who rewards us beyond our dreams.

And St. Gemma had plenty of suffering. She ran into houses afire time and again. In her letters, diary, autobiography and biographies the theme of suffering is consistent.

> I spoke with her about some of my desires, the most important one being that she should bring me with her to Heaven; this I said to her several times. She answered: "Daughter, you must suffer still more." "I will suffer up there," I wanted to say, "in Heaven." "Oh no," was her reply, "in Heaven there is no more suffering; but I will bring you there very soon," she said. She was near my bed, so beautiful, I contemplated her and could not get enough. I commended my sinner to her; She smiled: that was a good sign ... I further commended to her various persons who were dear to me, in particular those to whom I have a big debt of gratitude.[12]

And from her diary entry of August 30 we find,

> A little strength, a little courage comes to me when I feel Jesus at the hour when he places the crown of thorns on me and makes me suffer until Friday evening, because this I offer for sinful souls, especially my own [...] He [Jesus] placed the crown of thorns on my

> head, the cause of so much pain for my beloved Jesus, and left it there for several hours. It made me suffer a little but when I say suffering I mean taking pleasure. It is a pleasure, that suffering. How He was afflicted! And the cause: for the many sins committed, and the many ungrateful souls whom He assists, only to receive in return exactly the opposite.

The devil, of course, also recognized the efficacy of a holy soul suffering on behalf of sinners. Writes Fr. Germanus,

> Certainly Satan must have growled with rage at the zeal of this holy girl, finding how she snatched his choicest victims from him. He often appeared to her with eyes of fire and in threatening tones said: "While acting for thyself, do as thou pleasest, but mind, do nothing for the conversion of sinners; if thou attemptest it thou shalt pay me dearly for it."[13]

At this point, an objection may arise. "St. Gemma was a holy soul, and from a very early age. Is such a spirituality truly possible for all? Surely Our Lady at Fatima tells us to offer sacrifices, but can we who are not yet saints really do any good?" The answer to this comes directly after the above selection, and again comes as a temptation from the Father of Lies:

> "How and whence comes such presumption? Thou art laden with sins and all the years of thy life would not suffice to bewail and expiate them, and yet thou losest time about the sins of others...[14]

Jesus coming to visit her in an apparition, St. Gemma says concerning this psychological attack of the devil,

> Dost Thou know, Jesus, who has forbidden me to think about sinners? The devil. On the contrary, Jesus, I recommend them to Thee. Think of them, O Jesus, poor sinners, and teach me to do as much as possible to save them.[15]

In other words, no one is perfect, yet Jesus and Mary desire that this spirituality of coredemption be lived by all Catholics; it is the devil who tells people otherwise.

In sum, St. Gemma providentially anticipated by fifteen years what Our Lady would ask at Fatima. And truly, this is the greatest apostolate, so essential that Mary asks all to do what St. Gemma did just prior to Fatima—certainly not expecting all to bear the stigmata and fight the devil in a visible manner, but, as St. Gemma said to Jesus of souls in danger of Hell, "teach me to do as much as possible to save them."[16] *As much as possible*. St. Gemma phrased it once, "Tonight, O Jesus, I wish to suffer all; if You also wish to suffer, let us suffer together. Let me be one victim with Thee."[17] Every day souls sit on the precipice of Hell, not realizing or perhaps not caring that their souls will be required of them "tonight." Pulling to safety even one person perched at the edge of an abyss is the saving of a whole world, one of infinite worth. "Pray, pray very much, and make sacrifices for sinners, for many souls go to Hell because there is nobody to make sacrifices and to pray for them." The message at her last apparition reiterated this:

> "Men must correct their faults and ask pardon for their

sins." Assuming a sadder air, with a voice of supplication, she adds: "In order that they no longer offend Our Lord, who is already too much offended." These words remained strongly impressed on the children's minds. The sad look that overspread the Lady's face as she pronounced them will always be remembered. They were her last words, and they contained the essential point of the Fatima message.[18]

—Notes—

1. Pelletier, *The Sun Danced at Fatima*, p. 60
2. Chanoine C. Barthas, *Our Lady of Light*, p. 23
3. ibid, p. 30
4. ibid, p. 38
5. *Light, Love, Life, Elizabeth of the Trinity*, Conrad de Meester, ed. p. 123
6. Manelli, Stefano. "Mary Coredemptrix in Sacred Scripture," p. 65
7. Tertiary: that is, Jesus is the Redeemer (primary), and Mary with Him (secondarily, subordinate to Him) participates in objectively winning the graces of Salvation, and we with Mary and Jesus by our prayers and petitions, sacrifices and sufferings release those graces for others; so this is the third wrung, we are tertiary helpers.
8. Enrico Zoffoli, *La Povera Gemma*
9. ibid
10. Shakespeare, *As You Like It*, Act II, Scene 7
11. Shakespeare, *The Merchant of Venice*, Act I, Scene 1
12. *St. Gemma Diary*, August 4
13. *The Life of St. Gemma Galgani*, p. 285
14. ibid, p. 285
15. ibid, p. 285

16. ibid, p. 285
17. Amadeo, *The Biography of Saint Gemma Galgani*, chapter 16
18. Barthas, *Our Lady of Light*, p. 47

Chapter Four
Kibeho, Africa

The apparitions of Mary at Kibeho in Rwanda, Africa, which occurred in 1982-1983, are some of the most remarkable apparitions of Mary. In these visits Mary showed in detail what would happen if people did not change, and this change includes, again, us—how many people live in union with Mary and live what she asked at Fatima in order to make reparation for sin and save souls from Hell? The number is still relatively few. Mary showed the seers horrific visions of a river of blood, mutilated and headless corpses scattered all about unburied, and uncountable thousands hideously murdered. People did not change. On April 7th 1994, a genocide began that lasted a mere 100 days, but saw the gruesome butchery of around 800,000 people in Rwanda. Most were murdered by machete, and so many of these corpses were dumped into the river that it was a literal river of blood. Mary's warnings at Fatima were little listened to, and World War II broke out, just as she said would happen if people did not change their lives, and Rwanda was no different. At the recently approved apparitions from San Nicolas, Argentina, Mary said, "Everywhere in the world where my messages have been given, it would seem that one preached in the cemeteries. The response which the Lord expected was not there."[1] But we can give this response—Mary tells us how, to us thick-headed sheep:

> Are you orphans? Do you not have a God? Do you not have a heavenly Mother? It is time to purify yourselves, my dear children!... It would be only necessary for them to look toward the Mother of God, their Mother, and she would lead them to God. It would be necessary for them to introduce themselves into the heart of the Mother, in order to listen to the voice of the Lord. I do not hide myself; let no one avoid me![2]

There are two points pertinent to Mary as Beloved in this apparition. The first demonstrates, as in other apparitions, that one unites with Mary in saving souls from Hell. She needs our help, she says. While we are preoccupied with clothes, politics, inane television shows and movies, shopping, parties, good food, video games, pets, and so on, we neglect a basic reality that is directly before us: Mary as our Beloved and truly paying attention to her and making her and her little Son happy. But it's the last thing most people think about, while walking the dog is never neglected. The devil, the master of illusion, constantly works to get our minds off of the reason we are in this world and how very short this world is. In fact, "anything but God" seems to be the devil's motto. That's not to say we should never have any relaxation or enjoyment in this world; we're not literally able to be in an absolute and constant mode of penance—we require relaxation. Nevertheless, Mother weeps and people party on. In one of the appearances of Mary at Kibeho,

> ...she [Mary] sounded so forlorn that the girl thought her heart would break. "My child," the voice said, "I am sad because I have sent a message and no one will listen to my words as I desire... So many souls are running to ruin that I need your help to turn them back to my son. As long as you are on Earth, you have to contribute to the salvation of souls. If you will work with me, I shall give you a mission to lead those lost souls back from darkness. Because the world is bad, my child, you will suffer—so if you accept this mission you must also accept all the sufferings I send you with joy, love, patience."[3]

Sufferings with "joy, love, patience"! This is vastly contradictory to the world's view of reality, and again we must fly back to that foundational reality of Mary's arms:

> Listen and let it penetrate your heart, my dear little son. Do not be troubled or weighed down with grief. Do not fear any illness or vexation, anxiety or pain. Am I not here, I, who am your Mother? Are you not under my shadow and protection? Am I not your fountain of life? Are you not in the folds of my mantle? In the crossing of my arms? Is there anything else you need?

And this carefree, familiar, intimate language was present at Kibeho too, and it initially baffled those who witnessed Mary's appearances to the first seer, Alphonsine. How did Alphonsine talk to the Mother of God, the Queen of Angels and of Heaven and Earth, the Gate of Heaven, God's Beloved? She called Mary, "sweetie" and "darling":

> Who would call the Virgin Mary "sweetie" or "darling"? That's the way you talk to a girlfriend, not the mother of God! When asked why she used such familiar terms with the Virgin, Alphonsine responded, "Because she wants us to talk to her like she's our mom, not like she's our principal or boss."[4]

Venerable Fulton Sheen, as we saw earlier, calls Mary "The World's First Love." She is truly the "Sweet Heart" of each of us. She is "darling," the most darling girl who will ever exist. "Sweetie" and "Darling" seem to fit Mary and our relationship with her perfectly. When we receive suffering, it is not from the hand of a "boss" or a physically and/or emotionally distant Queen. Rather, it comes from the mind, heart, and hands of the one who after God knows each of us best, and loves each of us best. When it's one's darling mom asking or one's beloved girl, that makes all the difference! A boss may say, "paint the house, have it done by tonight." Generally, this is unpleasant. It certainly lacks sweetness. When it's one's mom or one's sweetheart, and certainly if the one asking is *both* mom and sweetheart, then the whole essence of painting the house changes—now it's done for love, and a love that is, moreover, requited. Only this sweetest of women can look at someone and ask for tough and even seemingly crazy things, and with a look, a smile, a gentle flutter of the eyelashes, a touch of her hand on one's cheek, a kiss, the promise of unspeakably gentle and wondrous rest in love after the ordeal, send one off to paint the house, clean a filthy toilet, sweep a spiderweb covered hall, lovingly accept a broken arm, or endure gruesome (but always temporary) martyrdom. And unlike a boss or any earthly queen, she gives the grace to *do* these things and to do them, importantly, *with love*; and after carrying our Marian-sweetened cross is reward beyond our dreams, with the Woman of our dreams, in Our Father's House, forever. There is nothing more glorious than this, to be able to say, "I belong all to Mary, and Mary belongs all to me."[5]

Let's end with this dialogue between Mary and Fernande, one of the seers in the final appearance of Mary at Beauraing, Belgium (1932-1933; 33 apparitions during six weeks); along with Mary telling them to be good and pray always, this is the heart of the message in these appearances, and it sums up this section—and this book—perfectly:

—"Do you love my Son?"
—"Yes!" the girl exclaimed.
—"Do you love me?"
—"Oh, yes!"
—"Then sacrifice yourself for me."[6]

True love is sacrifice, a total giving of self. She has already sacrificed herself for us.

A Consecration Prayer of Offering to Console Mary

Mary, my life and my sweetness, I give myself totally to you, I give my heart to you and take your Heart as my own. I want to console you in your sorrows, remove thorns from your Heart, love your Heart as dearer than my own, and in so doing place the balm of requited love upon your Heart.

Jesus, give me this grace: to truly requite Mary's love for me, and to console her in her sorrows. On my own, Jesus, I cannot; but if you and I are one, then I can, because then it is not I that live, but you that live in me and as one with me, and then she can lean upon me. "Who is this that cometh up from the desert, flowing with delights, leaning upon her beloved?" (Canticles, 8:5).

Not that Mary, the Strong Woman of Proverbs 31, needs to lean upon me—I need to lean upon her! ("She will feed him with the bread of understanding, and give him the water of wisdom to drink. He will lean on her and will not fall, and he will rely on her and will not be put to shame," Sirach 15:3-4). But let me console her, as her beloved, to whom she can look to and rely on for comfort in her sorrow.

So lean on me, my most precious Mary, who loves me with the purest love of every womanly love, with all the loves of mother, sister and spouse, you who were entrusted to me at the Cross by Jesus in his holy Passion as I was entrusted to you. Lean on my prayers, sufferings, mortifications and Holy Communions offered to you in penance for sins and to save souls with you.

Be comforted, my sorrowful Mary, because I love you with all my heart and mind and will, as Jesus loves you. Your love in me is requited! I am all yours, I love you as my Mother, sister and spouse, as you love me with all these loves ("She will come to meet him like a mother, and like the wife of his youth she will welcome him," Sirach 15:2), and I take you for all mine with praise and thanksgiving to Our Father.

May we and all those souls we save from Hell rejoice with him in his house forever more. Amen.

—Notes—

1. Joseph Pronechen, *National Catholic Register*, "It's Official: Major Apparitions of Mary Are Approved"
2. ibid
3. Immaculee Ilibagiza, *Our Lady of Kibeho*, p. 49
4. ibid, pp. 43-44
5. Cf. *True Devotion to Mary*, n. 179
6. *Pierced Hearts*, "Apparitions of the Virgin Mary in Beauraing, Belgium"

Bibliography

Academic Dictionaries and Encyclopedias, 2000-2013. Web. 16 April 2016. http://useful_english.enacademic.com/201356/ectype

Agreda, Mary. Fiscar Marison, trans. *The City of God*. Chicago: The Theopolitan, 1913.

Amadeo, Father. *The Biography of Saint Gemma Galgani*. Catholic Way Publishing, 2013. Kindle file.

Apostoli, Andrew. *Fatima for Today*. San Francisco: Ignatius, 2010.

Aquinas, Thomas. "Summa Theologica." *New Advent*. New Advent, 2008. Web. 4 April 2016.

Barthas, Chanoine and Pere Da Fonseca. *Our Lady of Light*. Milwaukee: Bruce Publishing, 1948.

Bastero, Juan. *Mary, Mother of the Redeemer*. Portland: Four Courts, 2011.

Benedict XVI, Pope. "Act of Entrustment and Consecration of Priests to the Immaculate Heart of Mary." *Libreria Editrice Vaticana*. Vatican, n.d. Web. 8 July 2016.

—*Saint Catherine of Genoa*. "General Audience, Wednesday, 12 January 2011." *Libreria Editrice Vaticana*. Vatican, n.d. Web. 22 June 2016.

Bergsma, John. *New Testament Basics for Catholics*. Notre Dame: Ave Maria Press, 2015.

Biela, S.C. *In the Arms of Mary*. Fort Collins: In the Arms of Mary Foundation, 2005.

Brown, Raymond, Joseph Fitzmyer and Roland Murphy, eds. *New Jerome Biblical Commentary*. Englewood Cliffs, New Jersey: Prentice Hall, 1990.

Brunelle, Jayson. "To Jesus Through Mary, in the Spirit of St. Joseph: The Wheat, the Rose, and the Lily." *Homiletic and Pastoral Review*. October 4, 2013. Web. 6 July 2016.

Caswall, Edward, trans. "Liturgia Horarum." *Preces-Latinae*. Michael Martin, 2016. Web. 17 April 2016.

Chapelle Notre-Dame de la Médaille Miraculeuse "The Apparitions of the Miraculous Medal." Official chapel website.

Cox, Dermot. *Proverbs*. Wilmington: Michael Glazier, 1982.

Dallaire, Glenn. "The last letter of St Gemma—A note of love and suffering to the Blessed Mother." *St Gemma Galgani*. n.d. Web. 28 June 2016.

Danielou, Jean. "The Sign of the Temple." *Letter and Spirit*. 2008. Web. 20 June 2014.

de Meester, Conrad, ed. *Light, Love, Life, Elizabeth of the Trinity*. Washington, D.C.: ICS, 2012.

De Montfort, Louis. *True Devotion*. Rockford: TAN, 1985.

De Sales, Francis. *Our Lady, Sermons of St. Francis de Sales*. Frederick, MD: Visitation Monastery, 1985.

Douay-Rheims Bible. Rockford: TAN, 1989.

Eudes, John. *The Admirable Heart of Mary*. New York: Kennedy & Sons, 1948. Kindle file.

Evert, Jason. *Totus Tuus*. Lakewood: Totus Tuus, 2014.

Fifth Marian Dogma. "Mary Coredemptrix Mediatrix Advocate: A Response to 7 Common Objections." *Vox Populi Mariae Mediatrici, Part 2*. n.d. Web. 8 July 2016.

Flannery, Austin, ed. "Lumen Gentium." *Vatican Council II, Vol. 1: The Conciliar and Postconciliar Documents*. Collegeville: Liturgical Press, 2014.

Frisk, M. Jean. "The Holy Spirit and Mary." *The Mary Page, Marian Meditations and Reflections*. IMRI University of Dayton, 2011. Web. 30 March 2016.

Gaitley, Michael. *33 Days to Morning Glory*. Stockbridge: Marian Press, 2013.

Galgani, Gemma. *Autobiography of St. Gemma.* Catholic Way Publishing, 2013. Kindle file.

—*Diary of St. Gemma Galgani.* Catholic Way Publishing, 2013. Kindle file.

—"The last letter of St Gemma—A note of love and suffering to the Blessed Mother." *St Gemma Galgani.* Glenn Dallaire, ed. n.d. Web. 28 June 2016.

Gambero, Luigi. *Mary and the Fathers of the Church.* San Francisco: Ignatius, 1999.

Garibay, Angel. Kalvelage, Francis Mary, ed. "The Spiritual Motherhood of Mary." *Handbook on Guadalupe*. New Bedford: Academy of the Immaculate, 2001.

Garrigou-Lagrange, Reginald. *The Mother of the Saviour, and Our Interior Life*.

Germanus, Father. *The Life of St. Gemma Galgani*. United States: TAN, 2000.

Graef, Hilda. *Mary, a History of Doctrine and Devotion*. Notre Dame: Ave Maria, 1965.

Haffner, Paul. *The Mystery of Mary*. Chicago: Hillenbrand Books, 2004.

Hahn, Scott. *A Father Who Keeps His Promises*. Cincinnati: Servant, 1998.

—*Consuming the Word*. New York: Crown Publishing, 2013.

—*Hail, Holy Queen*. New York: Doubleday, 2001.

—"The Angel and Mary: Scott Hahn Reflects on the Solemnity of the Immaculate Conception." *St. Paul Center for Biblical Theology*. 12 Dec. 2012. Web. 5 June 2014.

—*The Ignatius Catholic Study Bible, New Testament*. San Francisco: Ignatius, 2010.

Hoffman, Dominic, and Basil Cole. "The Canticles of Luke: Argument for Authenticity." *Our Sunday Visitor Newsweekly*, January 2012. Web. 13 March 2016.

Ilibagiza, Immaculee. *Our Lady of Kibeho*. New York: Hay House, 2008.

John Paul II, Pope St. *Crossing the Threshold of Hope*. New York: Knopf, 2005.

—"Dominum et Vivificantem." *Libreria Editrice Vaticana*. Vatican, n.d. Web. 4 April 2016.

—"Ecclesia De Eucharistia." *Libreria Editrice Vaticana*. Vatican, n.d. Web. 4 May 2016.

—"Mary's Motherhood is Linked to the Spirit." *Libreria Editrice Vaticana*. Vatican, n.d. Web. 15 March 2016.

—"Redemptoris Custos." *Libreria Editrice Vaticana*. Vatican, n.d. Web. 4 May 2016.

—"Redemptoris Mater." *Libreria Editrice Vaticana*. Vatican, n.d. Web. 12 April 2016.

—"Salvifici Doloris." *Libreria Editrice Vaticana*. Vatican, n.d. Web. 10 June 2016.

Johnston, Francis. *The Wonder of Guadalupe*. Rockford: TAN, 1981.

Judd, Naomi. "A Team of Two." *The Love Between a Mother and Daughter is Forever*. Boulder: Blue Mountain, 2014.

Keating, James. "Imagination, Prayer and the Spousal Gift." *Homiletic and Pastoral Review*. October 22, 2013. Web. 6 July 2016.

Kirby, Mark. "I Love Them That Love Me." *Vultus Christi*. 26 January 2009. Web. 22 July 2016.

Kreeft, Peter. *Everything You Ever Wanted to Know About Heaven*. San Francisco: Ignatius, 1990.

Laurentin, Rene. *The Meaning of Marian Consecration Today*. San Francisco: Ignatius, 1992.

Leo XIII, Pope. "Fidentem Piumque Animum." *Libreria Editrice Vaticana*. Vatican, n.d. Web. 13 July 2016.

Liguori, Alphonsus. *Glories of Mary*. Brooklyn: Redemptorist Fathers, 1931.

Longenecker, Dwight. "Mary, Mother of Salvation How to Explain the 'Co-Redemptrix' to Evangelicals." *Catholic Answers*. "Catholic Answers Magazine." n.d. Web. 8 July 2016.

Looney, Edward. "Call the Evangelize: The Story of Adele Brise and the Mariophany that Changed her Life." *Marian Studies*, Vol. 62. Article 10. 2011. *Ecommons.udayton.edu*. Web. 1 July 2016.

Machen, Gresham. *New Testament Greek for Beginners*. Toronto: Macmillan, 1951.

Manelli, Stefano. *All Generations Shall Call Me Blessed*. The Academy of the Immaculate, 2005.

—*Jesus Our Eucharist Love*. New Bedford: The Academy of the Immaculate, 2008.

—"Mary Coredemptrix in Sacred Scripture." *Mary Coredemptrix, Mediatrix, Advocate, Theological Foundations II*. Ed. Mark Miravalle. Santa Barbara: Queenship, 1996.

Manteau-Bonami, H.M. *Immaculate Conception and the Holy Spirit, The Marian Teachings of St. Maximilian Kolbe*. Libertyville: Franciscan Marytown, 1977.

Martin, Therese. Clarke, John, trans. *St. Therese of Lisieux, Her Last Conversations*. Washington: Institute of Carmelite Studies, 1977.

Miravalle, Mark. *"With Jesus": The Story of Mary Co-redemptrix*. Goleta, CA: Queenship, 2003.

—*Mary: Coredemptrix, Mediatrix, Advocate*. Santa Barbara: Queenship, 1993.

—"Mary Co-redemptrix and the Fifth Marian Dogma: Perennial Christian Truth; Contemporary Call of the Lady of All Nations." Address given at Amsterdam Conference, May 31, 2008. *MarkMiravalle.com*. 15 Sept 2008. Web. 31 May 2016.

Montague, George T. *Our Father, Our Mother: Mary and the Faces of God*. Steubenville: Franciscan University, 1990.

Most, William. *Mary in Our Life*. "Catholic Culture." *Trinity Communications*, 2016. Web. 5 July 2016.

Neubert, Emil. *Mary in Doctrine*. Dayton: Marianist, 1962.

—*Life of Union with Mary*. Juergens, Sylvester, trans. New Bedford Academy of the Immaculate, 2014.

Pelletier, Joseph. *The Sun Danced at Fatima*. Garden city: Image, 1983.

Pitre, Brant. "Jesus, The New Temple, and the New Priesthood." *Letter and Spirit*. 2008. Web. 20 June 2014. <http://www.scotthahn.com/download/attachment/2520>

Pius XI, Pope. "Caritate Christi Compulsi." *Libreria Editrice Vaticana*. Vatican, n.d. Web. 15 July 2016.

—"Ineffabilis Deus." Irondale: EWTN. Web. 6 June 2014.

—"Miserentissimus Redemptor." *Libreria Editrice Vaticana*. Vatican, n.d. Web. 4 July 2016.

Pius XII, Pope. *Munificentissimus Deus*. *Libreria Editrice Vaticana*. Vatican, n.d. Web. 4 July 2016.

Pronechen, Joseph. "It's Official: Major Apparitions of Mary Are Approved." *National Catholic Register*. 27 May 2016. Web. 15 July 2016.

Ray, Steve. "Mary: Ark of the New Covenant." *Catholic Culture*. Web. 20 June 2014.

Raymond-Barker, Mrs. F. *Bernadette*. London: Thomas Richardson and Son. 1882.

Revised Standard Version Catholic Edition Bible. San Francisco: Ignatius, 1966.

Richer, Etienne. "Immaculate Coredemptrix Because Spouse of the Holy Spirit." *Mary at the Foot of the Cross—IX: Mary: Spouse of the Holy Spirit, Coredemptrix and Mother of the Church*. New Bedford: The Academy of the Immaculate, 2010.

Roberto, D. *The Love of Mary*. Rockford: TAN, 1984. Print.

Scheeben, Matthias. *Mariology, Vol I, Vol II*. Trans. T.L.M.J. Geukers. Lexington: Ex Fontibus, 2014.

—*The Mysteries of Christianity*. Trans. Cyril Vollert. St. Louis: Herder, 1946.

Seifert, Josef. "Mary as Coredemptrix and Mediatrix of all Graces—Philosophical and Personalist Foundations of a Marian Doctrine." *Mary Coredemptrix, Theological Foundations II*. Miravelle, Mark, ed. Santa Barbara: Queenship, 1997.

Servants of the Pierced Hearts of Jesus and Mary. "The Miraculous Medal" 2006. *Pierced Hearts.* Web. July 11, 2016.

—"Apparitions of the Virgin Mary in Beauraing, Belgium." n.d. *Pierced Hearts.* Web. July 11, 2016.

Shakespeare, William. "The Merchant of Venice." *The Complete Works of William Shakespeare*. shakespeare.mit.edu. n.d. Web. 19 July 2016.

—"Romeo and Juliet." *The Complete Works of William Shakespeare*. shakespeare.mit.edu. n.d. Web. 19 July 2016.

Sheen, Fulton. *The World's First Love*. San Francisco: Ignatius, 2010.

—"Mary, Tabernacle of the Lord." *Mother of All Peoples*. 22 Sept. 2006. Web. 20 June 2014.

—"The Blessed Virgin Mary-The Woman I Love." *YouTube*, 2013.

Steinmann, Andrew. *Concordia Commentary: Proverbs*. Saint Louis: Concordia, 2009.

Strong, James. *The New Strong's Expanded Exhaustive Concordance of the Bible, Hebrew Dictionary*. Nashville: Thomas Nelson, 2010.

—*The New Strong's Expanded Exhaustive Concordance of the Bible, Greek Dictionary*. Nashville: Thomas Nelson, 2010.

Thayer's Greek Lexicon. "1982. episkiazo." at Biblehub (2011) at www.biblehub.com.

Trochu, Francois. *The Cure D'Ars*. Rockford: TAN, 1977.

—*Saint Bernadette Soubirous*. Charlotte: TAN, 2012.

USCCB. "The Marriage Vows." *For Your Marriage*. 2016. Web. 6 July 2016.

Von Hildebrand, Dietrich. *Aesthetics, Volume I*. Trans. Fr. Brian McNeil. Steubenville: Dietrich Von Hildebrand Legacy Project. 2016.

—*Marriage: the Mystery of Faithful Love*. Manchester, NH: Sophia Institute, 1991.

Wayant, Patricia, ed. *The Love Between a Mother and a Daughter is Forever*. Boulder: Blue Mountain Press, 2014.

Wilhelm, Joseph and Thomas Scannel. *A Manual of Catholic Theology Based on Scheeben's "Dogmatik", Vol II*. London: Kegan Paul, Trench, Trubner, 1901.

Zoffoli, Enrico. *La Povera Gemma*. Trans. Rita Dunn. *St Gemma Galgani*. Web. 30 December 2013. <http://www.stgemmagalgani.com/2009/03/mary-suffering-in-union-with-jesus.html>

CPSIA information can be obtained
at www.ICGtesting.com
Printed in the USA
BVHW081105180719
553800BV00002B/143/P